InspireHER

Embracing Change and Transformation

Hanna Olivas

Along with 22 Inspiring Authors

ISBN: 978-1-966798-12-5

CONTENTS

INTRODUCTION

Change is inevitable, yet it is often met with fear, uncertainty, or resistance. But what if we chose to see change as an opportunity—an invitation to grow, redefine ourselves, and step into our true power? *InspireHER: Embracing Change and Transformation* is a testament to the strength, resilience, and courage of women who have turned life's transitions into stepping stones toward success and fulfillment.

Within these pages, you will find the stories of remarkable women who have faced challenges, navigated career shifts, embraced personal reinvention, and overcome obstacles that once seemed insurmountable. Each chapter serves as both a mirror and a window—offering reflections of shared struggles and a glimpse into what is possible when we lean into transformation with confidence and purpose.

Beyond storytelling, this book provides practical strategies, thought-provoking insights, and actionable guidance to help you navigate your own journey of change. Whether you are facing a pivotal moment in your career, a shift in your personal life, or a season of self-discovery, *InspireHER* is here to remind you that transformation is not just about adapting—it's about evolving into the best version of yourself.

Let these stories inspire you. Let this wisdom empower you. And most importantly, let this book be a reminder that you are capable of embracing change with strength, grace, and unshakable resilience.

Welcome to *InspireHER*. Your journey begins now.

SHE RISES STUDIOS

Hanna Olivas

Founder & CEO

Author, Speaker, and Founder. Hanna was born and raised in Las Vegas, Nevada, and has paved her way to becoming one of the most influential women of 2022. Hanna is the co-founder of She Rises

Studios and the founder of the Brave & Beautiful Blood Cancer Foundation. Her journey started in 2017 when she was first diagnosed with Multiple Myeloma, an incurable blood cancer. Now more than ever, her focus is to empower other women to become leaders because The Future is Female. She is currently traveling and speaking publicly to women to educate them on entrepreneurship, leadership, and owning the female power within.

https://www.linkedin.com/company/she-rises-studios/
https://www.facebook.com/sherisesstudios
https://www.instagram.com/sherisesstudios_llc/
www.SheRisesStudios.com

Inspire Her

Embracing Change and Transformation

By Hanna Olivas

Transformation is a word that carries so much power. It means stepping into something new, something unfamiliar, and allowing yourself to evolve into the woman you were always meant to be. Change, however, can feel terrifying. It disrupts the comfortable and forces us into the unknown. But what I've come to learn is that change and transformation are necessary for growth. They are the bridges that lead us from where we are to where we are destined to go.

For me, the journey of embracing change has been one of the most transformative experiences of my life. And I say "journey" because transformation isn't a one-time event. It's not something that happens overnight. It's a process, often messy, filled with laughter, tears, breakthroughs, and breakdowns. But every step of the way is worth it because each moment of change shapes you, refines you, and molds you into the woman you were created to be.

There have been moments in my life when I've resisted change, holding on to what was comfortable, even when I knew it no longer served me. I would tell myself, "Just a little longer," convincing myself that staying in a place of familiarity was better than stepping into the unknown. But deep down, I knew that in order to grow, I had to let go. I had to embrace the discomfort, the uncertainty, and the fear of what might be waiting on the other side.

One of my favorite mantras is "Let go to grow." It's something I repeat to myself often, especially in those moments when change feels daunting. I've learned that transformation requires surrender. It requires us to release the tight grip we have on the way things used to be and open our hearts to the new possibilities that await us.

I remember a time in my life when everything seemed to be shifting all at once. My career, my personal life, my health—it all felt like it was spinning out of control. I felt lost, unsure of where I was headed. But in the midst of that chaos, I found peace. And that peace came from faith. Faith that even though I couldn't see the bigger picture, there was a purpose to the changes I was experiencing. Faith that God had a plan for me, and that this transformation was part of my journey.

I often remind myself of this truth: "God doesn't give you what you want; He gives you what you need to grow." There have been countless times when I've prayed for things to go a certain way, only to be met with a different outcome. And while it was hard to understand at the time, I now see that every change, every twist and turn, was leading me to something greater. It was pushing me out of my comfort zone and into a space where I could truly grow and evolve.

I've learned that transformation isn't always pretty. It's not always wrapped up in a neat little bow. Sometimes, it's messy. It requires you to face parts of yourself you've been avoiding. It asks you to confront your fears, your insecurities, and your doubts. But here's the thing: "Transformation doesn't happen in the safe places; it happens in the uncomfortable spaces." And the more willing we are to step into that discomfort, the more we allow ourselves to grow.

There was a time when I thought I had to have it all figured out before I could move forward. I thought I needed to know exactly what the next step was before I could take action. But what I've come to realize is that transformation requires faith—faith in the process, faith in yourself, and faith in the journey. "You don't have to see the whole staircase; you just need to take the first step." This has been a guiding principle for me as I navigate the ever-changing landscape of life.

One of the most beautiful aspects of transformation is that it's a journey we don't have to walk alone. There is power in community, in sisterhood, in the women who stand beside us and cheer us on as we embrace change. I've been blessed to have incredible women in my life who have inspired me, lifted me up, and reminded me of my strength when I couldn't see it for myself. And that's what InspireHER is all about—lifting each other up as we navigate the twists and turns of life's journey.

I believe in the power of shared experiences, the power of storytelling. There is healing in sharing our stories, in being vulnerable and real with one another. "When we share our stories, we give others permission to do the same." And in that sharing, we find strength. We realize that we are not alone in our struggles, that we all have moments of doubt, fear, and uncertainty. But we also realize that we are capable of overcoming those moments, of rising stronger than before.

I think about the times in my life when I've been faced with seemingly insurmountable challenges and moments when I questioned whether I had the strength to keep going. I remember crying tears of frustration, feeling like the weight of the world was on my shoulders. But then, something shifted. In the midst of those tears, I found laughter. I found joy. And I found the courage to keep moving forward.

Laughter has been such an important part of my journey. It's what keeps me grounded, what reminds me not to take life too seriously.

"Laughter is the sound of resilience; it's the melody of hope." Even in the darkest of times, finding moments of joy has helped me to navigate the changes life throws my way. And I encourage you to do the same. Don't forget to laugh, even when things feel heavy. Laughter is a gift, and it's one of the most powerful tools we have as we embrace transformation.

There's a lightness that comes when we embrace change with an open heart. When we stop resisting and start flowing with life's current, we allow ourselves to experience the beauty of transformation. "What we resist, persists. But what we embrace, transforms us." I've learned this lesson the hard way. The more I resisted change, the more difficult it became. But the moment I surrendered, the moment I opened my heart to the unknown, things began to shift.

Of course, there have been tears along the way—plenty of them. And that's okay. Tears are part of the process. They are the release that we need in order to make room for what's next. "Sometimes, the tears we shed are the water we need to grow." I've come to embrace my tears, to honor them as part of my journey. They are not a sign of weakness but of strength. They remind me that I am human, that I feel deeply, and that I am willing to face whatever comes my way.

Faith has been my anchor through it all. Without faith, I don't know where I'd be. It's been my guiding light, the thing that has kept me grounded when everything around me felt uncertain. "Faith is the bridge between where you are and where you are meant to be." I hold on to that truth every day, trusting that even in the midst of uncertainty, there is a greater plan at work. God has a purpose for my life, and even when I can't see the path ahead, I know that He is guiding me.

One of the most powerful lessons I've learned in this journey of embracing change is that transformation is not about becoming someone new; it's about becoming more of who you already are. It's about shedding the layers of fear, doubt, and insecurity that have been holding you back and stepping into the fullness of your potential. "Transformation isn't about changing who you are; it's about revealing who you've always been." You are already enough. You are already capable. You just need to believe it for yourself.

InspireHER is about that belief. It's about inspiring women to embrace their power, to trust their journey, and to step into their greatness. We all have moments when we feel like we're not enough, like we're not capable of handling the changes life throws our way. But I want you to know that you are stronger than you think. You are braver than you know. And you are more capable than you ever imagined.

As you walk this path of transformation, I want to leave you with this thought: "Change is inevitable, but growth is a choice." You have the power to choose how you respond to the changes in your life. You can choose to resist, or you can choose to embrace. You can choose to shrink, or you can choose to rise. The choice is yours.

And when you choose to embrace change, when you choose to see it as an opportunity for growth, you unlock a power within you that is unstoppable. You become a force of nature, a woman who is unafraid to step into the unknown because she knows that on the other side of that change is transformation.

You were made for this journey. You were made to rise, to evolve, to grow. And as you continue to embrace the changes in your life, know that you are not alone. We are all on this journey together, lifting each other up and inspiring one another to keep moving forward.

"Inspire her to believe in herself, to trust her journey, to embrace the changes that come her way, and she will transform not only her own life but the lives of everyone she touches."

So here's to you, beautiful woman. Here's to the changes you've already faced, the ones you're in the midst of, and the ones that are yet to come. Here's to your transformation, to your growth, and to the incredible woman you are becoming. Embrace the journey, trust the process, and know that you are exactly where you are meant to be. And remember: "You are always one decision away from a completely different life." Every moment, every choice you make, has the power to transform your life. Embrace the change. Trust the process. And know that every twist, turn, tear, and moment of joy is part of your beautiful transformation.

The world needs your light, your strength, and your resilience. Inspire others by walking boldly in your truth, by embracing every aspect of who you are, and by showing up for yourself, even when it's hard. There will be moments of doubt, of fear, of uncertainty. But through it all, you are becoming the woman you were always meant to be. You are transforming into a force of nature—unshakable, unstoppable, and full of grace.

And as you continue on this journey of change and transformation, I want you to hold onto this final thought: "She, who embraces change, embraces her power." When you open your heart to the possibilities that lie ahead, when you stop holding on to the past and start welcoming the future with open arms, you become a beacon of inspiration, not only for yourself but for everyone around you.

So go ahead. Embrace the change. Transform. And let your light shine brighter than ever before.

WILD DESERT WISDOM

Lindsey Pollock
Heart-Centered Healing Coach

Lindsey Pollock— One, loving, creative force to be reckoned with, blending my Leo Sun's fiery passion with my Libra Rising's gracious charm. As a writer, energy healer, & intuitive guide, I weave together words, wisdom, & heart-centered healing to empower others. With a deep connection to the mystical & a passion for transformative change, my work is infused with a sense of wonder & a commitment to helping others awaken to their true potential. My writing is a reflection of my soul - authentic, inspiring, & deeply personal. When not crafting compelling stories or guiding others on their journeys, you can find me dancing to the rhythm of my heart, surrounded by the beauty of nature.

https://www.facebook.com/t.shorty08
https://www.instagram.com/lindseypollock

Awakening Your Inner Avatar

Guided script & created to imprint

By Lindsey Pollock

When I first started my awakening process, I missed so many little details throughout, and when I started to truly reflect on those moments, I had not missed one thing because I needed each and every single thing that happened—to happen, because it was for me.

Through the betrayal of myself.

The despair and discouraging thoughts.

It all led me to where I am now.

In this book, I will share in a fun, playful way to take us back to a child-like world where the real fine print exists to leave a deeper imprint as we grow. That's what we want to do, right? Be a child again! Play!

I will teach you some soft, gentle lessons about how words are so powerful when we know them, feel them and embody them. Whether we choose to do that from an internal dialogue or an external dialogue. Those environments really reflect in such a multidimensional way as we begin to understand ourselves and those around us.

My personal divine awakening sparked at the end of 2019 and ignited in 2020.

After going through a wicked storm in my life, I started choosing me little by little. Shadow work. I chose to do four seasons of dating myself in my darkness. My grandmother always told me growing up, "Be with someone for four seasons, because they will change through them." As this is so true, what became even more true for me is that I also had to date myself in this way for the reason of the seasons, too. The dark dating culture was so exhausting with myself, but I kept digging deeper into why I hated myself. My body. My mind. I had a will of unshakable loyalty and strength running through my soul that kept me going, as well as reading books—I came across Eastern medicine in connecting with my mind and body. This also opened ways for a higher level of awareness. I was aware by acknowledging there was a certain line within me called, chakras. I had heard the term thrown around, but when I opened my first book on this subject, I went into another dimension of different origins in my body and mind could be connected with that would be a beautiful way to guide me through some really fascinating and failing parts in my journey of this human experience.

It did not stop at books. I started seeing them on the deck cards I purchased. The lovely board that was handmade by a local artist that I saved for TWO years to have as my own! It lit me up. What lit me up is something I knew I could be proud of incorporating into my daily routine however I saw fit… even my outfits. I will share that I enjoy wearing the color of the chakra I am feeling, or one that I would love to feel, so wearing that color helps me embody that to align my senses with that! On top of that—food. I also choose to have a colorful diet, and if I need alignment in an area of my chakras, I choose wholesome foods that are nutrient-rich for a balanced diet. This also helps with regulating my nervous system and it's dreamy.

So, what really inspired me?

What was it within all these choices I was making for myself through the process of being me that kept digging deeper?

Me. It was simply me.

What was it about me that found myself so deeply attached to this particular piece of work that kept calling me forth and also calling me out on some of my own personal shadows that were so alive and screaming to be known, seen, heard, voiced, felt, expressed in their creative, emotional empowering and needed me to support that within me to find peace?

That was it. Me. I simply needed to share those things with myself, in real truth, honesty, and integrity, with how I desired to give myself the best chance of success in my life.

I want to go through and give three words that point to what I have chosen to highlight within me to connect, guide, and authentically create my most valuable asset for support.

Fear • Faith • Freedom:

Diversity and the Earth are what we phase through when fear shows up on our faces, where we have to take a moment of silence to remember that the Earth is where we find ourselves to be in a more diverse place within.

Once there is clarity claimed within our hearts, this will be the forthcoming season where faith is more known to the awakening of awareness.

As you continue to keep choosing you, there is the sense of belonging, the feeling of being liberated in your heart that is the key, and there is nothing that contains the type of connection to freedom than YOU choosing YOU!

Awareness • Acknowledge • Accept:

Being aware of your presence of where you are in life is very important.

Stop what you are doing right now. Are you choosing to be aware of yourself, or did you choose to be aware of something externally that kept your attention and focus away from what you should be aware of, which is only you? I understand how hard that can be to control and instantly be in a position where when you pause, the person you are making sure is aware of themselves, first, and then other surroundings second is what is happening for you to be authentically aware.

Continue to practice with yourself on this. Start pacing yourself to a slower rate of being, and catch yourself returning your instant awareness to your own body, mind, and spirit to shift into the moment of you. Serve and return.

Following this, a beautiful part of keeping you in this awareness is acknowledging that your body will attempt to hijack you, and this is where you keep in mind: you have you, and you are going to tell yourself, "Hey! I am acknowledging myself in this moment of awareness for myself being as I am. My body is safe and [insert whatever it may be that you want you to be aware of] you got this!"

Acknowledging you with you is vital for the rest of the universe to understand that you have a new way forward with the way of choice in voicing within yourself all the things you keep bringing to your awareness.

Last, accept that your own feelings are valid with how everything shows up. Accept that some things can change in your life within a moment that seems like it would never matter, but you matter.

So, in this self-acceptance process, let it go. Let the body and mind flow through it all. Don't hold back. Be vulnerable in every cellular sense that comes to the surface.

YOU ARE ENOUGH

Intuition • Isolation • Integration:

Have you ever felt like your heart is welled up with emotions so deep with gratitude and love that could release tears? That's how I know my intuition is correct about what truth is from knowing, feeling, and embodying the sense of this.

Pace yourself with this, though.

The more it comes into tune with your Self, isolation from everything, or everyone around you becomes more present, as you become more aware of your presence to Self.

When you come to this moment, that is when you truly need to be in silence, to listen for all the wonderful awareness of truths that echo and flow through your body, mind, and spirit! Mm! It is inspiring and natural buzzing within, filled with authentic love for one's Self.

Transcend • Truth • Transformation:

Going beyond any direction can be the most satisfying experience. When you have met the parts of you that know where they're going, from where they have been, this is where you meet yourself in deep feelings and depths.

Trust what you feel, not what you think. Feelings let you know what the real energy of the dynamic is. Thoughts tend to lead you astray, always thinking there is a problem that needs resolution. Know how your authentic yes or no response comes from within you feeling it where your heart is.

Transformation is infinite. I have heard many express that, "There is no change in them!" When in all reality, this is true, but also, have you made changes within yourself to see the transformation clearly enough that it's always been happening all along? Humans are made up of 60% water on average, and that water plays a critical role in numerous bodily functions, such as regulating temperature, transporting nutrients, and removing waste. We are all transforming, constantly. It's natural. Be aware of your shifts. Deal, heal, and wheel your body, mind, and spirit as one before you go pointing energy somewhere or on someone else.

Hope • Help • Haven:

Hope is the chosen, middle name, for my daughter. It originated from her great-great-grandmother on my side and a first cousin, on her father's side, who had passed within a month, after birth from Trisomy 18, meaning there was an extra chromosome produced during conception. The middle name, Hope, fits my daughter, and she has been an angelic guardian being for me, who has taught me how to be a loving and virtuous Womban.

The help I have given and received has been the most encouraging find to be with having hope. Moments when I felt things would be the end, it truly was the beginning when I started being clear and speaking up, when I did, authentically need help, when it was life or death.

Speak up for yourself.

There WILL be an energy that will come.

This is what I call your Self Haven. The place of safety that does come from inside yourself. Seeking safety, security, stability, and sanity outside of yourself is honestly a cry for help. Learning how to handle the regulation of what a home is, inside yourself, is where the Self Haven naturally leads to.

Choice • Consideration • Connection:

Every movement made forward is always given the opportunity of a choice or choices.

I find that many, when faced with these, can feel a flare in their hands, which one do I choose and take hold of?

Choices follow with also taking accountability for the choice once you do make one. Which, for some, is the even greater difference in, once again, which one?

While sitting and playing out all the scenarios, I would love for humans to be open to choosing one, taking action, and seeing what happens!

I have a strong faith that no matter the choice, as long as you choose, you will always learn something either way, and that is the beauty in it all!

Consider yourself through this process. It is one of the major parts of respecting what you'll become of this choice.

Many miss this little part in the process of choices, and it is something I have learned in all aspects of choice is a huge privilege to give yourself.

Because in the end, it is you that should always be highly considered, and others will recognize you doing this, which leads to them choosing to consider themselves and it ends with everyone knowing what respect feels like as well!

Win! Win!

When all of this starts to happen, a connection will begin to come to light.

Connection with yourself is such a powerful feeling and intriguing thing that I love immensely.

For me, connecting with myself in all the aspects of character development is something I have grown from being able to relate with myself in the spaces that seem detrimental and the ones that are freely magical!

Who doesn't want to feel self-conscious and connected in all ways, dark and light, to then be able to meet someone where anything that they share with you, in all forms, you can truly feel yourself, where the connection blossoms?

It feels safe.

It feels secure.

It feels stable.

It feels sane.

It feels sound.

It feels solid.

Open • Observation • Ownership:

Opening doors after having them closed for so long can cause many turbulent conditions because deep inside, we are all on a path of creating new doors of opportunities to flow in. We must first discover what our hearts are calling in, be willing to breathe and deeply listen in order for this moment of truth with open doors, heart, mind, and spirit.

Observing this moment experienced has to be as open as possible within. I have learned that if I continue to observe everything outside of me, I begin absorbing it, and it takes me out of what is called, "homeostasis," by which living organisms maintain stable internal conditions, despite external changes. In essence, it is the body's way of keeping its internal environment balanced and functioning optimally. Go within. Observe how you are embodying. Absorb how you feel. Know it's time to release and renew YOU!

I love this part of being human! Claiming your ownership of YOU! Going through all these emotions of observing yourself where you are, opening up to the truth of claiming each part of where YOU, not anyone else, felt, but what you felt was taken from you, when in all existence, it was given for you to receive at the highest version of your SELF!

I choose to say daily, "I take back my power, release what does not serve me in energy, return to sender, and I claim me!"

Urges • Unique • Union:

It all comes rushing from all directions. Having urges can lead you to indicators within you that are calling to be connected with. The parts that dissolve the energy of attention when you choose to focus on the sudden urge when it arises.

It's all yours to be one with this. Keep asking yourself all the questions that make the appearance of you be known, felt, and seen for who you really are. As you continue to keep curious, while asking yourself what that is—you'll form something unique, specific for you!

When connecting the rushes of feelings, know the essence of what it will begin to feel as one, that togetherness of your being as an observer of you, that is within the union, and that divine will is sacred.

Righteous • Resistance • Remember:

Being conscientious, just, and virtuous. A feeling I choose to act with integrity, following committed rituals and doing what is true, even when it's difficult. In a spiritual sense, it can also mean being in a state of harmony with a higher power or the universe.

This also can come with the added pressure, which can lead to resistance. How many times have I had to keep my focus forward, taking a leap of faith, even when the tides of the currency seem higher than I can see through?

I have learned that calmer waters always flow through. This has come from choosing to find different ways with how I breathe, how I sound when I'm feeling, or when I am in a reflecting state that brings the air into my thought, that says, "Do you remember?" This follows with listening to the song, "A Reminder," by Trevor Hall. His music brought me through a lot of times when I needed to hear me again through song. I always listen to music as a reflection of my own soul versus attaching it to a moment in time with another.

Activate • Articulate • Accountability:

I have had to sit through many parts of myself where I never felt a thing. This can be excruciating for the nervous system. What changed? Me. I chose me. Instead of being triggered by everything that was so traumatic and transforming it to activate the brain cells to create something I felt, what was always inside of me, to begin with.

Finding these feelings was truly something I had to be clear on as I connected with me in my own way. Not every person has the same body, mind, and spirit. That was something that I also had to learn to articulate in the first instance as well.

Through this, I learned a valuable lesson to my own self-worth. It was a key part of my life; for every choice I made— I was held accountable for what happened. When you choose you, you choose to be accountable. Damn, it felt so igniting!

Give • God • Gratitude:

"What you give is what you get." This statement couldn't be more true. For me, "give," means allowing yourself to receive and accept the love, care, and compassion that you need right now. It's about surrendering to your emotions and letting go of the need to control or change the situation. By giving in to your feelings, you're giving yourself permission to heal, to feel, and to be vulnerable. It's a beautiful act of self-love and acceptance. Because what goes around, comes around, and I view all sides as a beautiful gift.

There was a moment in my life when I felt I couldn't even say, "God." I grew up in a community where it was written everywhere, yet if it was said, you're saying it "in vain." As I have grown, I had a once close friend who kept saying it in a way that I realized, "Oh, my community never taught me the difference in how you say God with your energy and learn to use in give, receive, and surrender." I had quite the spiritual awakening after I chose to accept how I know, feel, and embody God. God is within me. God is my heart. The strength I am given through each step I take is one I always receive enlightening gifts.

Energy • Efficiency • Enlightenment:

As a celestial bridge guide, I see energy as the vibrational frequency that surrounds and flows through everything in the universe. Spiritually, energy refers to the subtle, intangible forces that shape our experiences, emotions, and connections. It's the essence of life, the spark that animates us, and the thread that weaves us together. In a spiritual sense, energy is about the quality of our being, our intentions, and our resonance with the world around us. It's the unseen, yet deeply felt, dimension of our existence.

Being efficient within this, for me, can be a deep dive into accomplishing tasks with flair and precision. Being naturally attuned to the energies of creativity, passion, and self-expression. When you're working efficiently, you're likely tapping into your inner spark, channeling your energy into productive outlets. I can be more focused on tangible results and practical applications, which can help me stay grounded and motivated. I always realign my energy by asking, "How do you feel when you're in a state of flow, and your energy is aligned with your goals?" Because I want all my energy to be in a state of balance and harmony where it is flowing through me immensely!

Believe • Behavior • Boundaries:

It truly takes what you believe in for yourself with your values and worth to gain the trust you deserve from choosing to the depths of every part of your being as a human.

From the beginning of my remembrance, I recall the feeling that my life was filled with magic. That simple fact of knowing what I desire in life will always be there for me. It's wild in the sense of an experience that can shift that feeling of what you believe to where it has you completely abandoning the beliefs that you created in your mind.

This shift for me began around the age of 4–5 years of age. So young, resilient, and needing conscious guidance from a world that was intended for safety, security, stability, and sanity.

That wasn't the case, and I have learned that it was like this for most humans in my life that I have been in connection with to find that we all have a pivotal moment where that dis-easement comes in, and we have to find a way in our own to regulate.

Once again, this often never happens for most. Where they have an environment that supports regulation, co-regulation, or auto-regulation in a sense, their behavior can change and become very daunting to one's self.

It can turn into an emotional state that can cause you to lose your energy, believing you have a way of coursing your life in your purpose that brings you peace.

Those behaviors are created in a wide variety of situations that can cause your body and mind to become overwhelmed.

How far do we let this go?

I have been in sittings of this with myself and a massive scale.

What have I learned?

BOUNDARIES.

Not only within myself, but the ones I needed to start doing for myself with everything and everyone.

What do boundaries feel like?

This gets me into a space of my life where I really had to revert back to that inner child who existed and created magic, before I chose to abandon myself in the space where I lacked a proper sense of belief.

My nervous system had to adapt.

My body's nervous system had to believe that my behavior was different and that I could hold healthy boundaries physically, mentally, and emotionally first, before any other relationship with myself that was external could flow through in what I wanted.

It was not my position to change others.

It is alright if I say no.

It is alright if others say no.

My responsibility is me, and only me.

Others are their own responsibility.

I do not have to anticipate the needs of others.

Others do not have to anticipate the needs of me.

There is bound to be a difference of opinion; reciprocate this.

Because we both have the right to our own feelings.

We are enough as we are.

Empower • Evolve • Explore:

Confidence and self-assurance are key when building empowerment!

That gut instinct!

Being empowered means taking ownership of your life, choices, and emotions. It's about trusting yourself, your intuition, and your abilities.

Here are a few tips to help you feel more empowered: set clear boundaries, practice self-care, focus on your strengths, and celebrate your accomplishments.

Remember, empowerment is a journey, not a destination.

What's one area in your life where you'd like to feel more empowered, and what's one step you can take today to move towards that?

I have found that evolving from a place of empowerment means continuing to refine your self-awareness, letting go of limitations, and embracing new experiences. It's about recognizing that empowerment is not a fixed state, but a dynamic process that requires ongoing effort and commitment.

Here are a few tips to help you evolve from empowerment: practice self-reflection, challenge your assumptions, and seek out new knowledge and skills.

Remember, evolution is a lifelong journey, and it's okay to take it one step at a time.

What's one area in your life where you'd like to evolve from empowerment, and what's one step you can take today to move towards that?

This takes me to exploring from a place of empowerment and evolution. It means embracing your inner wisdom, trusting your instincts, and being open to new possibilities.

It's about recognizing that you're not limited by your current circumstances and that you have the power to create the life you desire.

Here are a few tips to help you explore empowerment and evolution: practice mindfulness, set intentions, and take bold action towards your dreams.

Daring • Dream • Destiny:

Let us begin with what daring means to me and that is being courageous, taking risks, and stepping out of your comfort zone. It's about embracing uncertainty and trusting that you'll grow and learn from the experience.

What's one area in your life where you feel the urge to be more daring?

This goes into the parts of the dream you have for yourself!

I am naturally inclined towards creativity and imagination. Dreaming more can mean allowing yourself to tap into your subconscious mind, exploring your deepest desires, and trusting your intuition. This brings things together in ways of being conscious and accepting things can become your reality!

What's one thing you'd like to dream more about or achieve in your waking life?

Your life's purpose and direction have an immense impact upon your awakening. For me, divine intervention leads to a greater destiny, which I refer to as the unique path you're meant to follow, the experiences you're meant to have, and the lessons you're meant to learn. It's about aligning with your higher self and fulfilling your soul's intentions.

Awakening • Avatar • Author:

What does it mean to awaken to your spiritual truth? Heavy question to sit with, but one you must. Wake up before the sun rises and then sit with the sun as it does. Awakening to the truth can be a profound experience, especially for me, who's naturally drawn to authenticity and honesty. It means shedding light on illusions, misconceptions, or unconscious patterns that may be holding me back. I know by choosing this path, I am awakening to a deeper understanding of my emotional needs and desires, and how they relate to my sense of security and comfort.

Ready for a fresh perspective, a new understanding, or a significant change. It's like a fruit that's ripe for picking—it's ready to be harvested, and its true potential can be revealed. This involves exploring the depths of your own psyche, confronting fears or insecurities, and emerging stronger and more self-aware. Connecting to the inner spark and creativity. Your avatar represents your highest, most authentic self—the embodiment of your passions, values, and soul purpose. Awakening your avatar means tapping into that inner wisdom, embracing your unique gifts, and unleashing your full potential. What does your avatar look like, and what qualities do you want to embody in your daily life?

Rebirth • Revealed • Released:

Rebirth is a profound experience, especially during spiritual awakening! It's like a phoenix rising from the ashes, where the old story of you is transformed, and a new, radiant one emerges. In my special moment, rebirth has felt like a burst of creative energy, a renewed sense of purpose, and a deeper connection to my inner golden light. You might feel like you're shedding old patterns, beliefs, or identities that no longer serve you, making way for a fresh, more authentic expression of yourself. The sense of authority, structure, and responsibility, aligning them with your higher purpose. It is essential and freeing.

As you emerge into this new, rebirthed version of yourself, many hidden aspects can be revealed! This emerging might uncover hidden talents, passions, or creative expressions that were waiting to be unleashed. You might discover innovative ways to structure your life, career, or relationships, bringing a sense of revolution and progress. This rebirth could also reveal deeper truths about your past, your relationships, or your sense of identity, allowing you to integrate these insights and move forward with greater wisdom and clarity. What secrets or surprises do you sense are waiting to be revealed as you emerge into this new chapter of your life?

I have asked myself to release the secrets that have been hidden. I know I do my best to keep them safe, but I feel there is a space between this and truly allowing yourself to let it go. Releasing the need for control or perfection can be a liberating experience, especially for me, and still, I have to be in alignment and refocus every moment. One way to start is by acknowledging that perfection is an illusion, and that it's okay to make mistakes. Focus on practical, tangible steps towards releasing control, like delegating tasks or surrendering to the natural flow of events. You could also try embracing the beauty of imperfection, celebrating the uniqueness and character that comes with being human. Journaling, meditation, or any type of creative activity has gotten me through some very interesting experiences of release.

Keep • Kind • Karmic:

KEEP YOUR CHIN UP! Staying in a humble awakening space is a beautiful intention, especially if you are naturally inclined towards growth and self-awareness! To maintain this space, you might focus on cultivating gratitude, recognizing the interconnectedness of all things, and staying open to new insights and perspectives. Prioritize self-care, nurturing, and emotional intelligence, allowing yourself to stay grounded and receptive to the present moment. What daily practices or rituals can you commit to, to keep yourself in a humble, awakened state, and stay connected to your heart and soul?

Choose to be kind. Choosing kindness is a beautiful path, the warmth and joy that you can experience within yourself that will help others can be life-changing and transform into big moments. Recognize that everyone is on their own journey and deserves love and support. You might also practice self-compassion, treating yourself with the same kindness and gentleness that you would offer to a dear friend. It's a circle of kindness, love, and respect.

Because when you have been through a lot in life, you learn the concept of karma! I have learned I am naturally drawn to the idea of cosmic balance and the law of cause and effect. Karmic refers to the idea that our actions, thoughts, and intentions have consequences, and that we must face the repercussions of our choices in this life or the next. Being particularly aware of the karmic debts you can accumulate, and the need to take responsibility for your actions and make amends when necessary. What karmic lessons or patterns do you feel you're currently working through, and how can you use this awareness to create positive change in your life?

There is love and light within each part of our unfolding hearts. As I send this message for you to open those parts up, know you are not alone, because we are, all one

— *Lindsey Pollock*

Awakened Avatar Author

HEART ENERGY X ME

Nikki Girard

*Founder and CEO, Visionary Entrepreneur,
2x Best-Selling Author & Exponential Transformation
Manifestation Expert*

Nikki Girard, a visionary entrepreneur, exponential transformation & manifestation expert, 2x Amazon & #1 international bestselling Author.

Founder and CEO of 'Heart Energy X Me,' she combines over 38 years of experience with neuroscience, psychology, coaching, and quantum energy engineering.

A Force Awards nominee for Top 10 Entrepreneurs to Watch in 2025, a 2-time Executive Contributor-now Senior Executive Contributor for Brainz Magazine, Expert Panelist, prestigious CREA Global Awards nominee, and 2-time Brainz Magazine 500 Global List awardee - standing alongside luminaries Les Brown, Jay Shetty, Marisa Peer, Oprah Winfrey, Rachel Pailing, Jim Kwik, Lewis Howes and more.

A sought-after speaker and creator of the groundbreaking 'High AF Advantage,' Nikki challenges industry norms with innovative methodologies. Her passion for empowering clients to achieve sustainable success is making a lasting impact, positioning her as a true pioneer and inspiration in the field.

https://highafadvantage.com/
https://www.linkedin.com/in/nikki-girard-962601207
https://www.facebook.com/nikki.girard.311

Manifestation on Steroids

Revealing the Untold Secrets with the 'High AF Advantage'

By Nikki Girard

As ambitious entrepreneurs, executives, or thought leaders, you understand the importance of maximizing productivity, enhancing resilience, and making strategic decisions.

Stay ahead of the curve in today's fast-paced competitive world and transform your journey with Nikki's expert guidance.

The *'High AF Advantage'* is specifically designed to meet the unique needs of driven individuals like you.

It provides a comprehensive holistic approach to manifestation and personal & professional growth.

By mastering the four pillars of the *'High AF Advantage,'* you'll unlock your full potential, allowing you to achieve extraordinary success and fulfillment in both your personal and professional life.

Embrace the *'High AF Advantage'* and transform your life today.

So…are you ready to shatter your limitations and unleash your true potential?

It's time to turbocharge your success and transform your reality.

Discover how to tap into your brain's full potential, smash through subconscious blocks, and skyrocket productivity by up to 500%.

With this innovative process, you'll master your emotions, cultivate resilience, and create meaningful connections.

Gain practical skills, cosmic alignment, and unparalleled success in every area of your life.

Start now & invest in yourself and your future with the *__High AF Advantage__* today.

Get ready to dominate your industry and transform your reality!

Place Your Cosmic Order: Unleash the Power of the Universe

Imagine turning your wildest dreams into reality. This is the world of cosmic orders, where intentions and alignment with universal forces manifest success and prosperity.

With the *__'High AF Advantage,'__* individuals harness their inner power by aligning with cosmic principles.

Understanding cosmic laws, such as the *Law of Vibration, Law of Attraction, and Law of Manifestation,* you can tap into limitless potential.

To place your cosmic order, set clear and focused intentions. Visualize your desired outcome, infusing positive energy and emotion. Release resistance, take aligned action, and trust the universe's support.

By aligning your cosmic order with the '*High AF Advantage*' method, you can manifest your dream life.

Enhance manifestation potential by integrating the **four key pillars**: *Igniting Peak Brain Performance, Flow State Sweet Spot, Cultivating Resilience, and Self & Success Mastery.*

_____

Impact of Change

Our words, thoughts are like brushstrokes on a blank canvas

A grand mosaic of voices, a symphony of vibrant and bold

A Collective wisdom,
a masterpiece of change, a story untold, waiting & wanting to unfold

Behold the path, which lays before us, within us

The Oasis, where minds gather, borders erasing

A global village, with our round table wide

Impact embraced, sparking the challenge, the change

For our future bright, a beacon of light, which we hold, our knowing guide

From every corner of this earth, we rise

A choir of voices, singing into existence the song, which moulds the progress, comes to the solace of mankind's prize

The dance of destiny, on a canvas of soul

Let our symphony, eternal, echo far and near, we hear

As the seeds of change, we plant and sow,

For in the Oasis, we seek,

A mosaic of progress, which we lead…

the - Impact of Change - *Written by Nikki Girard-2025*

____

Embracing the Transformative Power of the High AF Advantage: Harnessing Your Full Potential

In a world saturated with manifestation techniques, the **'High AF Advantage'** stands out as a *revolutionary approach* to achieving extraordinary success.

This innovative system harnesses four interconnected pillars, each designed to cultivate different aspects of personal and professional growth.

Combined with the **CSI-Quantum Style** fundamentals and the groundbreaking **Quantum Flex method**, these elements form a cohesive and transformative experience.

The **CSI-Quantum Style** process unifies the '*High AF Advantage*,' while **Quantum Flex** empowers individuals to confidently leap into their desired reality.

As you embark on this journey, expect tangible benefits from each component:

With the '*High AF Advantage*,' you'll unleash your true potential and revolutionize your path to success.

- **Igniting Peak Brain Performance**—*will grant you laser-like focus, enhanced mental clarity, and improved concentration, enabling you to tackle tasks with precision and efficiency.*

- **Flow State Sweet Spot**—*will help you access a state of heightened creativity and productivity, maximizing your time and energy for optimal results. Increase productivity by up to 500%.*

- **Cultivating Resilience**—*will equip you with the mental fortitude to overcome challenges, learn from setbacks, and adapt to any situation with confidence and determination.*

- **Self & Success Mastery**—*will empower you to gain a deep understanding of your unique strengths and abilities, enabling you to manifest your dreams and reach new heights of success and fulfillment.*

Get ready to embrace the life-changing power and transform your reality today!

Welcome to the 'Freedom Portal' with the 'High AF Advantage'

The '**Freedom Portal**,' is where the '*High AF Advantage*' empowers you to unleash your full manifestation potential.

As you explore this groundbreaking approach, discover a comprehensive method that transcends trends.

By integrating unique techniques, the **High AF Advantage** offers a path to self-mastery and success that is as potent as it is transformative.

Shatter limitations and manifest your boldest dreams.

With the '**High AF Advantage**,' you'll embark on a life-changing journey, tapping into manifestation's full power and realizing your true potential for remarkable achievements.

Meet Nikki Girard: Transformational Manifestation Expert and 'High AF Advantage' Creator

Nikki Girard, a visionary entrepreneur, is a transformational manifestation expert committed to helping others reach their full potential.

As a **Brainz Magazine Senior Executive Contributor, Expert Panelist and prestigious CREA Global Awards nominee,** standing alongside luminary figures such as Les Brown, Jay Shetty, Marisa Peer, Oprah Winfrey, Rachel Pailing, Jim Kwik, Lewis Howes and more. *Discover more: Brainz info*

As the **Founder and CEO of Heart Energy X Me**, Nikki has devoted over 38-plus years towards studying Human Behavior & Design, Consciousness, Manifestation Techniques, and more.

Driven by personal experiences, she's developed cutting-edge strategies to empower individuals and guide businesses to sustainable growth.

Nikki actively learns from thought leaders to stay at the forefront of her field. Invited to speak worldwide *from India to Paris, New York to Spain, and beyond* on topics like *Business Leadership, Entrepreneurship, Positive Psychiatry,* and more.

Her expertise combines methodologies, neuroscience, psychology, coaching, and quantum energy engineering.

Nikki's *'High AF Advantage'* empowers clients to achieve sustainable success and personal fulfillment through a transformational approach.

By *'stepping into their comfort zone,'* clients cultivate confidence and inner strength, fostering a sense of comfort alongside growth.

Her commitment to redefining personal growth and success establishes her as a leading authority and beacon of inspiration in the entrepreneurial world.

Experience the life-changing benefits of the *'High AF Advantage'* unlock your potential with Nikki Girard's guidance and expertise.

Nikki's always excited to join initiatives like the **Oneness Foundation**—*Magic School for Teens & Kids*—a *free online ascension platform.*

Force Magazine's: Force Awards Nomination—Top 10 Entrepreneurs to Watch for in 2025.

Forbes Magazine: The Entrepreneur of Impact Competition - *Daymond John, FUBU founder, and Shark Tank investor, alongside Mary Hagen, CEO of Colossal Fundraisers, supporting entrepreneurs while helping GENYOUth promote kids' well-being.*

Redefining the Comfort Zone: Entrepreneurship/Coaching

While traditional coaching often stresses *'stepping out of one's comfort zone'* to grow, Nikki Girard offers refreshing alternatives with her groundbreaking *'High AF Advantage'* approach.

Instead of pushing individuals beyond their limits, her method empowers them to *'step into their comfort zone,'* cultivating self-confidence and inner strength that propels them towards their highest aspirations and potential.

By focusing on balance and alignment within the *comfort zone* before venturing into new experiences and opportunities,

Nikki's approach prioritizes self-love, mental resilience, and coherence.

This shift in perspective allows clients to confidently step into the world, fostering personal growth and transformation.

Equipped with the necessary tools and techniques, individuals are better prepared to face challenges and pursue their goals with clarity and focus, transforming the **comfort zone** into a source of empowerment and progress.

Conquering Entrepreneurial Challenges with the High AF Advantage

Entrepreneurship presents unique challenges, requiring resilience and adaptability.

The *'High AF Advantage'* offers a powerful process to overcome these obstacles, with each pillar addressing crucial aspects of business growth and success.

Common challenges faced by entrepreneurs stem from unproductive thoughts and behaviors hindering growth.

Identifying these patterns is the first step to finding effective solutions, such as:

1. **Procrastination**: Entrepreneurs often struggle with putting off important tasks or avoiding difficult conversations, leading to missed opportunities and strained relationships.

2. **Rumination**: Overthinking and worrying about negative outcomes can paralyze leaders with indecision, affecting well-being and causing missed opportunities.

3. **Freezing under pressure**: Stress may cause business owners to freeze during critical presentations or negotiations, preventing them from showcasing their potential.

4. **Negative self-talk**: Internal negative communication can erode confidence and limit risk-taking abilities.

By applying the four interconnected pillars of the **'High AF Advantage'**, entrepreneurs can develop the necessary skills and strategies to tackle these challenges and create lasting success.

This combination bridges methodologies, including *four key pillars integration, along with the Conscious Success Integration*—**C.S.I Quantum Style** *foundational fundamentals, and the* **Quantum Flex** *method*.

Quantum Flex catalyzes transformation, embodying limitless potential and empowering clients to break through barriers and achieve extraordinary success.

Drawing on **Quantum Flex's** adaptability and strength, individuals can make **quantum leaps** into their desired reality, harnessing the full potential of their intentions and desires.

The **Conscious Success Integration** component unifies these elements into a cohesive, powerful system for clients to embark on a journey towards unparalleled abundance and personal fulfillment.

Quantum Bio Bites: Empowering Clients for Success

Nikki's dedication to helping clients tap into their full potential and achieve lasting transformation is evident within her coaching practice.

She showcases a strong commitment to empowering them and ensuring they have the tools necessary to thrive in all aspects of their success journey.

Nikki's coaching practice features innovative techniques like '**Quantum Bio Bites**,' combining practical exercises and self-awareness to unlock clients' mental potential.

These methods help individuals transition from **quantum possibility to quantitative abundance**, *aligning their internal world, enhancing intuition, and boosting self-awareness.*

Client success stories showcase the transformative power of Nikki's coaching and the '**High AF Advantage**' *elite VIP one to one experience.*

Here are a just few examples of clients thrilled with their success journeys:

- **Meet Ashley**, The Mompreneur Coach & Best Selling Author:

'Working with Nikki Girard has been a game-changer. Her extensive knowledge and expertise make her a literal walking encyclopedia.

'The 'High AF Advantage' elite VIP 1-1 experience provides valuable insights and methodologies, and the integration process is seamless and easy.

'Nikki's dedication to her clients' success is evident—she's there each step of the way. Connect with Nikki, and watch the transformation!'

- ***Meet Hysam***, Entrepreneur/Personal Development & Attraction Marketing:

'I praise Nikki Girard's deep understanding of the Quantum realm; I find that I can balance my personal & Business life with ease, with laser focus, and in alignment.

'I continue to achieve higher aspirations. Nikki's ability to resonate with each client at their level has catapulted my success, and I now consistently hit over 100,000 USD months!

'I recommend the 'High AF Advantage' elite VIP 1-1 experience for everyone looking to truly level up and reach crazy abundance.'

Discover more inspiring success stories and learn about the **'High AF Advantage'** *at* highafadvantage.com.

This approach revolutionizes manifestation, unleashing your innate ability to create your dream life.

The **'High AF Advantage'** rests on four pillars, each representing a vital aspect of the manifestation process.

In the next section, we'll delve into the first pillar, setting the stage for a deeper understanding of this powerful technique.

The journey begins with the exploration of the first pillar...

PILLAR 1: Peak Brain Performance—Boost productivity by up to 500%

The first pillar of the *'High AF Advantage,'* Peak Brain Performance, emphasizes the critical role our mental faculties play in the manifestation process.

Harnessing the power of mindfulness practices, cognitive-behavioral techniques, and energy work, individuals can optimize their mental capabilities and dissolve subconscious barriers hindering their manifestation efforts.

Through Nikki's expert guidance, clients learn to rewire their neural pathways and cultivate a mindset primed for manifestation.

As clients integrate Peak Brain Performance into their daily routine, they discover newfound potential within themselves, enabling their desires to take form with unprecedented ease and efficiency.

The **'High AF Advantage'** *hinges on the strategic integration of four key pillars.*

This is coupled with the robust foundation provided by Nikki's Conscious Success Integration **C.S.I-Quantum Style** *foundational fundamentals, and the dynamic force that is* **Quantum Flex.**

Quantum Flex serves as the catalyst for transformation, embodying the limitless potential and possibilities that lie within each individual.

As the secret weapon that supercharges manifestation, **Quantum Flex** equips clients with the necessary tools to break through barriers and achieve extraordinary success and abundance.

Drawing on the adaptability and strength cultivated through **Quantum Flex** *method*, individuals are empowered to make **quantum leaps** into their desired reality, harnessing the full potential of their intentions and desires.

Meanwhile, the **Conscious Success Integration** component acts as a unifying force, seamlessly binding the various elements of the **'High AF Advantage'** method into an interconnected cohesive whole.

This powerful fusion of techniques creates a launching pad for clients to embark on their journey toward unparalleled success and personal fulfillment.

PILLAR 2: Flow State Sweet Spot

Harnessing the **Flow State Sweet Spot** focuses on tapping into the powerful mental state where individuals experience heightened creativity, productivity, and focus.

Through Nikki's mentorship and guidance, individuals learn to cultivate this optimal state of consciousness, enabling them to channel their energies effectively and efficiently toward their goals and break down barriers that may have once seemed insurmountable.

As clients embrace the **Flow State Sweet Spot** as an integral part of their daily practice, they not only **manifest their desires** with greater ease but also experience a heightened sense of fulfillment and purpose.

As we delve further into the **'High AF Advantage,'** *it becomes evident that this groundbreaking approach provides a clear and* **comprehensive roadmap to manifestation success.**

Each pillar builds upon the last, creating a solid foundation for individuals to transform their dreams into reality.

Pillar 3: Cultivating Resilience for Manifestation Success

Building upon the previous pillars, resilience—the **third pillar** of this innovative method—equips individuals with the mental fortitude to face challenges and setbacks head-on during their manifestation journey.

Through Nikki's expertise and guidance, clients learn to cultivate resilience by embracing a growth mindset and developing essential coping strategies.

By **nurturing a growth mindset,** individuals learn to view adversity as opportunities for personal and professional growth, fostering adaptability and perseverance in the face of obstacles.

Nikki emphasizes the importance of **reframing challenges,** *practicing self-compassion, and seeking support from mentors or peers as essential strategies for building resilience.*

With a strong support system in place, individuals can overcome barriers with greater ease, turning setbacks into stepping stones on the path toward success.

The '**High AF Advantage**' stands as a testament to the power of a comprehensive, results-driven approach to manifestation.

INSPIRE HER

By integrating these powerful methodologies into their daily lives, individuals are empowered to achieve extraordinary success, turning their dreams into reality with unwavering determination.

Pillar 4: Unlocking the Power of Self and Success Mastery

By integrating the principles of all four pillars, individuals can cultivate the skills, mindset, and confidence necessary to propel their results to new heights.

Nikki challenges her clients to combine the foundational fundamentals of the *'High AF Advantage'* and unlock the secrets to manifesting a life of true abundance.

At the heart of this process lies a focus on self-awareness, emotional intelligence, and strategic action-taking.

*By honing these essential qualities and aligning them with their deepest desires, individuals can **tap into the full power of manifestation**, transforming it from an elusive concept into a natural and effortless part of their daily lives.*

Harnessing balance and alignment leads to increased resilience when faced with life's challenges, enhanced decision-making abilities, and improved overall well-being.

By focusing on creating a balanced '***Harmonic Balance Biosphere***,' individuals can experience positive transformations in all aspects of their lives.

Achieving a ***harmonious balance*** within oneself can lead to a range of benefits. With a focus on the ***interconnectedness of mind, body, and spirit,*** individuals develop greater resilience, make better decisions, and foster a strong sense of well-being.

As a result, they become better equipped to face challenges and seizing opportunities, ultimately driving exponential personal and professional growth.

The Power of Balance: Enhancing Personal Growth and Success

Harnessing balance and alignment can lead to increased resilience when faced with life's challenges, enhanced decision-making abilities, and improved overall well-being.

By focusing on creating a balanced **'Harmonic Balance Biosphere,'** *individuals can experience positive transformations in all aspects of their lives.*

This **holistic approach** *not only strengthens one's ability to navigate adversity but also contributes to overall personal growth and success.*

Achieving a harmonious balance within oneself can lead to a range of benefits.

Energy Flows Where Focus Goes

With a focus on the interconnectedness
and emphasizing the mind-body-spirit connection, individuals enhance resilience, decision-making, and well-being.

This increased capacity enables them to tackle challenges and seize opportunities, fueling personal and professional growth.

The Interconnected Path to Success: Coherence, Synchronicity, and Flow State

Achieving alignment begins with understanding and experiencing coherence, synchronicity, and flow state.

By embracing these concepts and cultivating an interconnected approach to personal growth and success, individuals can create a more harmonious and fulfilling life.

Coherence *refers to the state of internal harmony and order within an individual. It involves aligning one's thoughts, emotions, and actions to create a sense of unity and purpose.*

Synchronicity *describes the phenomenon of meaningful coincidences that occur in life, providing guidance and confirmation of one's path.*

These occurrences often act as signposts, indicating alignment with one's goals and intentions.

Flow State is the optimal psychological state where individuals become fully immersed in an activity, experiencing heightened focus and performance.

This state is often associated with feelings of enjoyment, creativity, and a sense of effortlessness.

Conscious Growth: The Path to Empowered Living

Developing self-awareness and a sense of empowerment is crucial for fostering a strong sense of purpose and direction.

By taking ownership of one's life, individuals can align with their true desires and aspirations.

This section highlights the importance of cultivating consciousness and personal empowerment in the journey toward personal growth and success.

1. ***Cultivating Self-Awareness:*** Self-awareness serves as the foundation of personal empowerment.

By understanding one's strengths, weaknesses, values, and beliefs, individuals can make informed decisions and take purposeful action.

Techniques such as meditation, journaling, and seeking mentorship or coaching can help increase self-awareness.

2. ***Embracing Responsibility:*** Taking ownership of one's life is key to personal empowerment.

This involves acknowledging one's role in shaping their experiences and being accountable for their actions.

Embracing responsibility empowers individuals to make conscious choices that align with their goals and aspirations.

3. ***Setting Purpose-Driven Goals:*** Clear, purpose-driven goals provide a sense of direction and motivation.

By aligning goals with personal values and aspirations, individuals can tap into their inner motivation and pursue meaningful achievements.

4. ***Building Resilience:*** Developing resilience allows individuals to face challenges with confidence and adaptability.

By learning from setbacks, embracing change, and maintaining a positive mindset, individuals can build resilience and persist in the face of adversity.

The 'High AF Advantage': The New Coaching Revolution

The '*High AF Advantage*,' with its unique blend of neuroscience, psychology, and energy work, can be *considered* **a game-changer in the industry.**

By addressing the evolving needs and challenges faced by individuals and organizations, Nikki's method offers a comprehensive and *holistic approach* to personal and professional growth.

As more people and businesses recognize the power of harnessing the **four key pillars** *of the '**High AF Advantage**,' it will become an indispensable tool for anyone looking to thrive in an increasingly complex and competitive world.*

*The '**High AF Advantage**' represents the pinnacle of personal development, empowering individuals and organizations to achieve their full potential and reach new heights of success.*

As Nikki's influence in the field of manifestation continues to expand, she is preparing to release highly-anticipated books—*The Heart of a Mother* in May 2025, the ***High AF Advantage*** solo book in July 2025 and *I Am Quantum One* : Humanity's Guide to Thrive releasing 2026

Stay informed about Nikki's work and access exclusive content by subscribing to her website, High AF Advantage.com

This platform offers invaluable resources for those on their manifestation journey.

Immerse yourself in the transformative power of the High AF Advantage by joining the Elite 1-1 VIP Experience or the upcoming exclusive Group program.

These programs provide practical tools and personalized guidance for extraordinary manifestation, backed by scientific methods.

As part of the *'High AF Advantage' community*, you'll connect with like-minded professionals dedicated to personal and professional growth.

Together, you'll explore limitless manifestation possibilities, break barriers, and create your dream life.

*'Nikki Girard is a truly exceptional coach, friend, and mentor.'—**Julie, Entrepreneur & Coach***

*'Nikki's 'High AF Advantage' is game-changing for business and personal growth.'—**Alex, Master Practitioner NLP, Trainer & Consultant***

*'Nikki's transformative coaching has been a life-changing blessing for me and my family.'—**Erik, Business Consultant***

'Nikki's strategies and tools are invaluable for leaders and entrepreneurs…'—**Chris, Entrepreneur & Corporate Sales**

The *'High AF Advantage'* empowers you to unleash your potential, defy limitations, and manifest your dream life.

In conclusion, the ***High AF Advantage*** is the epitome of personal development, enabling individuals and organizations to reach new levels of success.

It's a comprehensive guide for personal and professional transformation, providing a ***deep understanding of manifestation.***

With Nikki's guidance, clients gain the tools, knowledge, and confidence to overcome obstacles and achieve extraordinary results, ultimately *mastering manifestation* and creating their ideal lives.

Nikki's work is featured in various publications, including the #1 International Bestseller *Sassy Classy & Badassy*.

Stay updated on Nikki's work, exclusive content at *High AF Advantage.com* Unlock your full potential with the Elite *1-1 VIP Experience* or upcoming *Group program.*

Providing practical tools and personalized support to empower your manifestation journey.

With a focus on physiology and scientifically-backed methods, success is not only attainable but inevitable and repeatable.

Join the High AF Advantage community to explore limitless manifestation possibilities.

Connect with like-minded professionals, overcome obstacles, and create your ideal life.

Discover manifestation's full potential as a member.

Also, join Nikki's Podcast - The Round Table Oasis with co-hosts, Hector Brito, and Destin Scott,

Unveiling the Science and Data Behind—the 'High AF Advantage'

Nikki's work serves as a testament to the immense potential that lies at the intersection of understanding physiology, employing data-driven strategies, and harnessing the power of manifestation.

She adopts a scientific and holistic approach to personal growth, drawing upon cutting-edge research in neuroscience, psychology, and physiology to provide a clear roadmap for achieving extraordinary success.

Neuroscience and neuroplasticity play an integral role in comprehending time management and personal growth.

Neuroplasticity, referring to the brain's remarkable ability to adapt and change throughout one's life, enables the formation of new connections and pathways, facilitating the development of fresh habits and behaviors such as time management strategies.

Scientific studies substantiate that the brain can be trained to prioritize tasks and manage time more effectively.

Practicing sound time management techniques, like breaking tasks into manageable steps and establishing achievable goals, fortifies neural pathways associated with organization and focus.

This fosters enhanced efficiency in time management, brain performance, and overall productivity.

Nikki's methodology is deeply rooted in a comprehensive understanding of the body's stress response system and its impact on cognitive function, emotional regulation, and decision-making abilities.

By implementing scientifically-backed strategies to optimize these physiological processes, individuals can cultivate greater mental clarity, emotional intelligence, and overall performance.

Discover battle-tested methods that have been refined and validated to deliver pragmatic, real-world solutions.

Nikki's work expertly bridges the gap between empirical evidence and powerful manifestation practices, forging a unique and transformative path to attaining unparalleled success.

The *'High AF Advantage'* stands at the forefront of results coaching, offering a pioneering, revolutionary approach to personal and business development.

Unveiling the secrets to success long held by the 1%.

This methodology equips individuals with the tools necessary to transcend barriers and manifest their most audacious aspirations.

Unleashing Your Inner Quantum Power Ninja: The Path to Sustainable Success and Personal Fulfillment

The *secret to magnifying and multiplying your success* lies in recognizing and addressing the subconscious and energetic blocks that impede your true potential.

By pinpointing these hidden hurdles, you can tap into the transformative power of *'quantum jumping'* and turn your wildest dreams into *tangible realities*.

As esteemed **Law of Attraction teacher Abraham Hicks** *underscores, 'The most effective way to manifest your desires is to become a vibrational match to them.'*

In doing so, you open the door to the *infinite possibilities* of the universe and unleash your inner *'Quantum Power Ninja,'* setting the stage for a thrilling journey of self-discovery and unparalleled success.

Unveiling the Unseen: Unlocking Secrets Beyond 'The Secret'

Discover the **hidden insights** *that even the hit movie* **The Secret** *didn't divulge, and learn why clients are raving about the life-altering breakthroughs they've experienced under Nikki's expert guidance.*

As you embrace the transformative power of the **'High AF Advantage**,' you'll experience a remarkable boost in mental clarity, creativity, productivity, resilience, and self-mastery.

Simultaneously, stress will diminish, decision-making will become more precise, and **unparalleled abundance** will infuse every facet of your life.

To embark on your own **transformative journey,** connect with Nikki today at:
High AF Advantage.com and seize the opportunity for personal and business success.

As **renowned speaker and author Mel Robbins** *wisely advises, 'Stop hitting the snooze button on your life.'*

Instead, embrace the **quantum leap into a new reality**, where you'll become an unstoppable force, shaping your life on your terms and achieving extraordinary feats.

With Nikki and the **'High AF Advantage'** as your allies, the sky's the limit. Step into this life-changing methodology and watch your wildest dreams materialize before your very eyes.

Introducing an exciting new venture on the horizon.

Aura Sphere: Introducing a New Groundbreaking Venture

*Founded by the **dynamic duo of Nikki Girard and Nikolai Martin**, the visionary creators behind the groundbreaking **'Aura Sphere.'***

This **exciting venture** brings together a unique blend of expertise and passion for personal growth and transformation. **United by a shared mission**...

*Discover the **Aura Sphere**, founded by the unification of the **'High AF Advantage'**—Exponential Transformation methodologies and **'Mirror AI'**—advanced technological capabilities.*

*By harnessing the power of the **4 Key Pillars**: Igniting Peak Brain Performance, Flow State Sweet Spot, Cultivating Resilience, and Self & Success Mastery.*

We help individuals navigate every interaction through morals and ethics. *This **unique approach** improves their value and self-worth.*

This will also **revolutionize** the entrepreneurial and coaching landscapes, creating an unprecedented environment for growth, innovation, and transformation.

*Keep an eye out for the **Aura Sphere**!*

*Also discover **Cindy Witteman**, best-selling author and Founder & Editor-in-Chief of **FORCE Magazine**, sharing her expert recommendations for the High AF Advantage*

'Nikki Girard has a rare gift for blending science, mindset, and manifestation into a practical, repeatable system that truly works. Her insights on neuroplasticity, emotional intelligence, and productivity are incredibly powerful and easy to apply.'

* *"Upgrade your brain, align your energy, and dominate your destiny."*

* *"Manifestation isn't magic, it's science. Get the strategy that actually works."*

* *"Turbocharge your manifestation game and create success that sticks."*

Connect with Nikki Now and watch for the <u>High AF Advantage</u> podcast

ORGANIZATIONS BY DESIGN INC.

Nicole van Kuppeveld

*Entrepreneur, Leadership Researcher, Course Creator &
Facilitator, Women-Centred Coach, Influencer, Author,
Keynote Speaker*

Nicole Van Kuppeveld is a dynamic leadership expert with 25 years
of experience. As founder of Organizations by Design Inc., based in

Alberta, Canada, she has transformed organizations across multiple sectors, specializing in creating psychologically safe, high-performance workplaces where collaboration, learning and engagement thrive.

With an MBA in Leadership & OD and leadership experience in private, NFP, health care and post-secondary education, Nicole has developed training programs that help leaders build stronger teams and enhance organizational culture.

Her Leading Edge Leadership™ programs are aimed at managers, executive directors, COOs, and strategic human resource professionals. Her women's leadership series equips women leaders with tools, strategies and support to leverage their strengths, refine their leadership skills and navigate today's workplace challenges.

Let Nicole show you 'how to' develop leaders that are equipped to lead through change, challenge and complexity and to build teams that create innovative solutions and exceptional results, together!.

To contact Nicole or to learn more about their transformational leading edge leadership™ programs use their LinkTree: https://linktr.ee/organizationsbydesign

https://www.linkedin.com/in/nicole-van-kuppeveld-6371069a
https://www.facebook.com/organizationsbydesigninc/
https://www.instagram.com/organizationsbydesigninc/
https://www.organizationsbydesign.ca/ideal-clients/
https://www.wlsleadingedgeleadership.ca/

Unleashing Leadership Potential

Breaking Barriers, Building Leaders

By Nicole 'van Kuppeveld

Did you know that…

One in four Americans dread going to work every day.

Nearly half of American workers have thought about leaving their current job. They are probably at work right now, Googling or browsing LinkedIn to check out new jobs.

Over the past five years, the cost of workplace turnover in the U.S. has exceeded $223 billion.

These stats, from the Society for Human Resource Management, paint an ugly picture of today's workplace. When I speak to leaders, I ask them to picture their staff, whether there are 100, 500 or 3,500 of them. And I ask them: "Can you afford to lose 50 per cent of your team? Can you afford to lose your portion of that $223 billion?"

These are not just numbers; these are people. And this is not only impacting an employer's bottom line. It's impacting recruitment, retention and performance. Let's face it—today's workforce demands more from their leaders. They want transparency, authenticity, and cultures that align with the times.

I'm Nicole van Kuppeveld, the founding partner of Organizations by Design Inc., which provides leadership development and coaching for leaders and their teams. I am a creator and facilitator of transformational Leading Edge Leadership™ programs. My approach, curated over three decades, focuses on creating connections, collaboration and community in the workplace and why it matters.

Lessons Learned in the Trenches

I first became passionate about fixing toxic workplaces when I was a young occupational therapist working for a health rehabilitation organization where I counselled people who were off work on stress leave. Over 10 years in that job, I counselled more than 1,000 people.

I figured out that it was not just their workplaces that were making these individuals sick. Their bosses played a significant role in their burnout as well—or, more specifically, their bosses' leadership style and their lack of leadership training.

In my role with these individual clients, I met with their employers to gather a history of their on-the-job performance to better understand the issues and impacts the employee had in the workplace. Over the course of these interviews over that decade, a pattern started to emerge. Not only were my clients sick, but things that were happening in their workplaces were contributing to their poor health.

One client, who worked as a physician, was losing his eyesight due to a neuropathy. He shared how his employer showed no empathy, nor did he offer any opportunities for him to be a part of the team in a non-surgical capacity. A little kindness, care and creativity can go a long way in being able to honour the valued contributions of a long-standing team member. And there are ways to leverage transferable skills to maintain a valuable asset in your organization. With my assistance, we found an important mentoring and consulting role for this gifted surgeon. A win-win because no one wants a visually challenged surgeon.

The most disturbing repetitive pattern I saw was the complete absence of leadership skills, specifically people management skills. The employers' responses to my questions that addressed this area of leadership flabbergasted me. Surely, no human leading humans could think it was all right to say the kinds of things, in the ways they said them, to the people purported to be their greatest asset, could they? Not only did they say them, but they had little or no awareness of the impact they had, not only on my clients but their entire teams. Because, you see, people watch how the boss treats others and adjust their behaviour to avoid a similar fate, sometimes at the cost of their job satisfaction or their own health.

So, I started to ask another question as part of my assessment, for my own research, and the answer was consistently: "I have had no leadership development training." They reported that either their organizations did not have a budget for leadership training, or they did not see it as a priority. As a result, these managers often felt they had been thrown in the deep end and forced to figure it out themselves. Many of them, very competent in the technical aspect of their work, felt like they were drowning when it came to leading teams.

After almost three decades of leadership research, my conclusion: It's a myth that great leaders are born. Leadership is a skill that can and must, for the betterment of our teams, organizations and communities, be learned.

Learning to Be a Leader Myself

That decade was a learning laboratory in leadership and the impact that lack of leadership or leadership development can have on the confidence of individual managers. But more importantly, I came to understand the intentional or unintentional consequences it can have on the teams they 'lead.' It was then that I moved into roles that involved leading teams. Over the next two decades, I went into a different leadership learning laboratory and became a leader myself in a variety of capacities. I was a group psychotherapist. I led program teams in mental health at an agency. Then, at the provincial (state) level, I became a program director, leading a health portfolio that included four youth treatment facilities and a multi-million-dollar federal grant. Later, I was executive director of a provincial advocacy group, leading leaders. Then, I became manager of academic administration, working in the executive suite, at a local community college. I was the area director of a home health agency. And my last position, prior to opening my leadership consultancy, was as a member of an executive team leading a state-wide change initiative.

In the 'trenches,' I learned good leadership from great leaders, and how not to lead from a few horrible bosses. All along this journey, I consulted the best leadership sources, like the *Harvard Business Review*, and integrated them into my own leadership style. I knew it was important to put these best practices into 'practice' to be a great leader and to make the biggest impact on the people on our teams.

A significant experience was my Master of Business Administration (MBA), with a specialization in leadership and organizational behaviour. It was 2006, almost 20 years into my professional career, and I was ready to acquire knowledge and some missing pieces about the makings of great leadership. I wanted to learn about the best qualities in one's leadership style, how to establish the best teams, and the conditions that enabled them to do their best work. Many of the foundational pieces of my *Leading Edge Leadership*™ approach were acquired through this MBA program at Royal Roads University in Victoria, Canada.

I applied that learning to my leadership roles for another decade and then moved from being a leader of teams to going into organizations as an organizational development consultant. This allowed me to take a deeper dive and focus on organizational development. To see whole organizations and the impact of leadership on all stakeholders, especially their most valuable resources, their employees. This was another research laboratory to hone the art and science of humanistic leadership. During that time period, I attended hundreds of seminars and workshops and obtained two certificates.

I'd been introduced to Peter Senge through his book *The Fifth Discipline: The Art & Practice of the Learning Organization* in my MBA. In this seminal work, this brilliant leadership scholar from the Massachusetts Institute of Technology shared the pillars of his leadership theory: personal mastery, team learning, shared vision, mental models and systems thinking. One of my goals has been to make his approach to leadership accessible to my clients, and his leadership pillars underpin all of my transformational leadership programs. I have figured out how to put his theory into practice.

In 2019, I decided to dedicate myself full-time to working with clients who were forward-thinking and wanting to learn a proven way of leadership that would allow them to navigate in our increasingly complex world. And so Organizations by Design Inc. was formed.

If you are curious about why all this matters so much to me, it comes from a desire to create workplaces where people feel supported, valued, motivated, and they learn every day. I believe that if we can become leading-edge leaders and create these types of workplaces, we can change ourselves, our teams, our organizations and our industries. And we might be able to change the world!

Because, like those thousand clients I had counselled back in the 1990s, I, too, know what it's like to dread going to work. To actually feel physically unwell on my way to work every day. To have my human spirit dampened. It happened to me more than once over the years, but the time I remember that feeling the most was in the spring of 2015, when I was a member of a state-wide change management team. Our leader berated us at every opportunity, including advising us that "she should be cloned like Dolly the sheep," insinuating that we were all inferior and failing by her standards. Six weeks into that job, my employment was terminated. The HR director said to me: "Nicole, this has absolutely nothing to do with you!" Getting fired was the best thing that could have happened.

I knew there was a better way. Another way. A leadership approach that shows leaders how to create a work environment with employees who are fully engaged. Where employees say, "Hip Hip Hooray, I get to go to work today!"

How to Create Your Best Team

Do you remember your BEST team? Maybe you are working with them now. If so, lucky you. If it's not your current team, maybe it was a team you worked on in your last job. Maybe a team in college or in a community project. Can you remember what made it different? How you were all able to work together, leveraging each other's strengths and creating amazing results, in a seamless manner. Where there was energy and flow. What was it that was happening that allowed you to do that great work, together?

I know how to create those BEST teams. I know the conditions needed to allow leaders to learn their way forward, innovating and creating teams that deliver exceptional results. I am here to tell you that you can recreate that BEST team in your current team, using my approach.

Let's face it, in today's world of constant change, complex challenges and increasing complexity, leaders need teams that are able to meet challenges and find innovative solutions, more than ever before.

Leila Hormozi, whose company Acquisition.com generates $200M annually, says leadership is the single most important skill for organizations. And if you know how to do it, it's a skill that multiplies.

Peter Senge, the renowned leadership guru I mentioned earlier, says: "Leaders who are able to foster a culture of trust, learning and collaboration, create the conditions where individuals and teams thrive."

I like to say: "The right leadership style doesn't just solve problems— it creates a culture where teams are equipped with the skills to navigate change and resolve the toughest challenges together!"

Let's be honest. Current leadership models are not proving to be effective in managing the complexity of the challenges we face today.

The world is demanding a NEW kind of leadership. Leadership that values:

- Connection over control
- Collaboration over hierarchy
- Community over individualism

Ray Kurzweil, an inventor and futurist, predicts that we will experience the equivalent of a hundred years of change in the next decade.

If you don't take action now, to learn how to lead differently, you'll continue to struggle with the same challenges—team disengagement, lackluster results and high turnover. This may result in the real possibility that you and your organization will be left behind.

The Steps to Good Leadership

After spending the last three decades studying, curating and practising leadership, I have developed a three-step system that is all about how to become a leader for the future, today.

The first step is learning how to create a psychologically safe workspace. That's when as a leader, you lead with authenticity and vulnerability, meaning you show up as yourself and bring your unique skills and strengths to your team. Where you are able to make mistakes, ask for assistance, and show your humanness. You model the way, and in turn, allow people to bring their skills, capacities and fallibilities. When your team feels safe enough to speak up, take risks and share ideas without fear of judgement, that's where the magic happens. This is the foundation of innovation—a culture where people aren't just working *for* you, but *with* you, bringing their best selves to the table every day.

The second is to learn how to build a collaborative learning team: Your team's diversity is not just a fact—it's your greatest asset. Learn how to leverage those assets to create unprecedented results.

The third step is to design a culture of learning and growth: A true learning culture isn't a goal; it's a way of life—one that unlocks the diversity and collective potential of your team and your organization. My definition of diversity is welcoming differences of opinion, perspective, unique ways of thinking, world views and ideas about tackling the challenges and approaches to the work.

These last two steps are interconnected.

As a leader, your role is to create a space where learning never stops—a space where failure is just feedback, and every challenge is an opportunity to improve together. When you nurture this growth mindset across your team, you cultivate a culture of constant progress that delivers powerful, lasting results.

When we talk about learning, it's not just about learning stuff like how to use artificial intelligence or best hiring practices. As a leader, when you focus on growth, apply what you've learned, and share it across your team and organization, you create a culture of learning that drives outstanding results.

And when you know how, you can crush every challenge, achieve unstoppable success and navigate through change, complexity and challenges as a team, working together.

I have heard from clients how much my programs have helped them. In September 2024, in the wrap-up of a full-day leadership learning program with a client group, one of the psychologists participating shared this poignant commentary:

"As a psychologist, I feel very competent in my work with our clients, but you know they don't teach us about how to manage people and teams at university. Today's learning event gave us the skills to lead difficult conversations with the people in our teams and to set norms for expected behaviour. It will make me a better team leader, and us a stronger team. And because we did this training as a leadership team, this shared learning will become part of our way of leading. We need to do more leadership training like the one we did today with Organizations by Design Inc."

What About Women Leaders?

Let's talk more specifically about women in leadership.

It's a myth that all women leaders are great and that only women can provide the kind of leadership the world needs today. The reality is that poor leadership is not gender-specific.

In my experience, it was a man who hired me not once but twice who was the best role model and mentor for the leadership style I espouse today. He balanced the best of his masculine and feminine qualities, embodying connection, collaboration and a sense of community. He led one of my best teams. I have also been on a 'she led' team (the one I described earlier) and have endured a few female bosses who, instead of leveraging my capacity, perceived me as that woman they felt a need to 'compete' against. They felt threatened and took me out.

One of these female leaders fired me after I'd spent 18 months turning a home health agency around. And by that, I mean making it profitable, including securing its first-ever $250,000 client. Under my leadership, we addressed significant gaps during an intensive internal audit, resulting in significant improvements in quality and delivery of care.

You've probably had some experiences with 'bad bosses' who are women too.

It's more common than you think. Research shows that as a result of our evolution as women, we have a competitive streak that goes back to the beginning of time. That relational aggression, also known as mean girl behaviour, has been a part of young girls' socialization and experience for a long time, and sadly continues today. This behaviour can continue to play itself out in executive suites and at every level of leadership if we allow it to.

I've learned that there is another way. To evolve as women leaders, we need to lift one another up, amplify and sponsor one another. We need to ensure that when we rise as women leaders, we remember to take the elevator down and bring other women leaders up.

Here are four strategies for women to become better leaders:

1. Cultivate mentorship and sponsorship opportunities. Shift your mindset from competition to collaboration. Reinforce the importance of providing opportunities, facilitating networking or creating pathways for visibility and advancement.

2. Encourage a collaborative leadership approach. Instead of fostering rivalry, encourage women to lead with an 'abundance' mindset. And to see the value in collaboration versus individualism.

3. Support leadership development programs for women. Investigate programs, workshops and seminars, like our Women's Leadership Series, dedicated to breaking through internal and external barriers that are unique to women and offering training to develop leadership skills, specifically for women.

4. Encourage recognition and celebration of others. Create a culture where you actively celebrate the achievements of other women, rather than viewing success as a zero-sum game.

As a leader, I've embraced this approach to leadership. I am really good at leading teams. I know that using our leadership positions of power to foster an environment where all can rise together is essential. And that creating connections in and outside of the workplace with peers, power partners or Mastermind groups is beneficial as they resonate with how we learn as women in a community.

But to suggest that is all we need to do would be foolhardy because I know from my own experience and research, that is not enough. Beyond leveraging the full capacity of people on our teams and amplifying women in the workplace, there are two other important things to consider. One is the external environment and culture in our predominantly patriarchal workplaces—that proverbial 'glass ceiling.' And the other is internal, the 'inner glass ceiling.' I believe it's important to spend some time talking about both.

The Time for Change Is Now

For starters, patriarchal leadership models, based on achievement, have fallen short of allowing women leaders to flourish. Even women who have achieved these 'standards' are often left feeling unfulfilled. In a course on feminine power, a Supreme Court judge talked about how she had reached the pinnacle of her career. According to U.S. societal standards, she was living the American Dream. She had it all: the house, the car, the maid, the nanny, the country club membership, two kids and a designer dog. But she was not fulfilled. It's called the 'great breakup,' and it refers to a trend where women are more likely to leave their jobs to get their needs met (*Forbes*, 2023). Or more specifically, to find a way to self-actualize, release their inner power and reach their full potential, on their terms.

Another reason women leave the patriarchal-dominant workplaces is that they still feel as though they cannot thrive or work effectively in a workplace culture that disadvantages women for any time spent on family and requires them to continue to work 'the second shift.' It's not just parenting policies, pay equity or affirmative action that are going to level the playing field and ensure women are fulfilled at work and smash through those internal and external glass ceilings. It's so much more.

Take, for example, a workplace culture that does not value, lacks acceptance or suppresses a leadership style that does not align with 'the old boys' approach. How many women, when using their powerful feminine qualities in their leadership role, are shut down, unsupported or encouraged to do it another way or to hit the highway? Not asked, but being told to adopt a leadership approach that they know will never create the conditions for team members and their organization to survive and thrive. I have been one of those women who has shut down, unsupported and asked to hit the highway. I have learned some lessons that are worthy of sharing, and that are supported by my research. And I'm here to tell you some good news.

The masculine, patriarchal, authoritarian leadership models that once shaped our organizations are no longer effective. They are outdated and incapable of navigating the complexity of today's rapidly changing world. These old models prioritize control, hierarchy and individualism. The time for that type of leadership has passed. We're at a tipping point, where leadership grounded in safe workspaces, inclusion, diversity and a culture of learning and growth offers the key to not only surviving the seismic shifts we face but thriving in the future.

Dr. Claire Zammit, a leading authority on feminine power and leadership, says: "The steady rise of women in global leadership roles isn't just a trend—it's the foundation of a new era in leadership."

His Holiness the Dalai Lama says: "Western women will be the ones to provide the leadership that is needed to solve the complex problems in our world."

I like to say: "It's time for women leaders to unleash their inner power—to embrace a leadership style grounded in connection, collaboration and community."

Reimagine Leadership: Step Into Your Full Potential

If you want to take a deep dive and come out feeling more alive as a woman in leadership than you ever thought possible, then consider applying for our next Women's Leadership Series. Women interested in applying can follow the link in my bio. In this transformational 8-module program, you will:

1. Discover a new image of what it looks like to lead in these unprecedented times.
2. Follow a blueprint for what it looks like to influence, using your authentic leadership style.
3. Embrace a new way of being to step forward and have an even greater impact.
4. Awaken to power inside you that's untapped, and break through your inner glass ceiling once and for all.
5. Step into a much bigger and new possibility of what a leader aligned with feminine power can accomplish.

We equip women leaders with a framework for leadership that leverages feminine strengths, tackles internal and external barriers and leverages feminine presence and power. We use a woman-centred approach, and you will learn in a safe environment.

We will delve into concepts such as mastering paradoxes, executive presence and navigating workplace politics to overcome unique obstacles to women leaders. I will guide you on this transformational leadership learning journey.

This comprehensive series empowers women leaders to embrace their feminine power and presence and to navigate the complexities and challenges of today's workplaces.

A woman leader in our inaugural program said it all: "I want this women's leadership series to become an epidemic, for so many reasons!" I would like to make that happen with a squadron of women co-facilitators like you, that want to take this transformational women's leadership series into your communities and networks. This is your invitation to join us in becoming part of a way of leading that can change you, your business, your industry and maybe even the world! For more information reach out to me through my linktree or to info@organizationsbydesign.ca

To our forward thinking leadership learning!

ANNA K LAW / ANNA P. KROLIKOWSKA PC

Anna Krolikowska

Attorney at Law, Mediator, CEO & Founder

Anna Krolikowska is a seasoned family law attorney, published author, and empathetic advocate for individuals navigating life's most challenging transitions. As the founder of Anna K Law, a Past-President of the Illinois State Bar Association, and only the 5th woman elected to that role since 1877, and the Chair of the Board for ISBA Mutual Insurance Company, a lawyers professional insurance provider, Anna blends decades of legal expertise with a deep commitment to protecting what matters most family, stability, and peace of mind. Recognized by Best Lawyers, Super Lawyers, and Leading Lawyers, she's known for her sharp advocacy and compassionate, client-centered approach.

Anna's writing, including her heartfelt children's book "My Parents Are Getting Divorced", inspired by children navigating their family's divorce journeys, reflects her passion for supporting families with honesty, empathy, and hope. Her chapters in collaborative anthologies "Everyday Woman's Guide to Thrive in Your Busy Life" and "Iconic Woman's Guide to Empowerment" reveal her belief in resilience, growth, and the power of human connection, while offering readers relatable stories of courage, transformation, and personal empowerment.

Beyond her legal and literary work, Anna is a dedicated mentor to women, young professionals, and fellow business owners, encouraging them to embrace their potential while redefining what life-work balance means in today's fast-paced world. Whether advocating in court, guiding clients through complex collaborative divorce matters, mediating disputes, or inspiring others through her writing, Anna remains committed to helping others find clarity, confidence, and a path forward.

Learn more at www.annaklaw.com and
www.myparentsaregettingdivorced.com
https://www.linkedin.com/company/annaklaw
https://www.facebook.com/AttyKrolikowska
https://www.instagram.com/Annaklawchicago/
@Annaklawchicago
https://annaklaw.com/
https://myparentsaregettingdivorced.com/

Embracing Change

How Busy Moms Can Rediscover Themselves Without Losing Their Sanity

By Anna Krolikowska

Hey there, Supermom! Life's a bit nuts, huh? Between the school drop-offs, endless snack requests, and that ever-growing laundry pile finding time for yourself feels like a far-fetched fantasy. Like, sure, I'll schedule a relaxing bubble bath right after I solve World Peace and fold that mountain of laundry that's currently doubling as a jungle gym.

But here's the deal: You can create space for yourself, find more joy, and actually enjoy your life again without adding a total life overhaul to your to-do list. And no, you don't need a color-coded planner, a three-step miracle routine, or a week-long meditation retreat in Bali (although if someone's offering, I'll pack my bags with you).

Let's talk about how to embrace change in a way that fits into your real, messy, beautiful life.

Why Change Feels So Freaking Hard (and Why We Avoid It Like a Kid Avoids Veggies)

Change is weird. We say we want "more balance, more joy, more time to remember our own name," but when the opportunity comes along, we freeze. Why? Because even though life feels chaotic, it's predictable chaos. It's our familiar, slightly dysfunctional comfort zone.

Sure, we're running on caffeine and the prayers of a woman who can't remember what day it is. But it's what we know. And stepping into the unknown feels like willingly signing up for another layer of stress.

But here's the truth: Staying stuck is actually more exhausting than changing. It's like holding a beach ball underwater, doable for a while, but eventually, it's going to shoot up and smack you in the face.

The good news? You don't have to do this perfectly or all at once. Small, messy, imperfect steps count. Let's break it down into bite-sized pieces.

Step 1: Reintroduce Yourself to You

Okay, real talk: When was the last time you thought about yourself "not as a mom, a partner, or a chaos-tamer-in-chief" but as a person?

Somewhere along the way, we put ourselves on the back burner. And then that burner basically got turned off because, well, kids. Work. Life. Laundry. (So. Much. Laundry.)

But before you were a mom, you were a woman with dreams, passions, and an actual personality beyond knowing all the words to the "Bluey" theme song. It's time to find her again.

Here's a fun little exercise:

- Steal 10 minutes alone. (Yes, even if you have to lock the bathroom door and pretend you're having digestive issues. No shame.)
- Jot down answers to these questions:
  - What did I love doing as a kid?
  - What hobbies made me happy before life got busy?

○ If someone gave me a free afternoon with no responsibilities, what would I do?

And don't censor yourself. If your answers include "singing karaoke like I'm a pop star" or "napping for three hours straight," that's valid. Your passions "even the weird ones" matter.

Step 2: Give Yourself Permission to Want More (Without the Mom Guilt)

Ah, mom guilt. Our constant, uninvited companion. We feel guilty if we're with our kids 24/7 and guilty if we take a 30-minute Target run alone. It's like we signed an invisible contract that says: I hereby promise to feel bad about literally everything from now until eternity.

But here's what I want you to remember: Taking care of yourself isn't neglecting your family; it's equipping you to be a better, happier, more patient mom. Do you know that airplane oxygen mask analogy? Put yours on first so you don't pass out while trying to help everyone else.

So, how do you ditch the guilt? Start small.

- Schedule 15 minutes a day for you. Not chores. Not work. Just you.
- When guilt creeps in, remind yourself: Happy moms raise happy kids. You're modeling self-care for them and that's a life skill they'll thank you for someday. (Hopefully before age 30.)
- Stop apologizing for needing a break. No one questions when a phone needs recharging; why do we act like moms are supposed to run on empty forever?

Step 3: Set Goals but Make Them Non-Intimidating

The word goal can feel overwhelming when your current life goal is just to drink a cup of coffee while it's still hot. But trust me, you don't need a 17-page life plan. You just need clarity about what you want and a few simple steps to get there.

Try this:

1. Think about one area you would like to improve. More energy? More fun? Less hiding from your kids in the pantry?

2. Make the goal laughably simple. Like: I'll walk around the block three times this week instead of becoming a marathon runner by next month.

3. Track your progress in a way that feels rewarding. Gold stars? Chocolate? Dancing like a maniac when you hit your target? Go for it.

And remember, the goal isn't perfection; it's progress. Even baby steps count if they're headed in the right direction.

Step 4: Master the Art of Saying No (Without the Guilt)

- Hey, can you bake 200 cupcakes for the school fundraiser? No.
- Can you chair the PTA committee for the next 12 years? Absolutely not.
- Mom, can I have a pet tarantula? That's gonna be a hard pass.

We get so used to saying yes to everyone else that we forget how powerful it is to say no. But here's a wild thought: Saying no to stuff that drains you means saying yes to more of what matters.

So, let's practice:

- Say no to activities that make you groan when you see them on the calendar.
- Say no to people who only call when they need a favor.

- Say no to anything that doesn't align with your goals, values, or mental health.

And you don't owe anyone a long explanation. A simple "I can't commit to that right now" works just fine. Bonus: The more you say no, the easier it gets. It's like building a muscle, a strong, assertive, no-more-excess-BS muscle.

Step 5: Embrace the Mess Perfection Is a Scam

Repeat after me: Perfect is impossible and boring as heck.

Instagram might be filled with moms who seem to have spotless houses, color-coordinated closets, and kids who willingly eat kale. But let me tell you a secret: Behind that curated grid is probably a pile of laundry the size of Mount Everest and a kid screaming about the injustice of being served water in the wrong color cup.

Real life is messy. Embrace it.

When your toddler paints the dog purple, take a picture before cleaning it. When dinner turns into a burnt disaster, laugh and order pizza. Some of the best family memories are born from imperfect, ridiculous moments.

And as for the house? If your floors are sticky but your kids are happy, you're doing just fine.

Step 6: Find Your People and Don't Be Afraid to Ask for Help

Motherhood can feel isolating like you're the only one losing your mind while everyone else somehow has it together. (Spoiler: They don't.) The key is to find your people, the ones who get it, who don't judge, and who are willing to laugh with you about the chaos.

So, reach out. Text that friend you haven't seen in months. Join a local mom group (even if it's just to reassure yourself that other moms also wear yoga pants 90% of the time). And when someone offers help? Take it.

No one gets a gold medal for suffering solo. Accepting help doesn't mean you're failing; it means you're human.

Step 7: Make Room for Joy Even in the Chaos

Ever notice how kids find joy in the simplest things? A cardboard box. A puddle. A sticker. They don't overthink it; they just enjoy it.

We can learn a lot from them.

Joy isn't in the big, Instagram-worthy events as much as it's in the everyday moments we often rush past. So, slow down a bit. Dance in the kitchen. Sing loudly in the car. Eat the cake without calculating the calories.

And when life feels overwhelming, do a quick joy check:

- What's one thing I can appreciate right now?
- What's something small that makes me smile?
- How can I add a tiny bit of fun to my day?

Sometimes, the answer is as simple as blasting your favorite 90s playlist and dancing like you're at a middle school dance again.

Step 8: Celebrate Every Win No Matter How Small

Moms are experts at celebrating everyone else's wins: the potty-training successes, the A+ on the spelling test, the first goal at soccer. But when it comes to our own achievements, we shrug them off.

Let's change that.

- Did you drink water today instead of surviving solely on caffeine? Win.

- Did you not lose your mind when your toddler had a public meltdown? Huge win.
- Did you go for that walk you promised yourself? Win.

Celebrate it all. Dance party. Fancy chocolate. A nap. Whatever feels good to you. Recognizing your own success even in the tiny things builds confidence and reminds you that you're making progress.

The Truth About Change (Spoiler: It's Not as Scary as It Seems)

Here's the thing: Change isn't about transforming into a brand-new person overnight. It's about giving yourself permission to evolve, grow, and find more joy along the way. It's about realizing that you matter just as much as the people you care for.

- Will it be easy? Nope.
- Will it be worth it? Absolutely.

So, go ahead. Take that first tiny step. Reclaim a bit of time for yourself. Say no to the stuff that drains you. Laugh more. Worry less. And remember: You've got this, Supermom. Messy hair, sticky floors, and all.

Introduction

Hey there, Supermom! Life is a whirlwind, isn't it? Between shuttling kids to school, managing work deadlines, and trying to remember the last time you had a moment to yourself, change can feel like a far-off dream. But guess what? Embracing change and finding joy isn't just possible – it's essential. Let's take a friendly stroll through how you can rediscover yourself, embrace transformation, and strike a balance that brings happiness to your hectic life.

The Necessity of Change

We all know change is a part of life, but for busy moms, it often feels like an unwelcome guest. Our routines become our safe havens, even if they're filled with chaos. But here's the thing: Staying in one place might feel comfy, but it also means missing out on growth and happiness. So, let's start seeing change not as a disruption but as an exciting adventure waiting to happen.

Change is inevitable, and resisting it only makes life harder. Embracing change can lead to personal growth, new opportunities, and a renewed sense of purpose. Think about it: When was the last time you did something just for you? When did you last feel truly alive and excited about the future? Change can bring that spark back into your life.

Rediscovering Yourself

Remember the person you were before "Mom" became your main title? It's time to reconnect with her. Start with some quiet time (yes, I know, easier said than done). Grab a journal and ask yourself:
• What lights you up?
• What hobbies have you shelved?
• What dreams have you put on hold?

Writing down your thoughts can be a powerful way to find clarity. Think of it as a love letter to yourself, rediscovering what makes you, *you*. It's easy to lose yourself in the daily grind, but taking time to reflect on your passions and desires is the first step toward rediscovery.

Spend some time reflecting on your values and what truly matters to you. Often, in the hustle and bustle of daily life, we lose sight of our core values and what brings us genuine joy. Maybe you used to love painting, reading, or hiking but have pushed these activities aside due to time constraints. It's time to reintroduce them into your life. Start small; perhaps dedicate just 30 minutes a week to an old hobby. Gradually, you'll find ways to incorporate more of what you love into your routine.

Another effective method is to connect with your inner child. What activities made you happiest when you were young? Did you enjoy riding your bike, playing an instrument, or simply exploring nature? Reconnecting with these activities can reignite a sense of joy and wonder that adulthood often suppresses.

Embracing Transformation

Transformation isn't about flipping your life upside down overnight. It's a journey, and every step counts. Here's how to get started:

1. **Set Clear Goals**: What does change look like for you? Maybe it's a career shift, better health, or finally starting that side hustle. Clear goals are your map on this journey.
2. **Prioritize Self-Care**: Self-care isn't selfish – it's necessary. Find time each day for something that recharges you, whether it's a bath, a book, or just a quiet cup of coffee. You deserve it.
3. **Seek Support**: Don't go it alone. Lean on your tribe – friends, family, or even online communities. There's strength in numbers, and sometimes, a good laugh or a shared tear can make all the difference.
4. **Adopt a Growth Mindset**: Embrace the idea that you can grow and improve. See challenges as opportunities. Celebrate your small wins because they're stepping stones to bigger victories.

Setting clear goals is crucial for any transformation. Without goals, it's easy to lose direction and motivation. Start by identifying what you want to achieve. Make your goals specific, measurable, achievable, relevant, and time-bound (SMART). For example, instead of saying, "I want to be healthier," set a goal like, "I will walk for 30 minutes three times a week."

Self-care should be a non-negotiable part of your routine. It's easy to neglect yourself when you're busy caring for everyone else, but remember, you can't pour from an empty cup. Self-care doesn't have to be elaborate or time-consuming. Simple activities like reading a book, taking a bath, or meditating can do wonders for your mental and physical well-being.

Seeking support is also vital. Talk to your partner, friends, or family about your goals and ask for their encouragement and help. Join communities or support groups where you can share experiences and gain motivation from others who are on similar journeys. There's no shame in asking for help, and having a support system can make a significant difference in your journey.

Adopting a growth mindset is about believing in your ability to change and improve. It's understanding that setbacks are part of the process and not a reflection of your worth. Celebrate your progress, no matter how small, and use challenges as learning opportunities.

Finding Joy in Life

Joy is often found in the little things. Here's how to sprinkle some happiness into your daily grind:
1. **Be Present**: Try mindfulness. Be fully present, whether you're working, playing with your kids, or enjoying a hobby. It makes the moment more meaningful and less stressful.
2. **Cultivate Gratitude**: Keep a gratitude journal. Write down three things you're thankful for each day. It's amazing how this simple act can shift your perspective.

3. **Pursue Passions**: Make time for activities that ignite your passion. Whether it's painting, dancing, or gardening, do what makes your heart sing.
4. **Build Meaningful Relationships**: Invest time in the relationships that matter. Surround yourself with positive, supportive people who lift you up.

Being present is challenging in a world full of distractions, but it's a powerful way to find joy. Practice mindfulness by focusing on the here and now. When you're with your kids, really be with them. When you're working, immerse yourself in the task at hand. Mindfulness reduces stress and increases satisfaction in whatever you're doing.

Gratitude is a game-changer. Keeping a gratitude journal helps you focus on the positives in your life, no matter how small. It's a reminder that even on tough days, there are things to be thankful for. This simple practice can drastically improve your outlook on life.

Pursuing passions is essential for a fulfilling life. Don't wait for the perfect moment to start; just begin. If you love dancing, dance in your living room. If gardening brings you peace, plant some flowers in your backyard or even start a small indoor garden. Engaging in activities you love brings joy and a sense of accomplishment.

Building meaningful relationships requires effort but is incredibly rewarding. Make time for friends and family who uplift and support you. Share your goals and dreams with them. Their encouragement can be a powerful motivator. Also, don't hesitate to cut ties with negative influences. Surrounding yourself with positivity makes a huge difference in your journey toward happiness.

Balancing Personal and Professional Life

Balance is the key to not losing your marbles. Here's how to juggle it all without dropping the ball:

1. **Set Boundaries**: Make clear distinctions between work and personal time. Let your boss and family know your limits. It's okay to say no sometimes.
2. **Delegate**: You don't have to do everything yourself. Share the load at home and work. It's okay to ask for help – it doesn't make you any less capable.
3. **Flexible Planning**: Plan your day, but stay flexible. Life loves to throw curveballs, and being adaptable helps you catch them without losing your cool.
4. **Regular Reflection**: Take time to reflect on your progress and adjust your plans as needed. Reflection helps you stay aligned with your goals and make necessary tweaks.

Setting boundaries is crucial for maintaining balance. Clearly define your work hours and personal time. Communicate these boundaries to your employer, colleagues, and family. Don't be afraid to say no to additional tasks that can overwhelm you. Respecting your own time sets a precedent for others to do the same.

Delegation is another key aspect of balance. At home, share chores and responsibilities with your partner and children. At work, delegate tasks to colleagues when possible. It's not a sign of weakness but of effective time management. Trusting others to help you can lighten your load significantly.

Flexible planning means having a plan but being willing to adjust as needed. Life is unpredictable, and rigid schedules can add unnecessary stress. Prioritize your tasks, but be open to shifting them around as circumstances change. This adaptability helps maintain balance without sacrificing productivity or personal time.

Regular reflection is essential for staying on track. Set aside time each week to review your progress and adjust your plans. Reflection helps you identify what's working and what's not, allowing you to make informed decisions and stay aligned with your goals.

Embrace Change

Embracing change and transformation might feel daunting, but it's a journey worth taking. For busy working moms like you, it's about finding a balance that lets you thrive in every aspect of life. By rediscovering yourself, setting clear goals, prioritizing self-care, and finding joy in everyday moments, you can transform your life into one of balance, happiness, and fulfillment. Remember, every journey starts with a single step. Take that step today and embrace the wonderful possibilities that change can bring.

Change is a process, and it's okay to take it one step at a time. Be patient with yourself and celebrate your progress, no matter how small. Embrace the journey, knowing that each step brings you closer to a more fulfilling and balanced life.

Embracing Change in Your Career

For many working moms, career growth and job satisfaction are integral parts of life. However, balancing career aspirations with family responsibilities can be challenging. Here's how you can embrace change and foster growth in your professional life while maintaining harmony at home.

1. **Identify Career Goals**: Reflect on where you are in your career and where you want to be. Are you looking to climb the corporate

INSPIRE HER

ladder, switch fields, or start your own business? Clearly defining your career goals will help you create a roadmap to achieve them.

2. **Seek Professional Development**: Continuously seek opportunities to learn and grow. This could be through online courses, workshops, or certifications related to your field. Staying updated with industry trends and skills not only enhances your job performance but also opens up new opportunities.

3. **Network Actively**: Building a strong professional network can provide support, advice, and opportunities for growth. Attend industry events, join professional organizations, and connect with colleagues on platforms like LinkedIn. Networking helps you stay informed and connected, which is crucial for career advancement.

4. **Balance Work and Home Life**: Use strategies like setting boundaries and delegating tasks to balance your professional and personal life. Flexible working arrangements, such as telecommuting or flexible hours, can also help. Don't be afraid to discuss these options with your employer to find a setup that works for you.

5. **Embrace Flexibility**: Career paths are rarely linear. Be open to exploring new roles, industries, or entrepreneurial ventures. Flexibility can lead to unexpected opportunities and growth.

Transformation in Personal Life

Personal growth and happiness are just as important as professional success. Embracing change in your personal life can lead to a more fulfilling and joyful existence.

1. **Reignite Relationships**: Relationships often take a backseat in the hustle of daily life. Make time to reconnect with your partner, friends, and family. Plan regular date nights, family outings, or coffee dates with friends. Strong, supportive relationships are essential for emotional well-being.

2. **Pursue New Hobbies**: Trying new activities can be exhilarating and refreshing. Whether it's taking up a new sport, learning to cook a new cuisine, or starting a creative project, pursuing new hobbies can add joy and excitement to your life.

3. **Focus on Health and Wellness**: Prioritize your physical and mental health. Regular exercise, a balanced diet, and sufficient sleep are foundational to feeling your best. Additionally, consider practices like yoga, meditation, or therapy to support your mental and emotional health.

4. **Simplify Your Life**: Declutter your physical and mental space. Let go of possessions, habits, and even relationships that no longer serve you. Simplifying your life can reduce stress and create room for what truly matters.

5. **Set Personal Goals**: Just like career goals, personal goals give you something to strive for. Whether it's reading a certain number of books a year, learning a new language, or improving your fitness level, personal goals keep you motivated and focused.

Balancing Parenting and Personal Growth

Parenting is a full-time job, and it's easy to lose yourself in the demands of raising children. However, personal growth and self-care are essential for being the best parent you can be. Here's how to balance parenting with personal development:

1. **Involve Your Kids in Your Interests**: Find activities that you can enjoy together with your children. Whether it's cooking, gardening, or exercising, involving your kids in your hobbies allows you to spend quality time together while pursuing your interests.

2. **Set a Good Example**: Show your children the importance of self-care, lifelong learning, and pursuing passions. Your actions speak louder than words, and demonstrating these values will teach your kids to prioritize their own growth and well-being.

3. **Create Family Rituals**: Establish family rituals that everyone can look forward to, like weekly movie nights, Sunday morning walks, or monthly game nights. These rituals strengthen family bonds and create cherished memories.
4. **Communicate Openly**: Talk to your children about your goals and why they are important to you. Open communication fosters understanding and support from your family, making it easier to balance your aspirations with parenting duties.
5. **Make Time for Yourself**: Carve out regular alone time, even if it's just a few minutes a day. Use this time for activities that recharge you, whether it's reading, meditating, or enjoying a cup of coffee in peace. Personal time is crucial for maintaining your identity and energy.

Embracing Emotional and Spiritual Growth

Emotional and spiritual growth are integral parts of embracing change and transformation. These aspects of growth help you develop resilience, find deeper meaning in life, and maintain a positive outlook.

1. **Practice Mindfulness and Meditation**: Mindfulness and meditation can help you stay grounded and present. These practices reduce stress, enhance emotional regulation, and improve overall well-being. Start with just a few minutes each day and gradually increase the duration.
2. **Explore Spirituality**: Whether it's through religion, nature, or personal reflection, exploring spirituality can provide a sense of purpose and connection. Find what resonates with you and incorporate it into your daily life.
3. **Seek Therapy or Counseling**: Professional support can be invaluable for emotional growth. A therapist or counselor can help you navigate challenges, understand your emotions, and

develop coping strategies. There's no shame in seeking help; it's a sign of strength and commitment to your well-being.

4. **Journal Regularly**: Journaling is a powerful tool for self-reflection and emotional processing. Write about your thoughts, feelings, and experiences. This practice can help you gain insights, release pent-up emotions, and track your growth over time.

5. **Cultivate Compassion and Kindness**: Practice kindness and compassion towards yourself and others. Recognize your efforts, forgive your mistakes, and celebrate your successes. Being gentle with yourself creates a positive inner dialogue and fosters a supportive environment for growth.

Overcoming Fear and Self-Doubt

Fear and self-doubt are common barriers to embracing change. They can paralyze you and prevent you from taking the steps needed for transformation. Here's how to overcome these obstacles:

1. **Acknowledge Your Fears**: The first step to overcoming fear is acknowledging it. Identify what you're afraid of and why. Understanding the root of your fear can help you address it more effectively.

2. **Challenge Negative Thoughts**: Self-doubt often stems from negative thinking patterns. Challenge these thoughts by questioning their validity and replacing them with positive affirmations. For example, if you think, "I can't do this," counter it with, "I am capable and strong."

3. **Take Small Steps**: Break down your goals into smaller, manageable steps. This makes the process less overwhelming and builds confidence as you achieve each milestone. Remember, progress is progress, no matter how small.

4. **Visualize Success**: Visualization is a powerful technique used by athletes and successful individuals. Spend a few minutes each day

imagining yourself achieving your goals. Visualizing success can boost your confidence and motivation.

5. **Seek Support and Encouragement**: Surround yourself with positive, supportive people who believe in you. Share your fears and doubts with them. Their encouragement and perspective can help you see your potential and keep moving forward.

Creating a Sustainable Routine

Creating a sustainable routine is essential for maintaining the changes you've embraced. A well-balanced routine ensures that you continue to grow and thrive without feeling overwhelmed.

1. **Establish a Morning Routine**: Start your day with intention. Whether it's through meditation, exercise, or a healthy breakfast, a positive morning routine sets the tone for the rest of the day. Find what works best for you and stick to it.

2. **Prioritize Your Tasks**: Use a planner or digital calendar to prioritize your tasks. Focus on the most important and urgent tasks first. This helps you manage your time effectively and reduces stress.

3. **Incorporate Breaks**: Schedule regular breaks throughout your day. Short breaks can boost productivity and prevent burnout. Use this time to stretch, take a walk, or practice deep breathing exercises.

4. **End Your Day with Reflection**: Spend a few minutes at the end of each day reflecting on your achievements and what you're grateful for. This practice fosters a positive mindset and helps you wind down for a restful night's sleep.

5. **Adapt and Adjust**: Be flexible with your routine. Life is unpredictable, and it's okay to adjust your plans as needed. Regularly review and tweak your routine to ensure it remains effective and aligned with your goals.

The Power of Positive Affirmations

Positive affirmations are statements that can help you overcome negative thoughts and self-doubt. Incorporating affirmations into your daily routine can boost your confidence and foster a positive mindset.

1. **Create Personalized Affirmations**: Write affirmations that resonate with you and address your specific fears and goals. For example, if you struggle with self-doubt, an affirmation could be, "I am confident and capable."

2. **Repeat Affirmations Daily**: Start and end your day with affirmations. Repeating them regularly helps reinforce positive beliefs and gradually shifts your mindset.

3. **Write Them Down**: Write your affirmations in a journal or on sticky notes placed around your home. Seeing them throughout the day serves as a constant reminder of your strengths and goals.

4. **Visualize the Affirmations**: As you say your affirmations, visualize them coming true. Imagining yourself living out these positive statements can strengthen their impact.

5. **Believe in Your Affirmations**: Trust the power of your words. Believing in your affirmations is key to their effectiveness. Even if it feels forced at first, continue practicing until it becomes a natural part of your thought process.

Nurturing Your Mind and Soul

Taking care of your mind and soul is just as important as nurturing your body. When you prioritize mental and emotional well-being, you create the foundation for sustained growth and happiness. Here's how you can ensure your mind and soul are well-nurtured:

1. **Practice Gratitude Daily**: Gratitude isn't just a buzzword; it's a powerful practice that can shift your mindset and enhance your overall outlook on life. Start or end each day by jotting down three

things you're grateful for. Over time, you'll find it easier to spot the positive aspects of your life, even on tough days.

2. **Spend Time in Nature**: There's something undeniably therapeutic about being outdoors. Whether it's a walk in the park, sitting by a lake, or simply breathing in fresh air on your patio, connecting with nature can calm your mind and help you feel grounded.

3. **Read and Learn**: Feed your mind with inspiring books, articles, or podcasts. Whether it's self-help, fiction, or professional development, learning something new keeps your mind engaged and your curiosity alive.

4. **Journal Your Thoughts**: Beyond just gratitude, use journaling as a tool for emotional release. Write about your day, your dreams, or even your frustrations. It's a safe space to process emotions and gain clarity on what's truly important to you.

5. **Give Yourself Permission to Rest**: It's easy to feel guilty about slowing down, but rest isn't a luxury—it's a necessity. Take time to relax without any agenda. Whether it's watching a favorite show, napping, or doing absolutely nothing, rest helps recharge your spirit.

The Role of Humor in Transformation

Let's face it: life can be downright absurd sometimes. Learning to laugh at life's quirks and even at yourself can be a powerful tool for transformation. Humor isn't just a way to lighten the mood; it's also a way to release tension, connect with others, and maintain perspective.

1. **Laugh Often**: Watch a funny movie, scroll through hilarious memes, or recall silly moments from your past. Laughing releases endorphins, which are your body's natural stress relievers.

2. **Don't Take Yourself Too Seriously**: Let go of the need to be perfect. Whether it's a messy kitchen, a forgotten deadline, or a

toddler's artistic masterpiece on your wall, find the humor in the chaos. It's all part of the journey.

3. **Surround Yourself with Joyful People**: Spend time with friends or family members who make you laugh. Their energy will uplift you, and their humor will remind you that life doesn't always have to be so serious.

4. **Embrace Mistakes**: We all mess up—sometimes hilariously so. Instead of dwelling on errors, laugh at them and move on. Life's bloopers often make the best stories.

5. **Celebrate Small Wins with a Smile**: Got through a crazy day without losing your cool? Celebrate it. Managed to find your keys in the chaos of the morning rush? That's a win! Celebrate the little victories with humor and joy.

Celebrating Your Journey

Transformation is not about the destination; it's about the journey. Each step you take, no matter how small, is worth celebrating. Recognizing your progress helps you stay motivated and builds a sense of accomplishment.

1. **Create a Progress Journal**: Document your milestones, big or small. Whether it's finishing a book, hitting a fitness goal, or managing a tricky work project, seeing your achievements written down is incredibly validating.

2. **Reward Yourself**: Treat yourself for the effort you've put in. This could be something as simple as a favorite snack or as elaborate as a spa day. Rewards are not just indulgences; they're reinforcements of your hard work.

3. **Reflect on How Far You've Come**: Take time to look back and appreciate your growth. Compare where you are now to where you were a year ago. It's easy to focus on what's next, but pausing to acknowledge progress can be deeply satisfying.

4. **Share Your Wins**: Share your accomplishments with trusted friends or family. Celebrating together strengthens bonds and inspires others to pursue their own goals.
5. **Reframe Challenges as Growth Opportunities**: Even when things don't go as planned, celebrate the lessons learned. Challenges and setbacks are inevitable, but they're also crucial for growth.

Moving Forward with Confidence

As you embrace change and transformation, know that confidence is something you build along the way. It's not a prerequisite to start—it's a byproduct of action, learning, and perseverance.

1. **Trust the Process**: Change takes time. Trust that the effort you're putting in will yield results, even if you can't see them immediately. Patience and consistency are your allies.
2. **Embrace Your Unique Journey**: Everyone's path looks different. Avoid comparing yourself to others, and focus on your personal growth. Your story is uniquely yours, and that's what makes it powerful.
3. **Lean Into Discomfort**: Growth happens outside of your comfort zone. Embrace the uncertainty and remind yourself that discomfort is a sign you're moving in the right direction.
4. **Celebrate Your Strengths**: Acknowledge what you're good at and use those strengths to propel yourself forward. Confidence grows when you focus on your abilities rather than your limitations.
5. **Visualize Your Success**: Spend time picturing the life you're working toward. Visualization is a powerful tool for building confidence and maintaining focus on your goals.

Conclusion

Busy moms, you are extraordinary. Life's demands may be relentless, but you have the power to embrace change, rediscover yourself, and transform your life in ways you never thought possible. It's not about perfection; it's about progress. It's about finding joy in the little moments, laughing through the chaos, and celebrating every small win along the way.

Remember, you're not alone in this journey. Seek support, stay flexible, and above all, be kind to yourself. Transformation isn't a one-time event—it's a lifelong journey. As you move forward, know that every step you take brings you closer to a life of balance, happiness, and fulfillment.

So, go ahead—take that first step. Embrace the beautiful mess that is life and watch as it transforms into something truly magical. You've got this, Supermom!

DK HILLARD ART, LLC

DK Hillard
Owner & Artist

Debra is a creator. It is how she lives and what she does in her work. Her art has been a consistent thread throughout her life, whether it be painting, writing or working with others. It is based in her spiritual journey, her Shamanic practice and her connection to nature.

For 20 years she was a life coach and personal trainer, a career that evolved out of her experience transforming her life through bodybuilding. During that time she developed a 12 week program using the body as a vehicle for transforming your entire life.

She transforms her paintings into sensual, luxurious fabrics-clothing, blankets and pillows called "Wraptures", bringing the energy of her artwork into forms you can touch. They are filled with the love that she puts into everything she creates. She works with individuals and small groups using many of the interactive processes she developed while teaching her program.

https://www.linkedin.com/in/debra-hillard-93526913/
https://www.facebook.com/dkhillardart/
https://www.instagram.com/dkhillard/
https://www.dkhillard.com
https://www.dkhillardart.com

Change Is Inevitable

Transformation Is Not

By DK Hillard

"The more life I have behind me, the more acute my true eyes have become. I perceive with more of my senses. I have danced in my youth the way most young people dance, with a vibrant energy only available in the young. But learning to dance when the world is whistling around me, throwing me off balance, is another kind of dance altogether. It requires a grace cultivated over time. It doesn't always look as elegant as it did when I was young, but it is a dance of abundant resilience, drawing upon all of the inner jewels gathered over a lifetime—a dance more beautiful to my aging eyes than anything else."

I wrote this years ago when the words felt as if they were emanating from the wisdom of age. They were, but what I didn't realize at the time was that there was a layer to this process of aging that only true faith, trust, and the courage to surrender, would reveal. Since those days when the words flowed effortlessly through my hands onto the page, I have had the privilege of added years and experience. I say "privilege" because I am acutely aware that aging is just that, and not everyone gets to experience it. Some pass from this world without the benefit of the challenges and the rewards of the wisdom that only experience can bring.

Though I'll admit the process of aging is not an easy one, it has its advantages. With each new season of my life, I find myself wiser, stronger in spirit and with a greater ability to surrender that which is out of my control. Like the cycles of nature's seasons, the passing years bring change. And now, in the winter of my life, I am faced with both the changes that age has left on my doorstep and the reality that little of it was under my control. I cannot turn back the clock. I cannot reverse the effects that my life has had on my body. I can only let go and embrace having changed into a woman of a certain age. I will never be or look the same again. I will never enjoy the youthful energy or exuberance of my early years. The changes happened without my intervention; however, transformation is another story altogether.

Change is inevitable. Like day turning to night, and summer shifting to autumn, our lives naturally change with time. We take for granted that the sun will rise again in the morning and that the chill of winter will be met with the first warm breezes of spring. It's not something we attempt to control because we trust these cycles. They have proven time and time again to bring similar results without our intervention.

We all change, but not all of us transform. Transformation requires a certain level of awareness and commitment. Unlike change, it is something we do have a say in, but it is not a given with the passing years. It is transformation at a very core level that has guided me throughout my life, a desire to become more of who I truly am, separate from the outward appearance of who I seem to be. The process is a bit like alchemy, turning lead into gold. In this process we become something more than who we were previously, not simply an evolution of aging, but a new entity altogether out of choice and surrender.

As a creator, a visionary, and a mystic, the creative process of transformation is one I know well. When I paint, what began as simple colors in jars magically become images speaking a language all their own. They dance off the canvas as if I have infused them with the spirit to live their own lives. In a way, that is exactly what this magical process has given birth to. I am creating something that never existed before and giving it the wings to embark on a journey that is now out of my hands. I have transformed inanimate objects into a new entity with the ability to touch and inspire others, a work of art whose path I cannot foretell.

When I design fabrics from these images, the pieces transform from something my eyes see to something my body responds to with all of its senses. I feel enveloped in the energy of this creation and I, myself, am transformed by the experience. It is through my Shamanic work as Shaman and Priestess that I have experienced myself shed the skin of who I was, to become the dream that lived within me. I have experienced death and birth all in a matter of hours, transforming before my eyes into someone new. Whether it is a work of art or my own life, the transformative process is similar, and when the transformation takes place, I am no longer in control of its destiny.

Transformation requires complete surrender of all that has been. Beliefs about who you are, the way you go about your life, relationships that no longer serve who you are becoming, and even the thoughts that occupy your mind on a daily basis—all surrendered to this magical process of becoming something new. Not a version of who you were, but the evolution of all that has gone before mixed with a hint of magic dust.

Each time I go through another transformation, I am easily fooled into thinking I have finally reached some destination where I will remain for the rest of my days. The illusion doesn't last as long now, but in the moment, when it first becomes real to me, I have a flash of momentary peace: Ah, now I've arrived. No more real challenges. I've met the hardest ones. I've been through enough. I made it.

And then, in a very brief time, I am faced with the reality that transformation never ends for those of us on this path. At least not until we are ready to pass from this earth and transform back into the energy that created us once again. In those brief few moments of newness, there is both elation and supreme peace, because the journey of transformation is not an easy one, and the rest is a welcome respite.

I've often said that I have lived multiple lifetimes in this one incarnation. There have been instances when I have felt myself pass from one to the other. Not in hindsight, but in the moment itself as I shift from one being into another.

I believe most of us are familiar with the process a caterpillar goes through to emerge as a butterfly. It has been referred to in every way, shape, and form possible. For me, it is a very real experience. A caterpillar doesn't know it's a caterpillar. It simply goes about eating as much as possible to store fuel for the transformation it's about to go through.

I have done something similar in my life, consuming as much life experience as possible and feeding myself with all of it so that when it was time to cocoon, I would have all of that to draw upon. In the cocoon, the caterpillar begins to eat itself alive, turning its caterpillar form into a mush-like state. It's a state of being nothing in particular on its way to becoming who it was meant to be. Like the caterpillar, I have had to cocoon for a very long time, not being one thing or another. The difference is that as a human, I have had to pretend to be something, because, in our culture, being something is the only acceptable identity to have. People will ask you what you do, who you are, and if you say you don't know, well, that just makes you sound even worse than nothing. How can you be an adult and not know who you are?

During one such shift in my life, I painted a series of images entitled "Metamorphosis." I was deep in the process myself and feeling the same things I imagine a caterpillar might feel if it had the awareness that I do. Speaking of myself as "goo," no solidity to me any longer, I was acutely aware of the disintegration of who I had been. I felt myself dissolving into nothingness long before I had any sense of solid form returning. As I said, the process of transformation is unsettling at best, totally unnerving, and anxiety-inducing in many instances. You cannot transform into something new without letting go of what has been, and the in-between stage, the place of being nothing, can feel like death.

Looking back over the past few decades of my life, it's apparent that I've been in this state on and off multiple times without identifying it as such. In my 50s, I left an identity as a hard-core bodybuilder, trainer, and coach, not knowing what was to come next. I was forced from this safety of believing who I was by sudden illness. It ripped me from myself as if disrobing me from all that I knew without my consent. Often, that's precisely what it takes to precipitate the death, the release of illusion. Though I clung to shreds of this identity for far too long, it's clear in retrospect that it was the clinging that made it all last so terribly long. If I could have let go fully, perhaps the process would have gone faster and more smoothly.

Hanging on is an old pattern and one that is natural for many of us when faced with such change. Leaving behind something, even if it's not right for us any longer, can feel a bit like jumping off a cliff with no sense of the ground below. Our cocoon is safe, but stifling, and for me, pretending to be something I wasn't in order to remain inside, became untenable. My mushy self was beginning to take form, and there wasn't enough room for me in there anymore. I was bursting at the seams, but first, I had to embrace being nothing at all with no assurance that I would ever be anything of worth again.

To transform, one must embrace death, surrender ego, and, sometimes, life itself. The caterpillar becomes pure goo, no form at all, before it ever has wings to fly. It must release everything for the possibility of being who it was meant to be. She embraces that naturally. It is simply the way of her life and there is no question about whether to dissolve or not. For us, humans with egos, it is a supreme struggle tinged with terror. We have forgotten that it is also a natural process for us because our egos are committed to survival at all costs. It doesn't matter to our ego that what we are protecting is not our highest potential of being. Egos are designed to hold on to the familiar, not to surrender to nothingness, not even for the hope of something greater.

I'll share a story from my own life, one that will sound unbelievable to most. It is still a bit like that for me, and I know it's real. It is a story of transformation that required absolute surrender, to the point of death. And it all happened after seventy years of journeying and peeling away layers of illusion to become the person I had been in search of my entire life.

I was nearing my seventieth birthday. All of the Shamanic work I had been engaged in up until this point was coming to a crescendo. Something inside told me that I was about to undergo one of the most important transformations of my life so far. The paintings coming through me foretold of birth, and I could feel something growing within me. My life had been dedicated to this journey of remembering and embodying who I truly am for so long that this juncture felt like the culmination of my life's quest, but I had no idea what was actually in store.

On my birthday, I created a ceremony around the medicine wheel in front of my studio, one I had built years ago. The people closest to me were there to witness the declaration I was about to make. When the time came, I had no idea what I was going to say, but as the ceremony began, the words came naturally, and I found myself declaring aloud a truth that had been welling up for decades. I spoke the words that would set the next nine months in motion. It was January 13, 2023.

Speaking the truth of who I am took courage. Knowing it had required acceptance of something that challenged all sense of the reality that had been handed down to me as a child. But once I accepted it, the courage welled to the surface, and I found that speaking it in front of others had a different effect than I expected. No one questioned my sanity. They heard me and honored the sanctity of my words. That was the first step.

The next nine months were ripe with the sensation of pregnancy. Having never been physically pregnant, I had the sense that I had been saving that experience for this very time in my life. I knew that I was the person I was supposed to give birth to and that my entire life had been leading up to this. I spent my days creating a safe haven, speaking truth to the child growing within me, and painting images that were the unspoken language between us. I found myself nesting as I imagined pregnant women did, creating a home for my child to be born into. I was clearing space, both literally and figuratively.

Almost nine months to the day, on Sept 9, 2023, I took part in a sacred ceremony with the Shaman who had been helping me to prepare for this transition. In that final week leading up to the ceremony, we continued our work together—clearing, shifting, moving me closer to the state I needed to be in for this to happen.

As the days passed and the hour drew near, we both attuned ourselves to the subtle shifts in energy and the messages coming from our guides. The timing of this was not mine nor his. Everything had to align perfectly, and there was no way to know when that would be. On the day of the ceremony, I fasted and prepared myself in every way I knew how. The hours passed, and the sun set. It was still not time. Alone in my loft, the sanctuary I had created for myself to do my spiritual work, I closed my eyes to sleep. The Shaman told me to wake him when I knew the time was right. Each hour, I awoke from my dreamless sleep but closed my eyes again when I realized that it was not yet time. Time after time, I awoke only to find myself hesitating. It was late that night when something woke me to let me know that whatever needed to align, had done so, and I was ready.

We gathered under my tree, my sacred tree. It was the spot I chose to take this journey as it had special meaning for me. This tree and I have a relationship of mutual love, and I have used her roots many times to take me on journeys to the lower world.

Under her sweeping branches, I drank a brew of the cactus that would help facilitate my transformation. It was prepared with the greatest care and love. The bitter taste was hard to take, but it also reminded me that nothing about this was easy. It was a conscious choice, made with the full knowledge that whatever was to happen would be for my highest good. It might not be what I thought I wanted, and it might be a difficult pill to swallow, but it would be spirit-given and exactly what I would need for the next phase of my evolution.

It was hours later, after experiencing both the depths of tragedy and despair and the majesty of beauty beyond words, that spirit graced me with the gift of death. The night was warm, with the last hint of summer in the air. The stars blanketed the sky, shining through the branches above me. The air was still, and all I felt was the earth breathing beneath me. Suddenly, the branches began to descend and transform into the wings of angels. A light, brilliant and penetrating, filled my awareness. I felt myself held in these wings, and the light permeated my body and mind. I was filled to the edges of my being and beyond. No words were said, but the message was clear. Everything I had ever known was true; all that I knew myself to be was actually real.

The lies I had been told about myself as a child and the horrors I had witnessed and absorbed, were not mine. I was not only OK, but I was blessed, I was loved, and I was more than I ever imagined. I knew love in that moment like I had never known love. I felt myself dissolve into nothing and become light, and it was bliss. It was in those moments, held in the arms of angels and graced by the hand of the spirit, that I passed from this earth as who I had been and was born into this world as the One I had declared myself to be.

There are no adequate words to communicate this—the ones I've chosen will have to suffice.

Throughout my life I have transformed many times. I have facilitated transformations in others through the work I've done with them. I have painted and created, thus transforming one material into another through my art. But this? This was a total transformation that left me speechless and new. I arose from the ground under that tree a new person, having left behind all that was. I couldn't relate to being the person I had been for the first seventy years of my life, and after a few days, I wound up calling her my "mother." She was the person whose quest brought me to life and gave me the chance to live as the person she could not. She knew who she was, but without dying to it all, all of the lies and trauma she had endured, she was unable to make room for the truth.

That night, I experienced death. Now, I know what that is like and I have no fear of it any longer. I am, in the last chapter of my life, a baby just learning how to live my truth. And like a young child, my legs are not yet steady, my mind is deciphering my own thoughts from "hers." When we speak of transformation and change, this is the best example of the difference between the two that I have ever experienced. It's so clear to me that I have not simply changed, but transformed. The true transformation leaves no remnants behind. One might glimpse flecks of stardust in the new creation, signs of its origin. But it is not the star itself. It is a new entity altogether.

In the wake of such a miracle, there is now the task of creating a new life. The transformative act took courage. The next stage calls for boldness. I have found myself tentative at times in making the cuts that will allow me a life separate from what has been. Without a blueprint, how do I know if I'm cutting away something important? What do I want to keep, if anything? And what in the world is going to replace whatever my knife eliminates?

I began the process of cutting away and found myself to be the same tentative artist who took a sculpting class so many years ago. I began by whittling, afraid to eliminate too much. After hours of reviewing my results, the awareness hit me that I had been approaching the process with the wrong mindset, asking questions that could not bring me the result I was after.

I was asking what I liked that was already there, rather than asking what I needed to remove to make space for myself to show up. This might sound like a small distinction, but it makes all the difference in what I remove. If my motivation is to make space for something to appear, then I will have to remove more rather than less. I will need to take out big chunks of stone and cut away even those pieces that could possibly be useful at some point. There are parts of the stone that are beautiful in their raw state. There might be veining or colors that are particularly appealing, but the question is, are they part of the final piece of art? Do they hinder or reveal more of the truth?

I went back at the process with this new mindset and found that I was able to eliminate much more than I did on that very first pass, but I knew that I was still too tentative in my approach. What if I got rid of something that, down the line, I wished I had kept? What if I took away too much and then couldn't replace it? That is the part that requires courage, boldness, and vision.

You see, when I paint, I do not have a vision of a finished piece. My process of painting is quite different and unique. It is a process of listening and allowing my hands to be guided as the message is revealed before my eyes. Most of the time, I have no idea what it is until the painting is complete, and I've had time to sit with it and let it speak to me. I add paint, color, line, and texture, and it is a continual process of adding and subtracting, moving, and dancing with the materials until something is revealed. But in sculpting, unlike painting, those first strokes are ones of elimination, not addition. Facing a blank canvas has its own challenges, and they are not for the faint of heart, either. But facing a solid block of stone, with no going back once those cuts have been made, means that there has to be a vision guiding me first. I have to have some idea of where the lines of demarcation are before I begin.

After some time of cutting away, some strokes bolder than others, I was ready to go back to work with more courage than I was able to muster before. So, what if I get rid of things that are beautiful and possibly useful at some later point? That's part of the process. It's not about keeping everything that is beautiful. It is more about making space for the unique beauty that is mine to reveal. It cannot be seen unless its lines are clearly defined, and it is free to be fully itself, separate from what lived before it.

My "mother" had her own beauty, and I honor and cherish so much of what she left me. But it's not mine. It's now up to me to choose which pieces to carry forward and which to leave as hers and hers alone, not diminishing either, but allowing space for each to shine in its own spotlight.

As I mentioned previously, a sculptor needs a vision of what lies within the stone before making the first cuts, and releasing an old vision is part of the process of cutting away. There is a reason I wasn't a good sculptor. The vision wasn't clear to me at the time and I was hanging onto old beliefs and ideas of who I should be. But when it comes to my vision of who I am now and what this new life is, something different is required. I must be willing to cut away even the beautiful pieces of myself and the life I've lived. They might have been there for decades, but if they are no longer part of the truth of who I am, they must go. Unlike my personal process of painting, where the paint leads me to the vision, this must be guided by a connection to spirit and to myself, because this is the most important creative act of my life. It is my life itself.

Once transformed and tasked with the work of creating a life fit for who I say I am, rooting myself in that truth is paramount. The spiritual work, the dedication to remaining true to myself no matter the external pulls in other directions, becomes the guiding force for further transformation.

Some change is required in the ways I choose to live and work. Seeing myself as this new person instead of who I had always known myself to be spurs further transformation in my belief system, my thoughts, and, eventually, the actions that arise from both. Living in a new way, not from the fear that used to color all of my choices, but from the awareness that I am graced, blessed, and always provided for, naturally transforms the landscape surrounding me. My life cannot look or feel the same when created from love instead of fear.

Change is inevitable. It is not easy for most of us, but to be expected as the years pass.

Transformation is a gift given to those who do the work required. It is the reward for the courage it takes to seek truth and surrender all else. Though not easy, it is also a natural process, like the caterpillar and butterfly. If we do not turn a blind eye to the truth in front of us, rather than heading straight for it in spite of the challenges it presents, we can be like the caterpillar, naturally trusting that our wings will sprout out of nothingness. We can transform over and over again throughout our lifetimes, becoming more of who we were born to be—eventually, with a touch of grace, spreading our newly evolved wings and taking flight.

AVANT HOMES & SAFE HARBOR COUNSELING INSTITUTE

Joyace Reyes Silva

Business Intelligence Expert & Founder

Joyce has over 15 years of Sales experience, 7 specializing in Growth Marketing teaching topics such as marketing, communication, sales, conversion optimization and technology for business.

She's now the Business Intelligence expert in a group of over 700,000 **women entrepreneurs, a Growth Strategy Engineer and forward-thinking marketing specialist.**. Joyce harnesses her experience in sales, behavior and technology into creative, high-impact solutions. She thrives in a culture of innovation and enjoys making a difference.

Joyce is also Board of Director at Safe Harbor Counseling Institute, a mental health nonprofit making a difference to underserved populations, was honored with an award on the Orange County list of 40 Under 40 Most Influential Leaders Making An Impact.

After 3 degrees and 4 certifications, she studied Technology for Business at Harvard University. She now works with corporate teams to implement effective Marketing, Communication and Productivity-boosting tech tools like apps for business use and Ai.

https://www.linkedin.com/in/joyce-odette/

https://www.facebook.com/joyce.odette.tech.queen/

https://www.instagram.com/the.tech.queen

https://sales-buddy.app/

https://strategicgrowthxp.com/

You Are The One That Will Save You

By Joyace Reyes Silva

You Are The One That Will Save You

To the woman standing at a crossroads of uncertainty, grappling with doubts and fears that whisper of inadequacy and limitation, I offer you this truth: within you beats the heart of a warrior, the soul of a dreamer, and the spirit of a trailblazer. Your challenges, your fears, your doubts—they are not barriers but stepping stones. Guiding you towards a future defined by courage, resilience, and unyielding determination.

The lessons learned through the crucible of adversity are not meant to break us but to shape us. To mold us into beings of strength and fortitude. Each obstacle overcome, each fear conquered, each doubt silenced, is a testament to the power that resides within you. The power to rise above, to transcend, to transform.

As you navigate the complexities of life, facing challenges that test your resolve and fears that threaten to paralyze your spirit, remember this: You are not defined by your circumstances, limited by your past, or constrained by your doubts. You are a force of nature. A beacon of light, a warrior of the soul, capable of achieving greatness beyond your wildest dreams.

As I reflect on the chapters of my own life, each page turned reveals a tapestry woven with threads of resilience, courage, and, as I now look back—unwavering perseverance. The journey from doubt to determination, from fear to freedom, mirrors the struggles and triumphs we all face in our own unique narratives. In sharing my story, I hope to illuminate the path of possibility and empowerment that lies within each of us, waiting to be unearthed and embraced.

In my journey from doubt to determination, from fear to freedom, I discovered the transformative power of self-belief, the courage to defy the odds, and the resilience to weather life's storms. These lessons, hard-earned and deeply cherished, are not mine alone but gifts to be shared with you, my fellow traveler, on this path of self-discovery and empowerment.

Whispers of dreams yet to be realized? I had those, too. Too often. They almost drove me wild. It wasn't until I let the dreams seep into reality that I finally gave way to the momentum for growth.

It was a time of innocence and uncertainty, of budding ambitions. Teachers, with their well-intentioned but misguided advice, unwittingly became the architects of doubt in a young girl's heart.

Picture a classroom bathed in the soft glow of afternoon sunlight, where I sat perched on the edge of my seat, eager to absorb the wonders of science and the mysteries of literature. Yet, as the days turned into weeks and the weeks into months, a shadow of doubt began to creep into my mind. The words of my two teachers, delivered with a mix of concern and condescension. "Science isn't your strong suit," they said. "Writing is beyond your reach."

But they had no idea their shallow critique laid a simmering determination beneath the surface of my skin, a quiet rebellion that sparked, and I refused to let someone who didn't even know me well tell me what I could and could not do. I was a girl with a newfound fire in her veins. A spirit that refused to be tethered by the limitations imposed upon her. So, I rolled up my sleeves, tightened my grip on my dreams to help people, and embarked on a journey of self-discovery and defiance.

You see, life outside the classroom at that time was a struggle and full of sacrifice, resilience, and growing up too soon to help the family stay financially afloat. After the final school bell tolled, I would rush to my job at a retail store. Where the hum of fluorescent lights, rude customers, and the constant rustle of clothing formed the backdrop to my after-school routine. While other high school students were hanging out with friends and joining sports, I was balancing textbooks and making sales, homework, and customer service. I navigated the two worlds of high school academics and financial responsibility.

The 2008 housing crash shook the very foundations of my family's stability. We lost our house, and I found myself helping to pay bills as my parents faced the loss of their beloved home. We had finally settled in a good neighborhood after moving countless times, starting from a cramped, infested apartment in Downtown LA, slowly moving west toward the suburbs and safer neighborhoods as my parents found better jobs and were involved as leaders in church prayer groups.

It was a time of constant uncertainty, financial strain, resilience tested and courage found. Being good at art since it was my escape, I even received a scholarship from the Hispanic Chamber of Commerce of Corona, and I gave the full amount to my parents when they didn't have enough to pay the rent without being asked and with no hesitation.

The challenges of those days were no match for the strength forged in the crucible of adversity. When my father lost his job, the weight of financial uncertainty settled heavily upon our family. The burden of supporting the family suddenly fell upon my older brother's and my shoulders, and we embraced it with a fierce determination born of love and duty. Each shift at work, each dollar earned, was a testament to the unbreakable bond of family and the unwavering spirit of resilience.

As a child, I dreamed of service jobs like being a doctor, a teacher, a nurse, and an architect, helping people design their dream homes. Something about helping others always pulled my soul, and maturing into the real world, I realized nursing would be a lucrative way to help others. Halfway through the nursing requirements, however, I realized I could not handle seeing people in pain. It was almost like I could feel the pain with them, and I could not stand it.

Then when I became a mom at such a young age, I made working a priority and left it up to destiny to see what I would encounter and what the future would hold for me. Graduating at a very bad economic time made being low-income a struggle, compounded by the responsibilities of being a young mother. Blessed with being married to my high school sweetheart, the family became my everything.

As the years unfolded and the pages of my story turned, I found myself at a crossroads—a pivotal moment of choice and consequence. The financial world called me, with its promises of stability and success, but also came its rigid rules and stifling expectations. Within those hallowed halls, I encountered a new set of challenges, a fresh set of doubts that tested me to my limits.

In the corporate world I was seduced to, I found challenge after challenge, one glass ceiling after another as a woman of color. Being overworked and overlooked became a constant theme that would find me. Training people hired at higher rates or above my level brought the constant question of why not me if I was the one with more knowledge, better performance, and experience.

But so many rules and so little growth—was always a sign of the need for   change.

The nail in the coffin that buried my old life was when my father passed away from COVID. Deep within me, a spark of defiance flickered. In the corporate world, even hair with a gentle expression of color and creativity was a distraction. A deviation from the norm that could not be permitted. They said conformity was key, and uniformity was essential.

A rebellion against the boxes they sought to confine me within. And so, in a moment of bold assertion and unapologetic self-expression, I dyed my hair purple—a symbolic act of reclaiming my identity and asserting my autonomy in a world that sought to diminish my light.

The decision was more than a mere change in appearance; it was a declaration of independence, a proclamation of self-worth, a testament to the power of authenticity in a world that demanded conformity. In that single act of defiance, I found liberation, empowerment, and a renewed sense of purpose that would shape the course of my journey in the years to come.

Fast forward to today, and I stand before you as a woman transformed by the crucible of unrelenting experience, the forge of adversity, and the wellspring of resilience that flows deep within my soul. Armed with 3 degrees, one being in Computer Science, four certifications, and a wealth of experience in the realms of sales, technology, marketing, and even writing press releases that have been featured in major publications and business plans. I do the very things they said I couldn't and shouldn't—every day of the week.

I have navigated the turbulent waters of innovation and disruption with grace and tenacity. My journey has been a testament to the transformative power of perseverance, courage, and unwavering self-belief in the face of insurmountable odds. I've been through the deepest pits of the mind, I've almost died three times, one of our homes was broken into, and I've made some serious mistakes I will never be able to take back, but I have also learned how strong I really am. The biggest lesson is how there is extraordinary power in good intentions, focus, confidence, action, perseverance, and determination.

As I weave my story into this anthology of inspirational stories from amazing women, I do so humbly. Not to serve as another story of struggle but as a message from a sister, a friend, a mother—a woman who has walked a tough path of self-discovery and empowerment, maybe similar to you.

Life is not perfect, but it is beautiful.

Life is a journey of shared experiences and collective growth, where the echoes of our past reverberate with the promise of a brighter tomorrow.

Life, with all its twists and turns, its joys and sorrows, is a grand tapestry woven from the threads of our shared experiences. Each chapter, each verse, tells a story of resilience, courage, and determination in the face of adversity. As we turn the pages of our lives, remember that we are the authors of our destinies, the architects of our dreams, and the champions of our own narratives. You can choose to continue your story as it seems it will play out, or you can decide to flip the script at any time.

Every Day Is a New Day

Every day is a new chance to know better, do better, and be better.

So, as you embark on your own quest for growth and transformation, know that I am here beside you, cheering you on, rooting for your success, and believing in the infinite possibilities that await you.

Now as the CEO of Avant Homes, a real estate development company dedicated to building smarter to provide new housing in California amid a major shortage crisis, I stand as a testament to the power of perseverance, vision, and unwavering belief in the face of adversity. Engineering AI tools while studying Technology for Business at Harvard University, helped hundreds of businesses grow.

However, what is closest to my heart is helping my parents establish Safe Harbor Counseling Institute, a non-profit organization after they graduated as Psychologists and organized with 8 other experts in mental health to help low-income and uninsured families get access to mental health. I've also given masterclasses to over 700,000 Women Entrepreneurs and as a Business Intelligence Expert.

Each brick laid, each foundation poured, echoes the story of transformation and growth that defines not only my journey but the journeys of all who dare to dream, to defy—to rise.

You Are The One That Will Save You

So, my fellow warrior of the soul, I offer you this call to action: do not wait for someone to save you, to lead you, to guide you. Step into your power, embrace your potential, and rise as your own hero. The challenges you face, the fears you confront, the doubts that linger—they are not obstacles but opportunities, begging you to seize the moment, to claim your destiny, to write the next chapter of your story with courage, resilience, and unwavering self-belief.

Don't let your fears hold you back, let them propel you forward.

Don't let doubts dim your light, let them ignite your fire.

Don't let challenges defeat you, but let them strengthen you.

For within you lies the power to transform, to grow, to rise above the limitations that seek to confine you.

Don't be afraid to take on your journey of self-discovery and empowerment, where the echoes of our dreams once whispered now reverberate strongly in goals with the promise of a brighter tomorrow.

Know that as long as your intentions are good, faith strong, confidence high, and actions consistent—you are unstoppable.

You are a force to be reckoned with.

Maybe all you needed was a reminder of the spark in your soul.

Maybe all you needed was to hear a story of someone who overcame the odds so you could realize what is possible: anything you set your mind, focus, and actions to.

But at the end of the day, no one else will bring success—you are the one who rises to the occasion when you are ready.

Your time is now.

You Are The One That Will Save You

RAFA TADIELO - LIFE COACH & HYPNOTHERAPIST

Rafa Tadielo

Founder

Rafa Tadielo is a big believer that by changing your mind, you can change your life.

After a fast awakening sparked by hitting rock bottom, she discovered that hypnosis and life coaching held all the tools and strategies she needed to create a life she loves.

Now, she blends neuroscience, hypnosis, and a dash of "woo" to create a down-to-earth approach that helps women reach their full potential and become the best version of themselves.

Rafa believes we are mind, body, and soul, and true transformation requires a holistic approach.

She's passionate about guiding women to become the best version of themselves.

Her philosophy is that life should be like the dreams they were once told were too big—bold, fearless, and unapologetically authentic.

Through her work, Rafa inspires others to rewrite their stories, embrace their truth, and build the life they truly deserve.

https://www.linkedin.com/in/rafa-tadielo-448b37281/
https://www.facebook.com/rafatadielo
https://www.instagram.com/rafatadielo/
https://www.rafatadielo.com/

Be Bold

My Path to Freedom, Power, and Purpose

By Rafa Tadielo

Hi, I'm Rafa, and I'm a big believer that changing your mind can change your life. But it wasn't always like that. At least for the first 40 years of my life.

Life wasn't easy growing up in Brazil, despite having a good family with great conditions. My parents were loving but in their own way. They weren't people with much knowledge of how to raise a child to feel empowered, safe, or "good enough." From a young age, I was taught that life was hard, and there was no room for softness, vulnerability, or weakness. I quickly learned that emotions and feelings weren't something to be valued or nurtured; instead, they were to be pushed down, ignored, and suppressed. From the moment I could remember, I was taught that the world didn't have time for emotionality. I had to be tough, resilient, and relentless. It was a culture of "suck it up and get on with it." Your worth was based on what you could do, how hard you could work, and how much you could achieve—not on how you felt or who you truly were.

I grew up hearing phrases like, "Be a good girl." And though this may sound harmless, it became the foundation of everything I did and didn't do. "Be a good girl" meant being quiet, doing what was expected of me, never making waves, and always putting others' needs ahead of my own. It meant suppressing my voice and desires, and prioritising approval over authenticity. It led me to become a people-pleaser, someone who constantly sought validation from the outside world, afraid to express the real me. Over time, I found myself bending and twisting into a version of what others wanted me to be. But deep down, something inside me kept whispering that I didn't fit the mould, that I was meant for more than just following the rules and staying in the background. Yet, I couldn't hear that voice clearly through the noise of expectations and self-doubt.

Isn't it incredible how the magic of being a child can vanish the moment the world tries to fit us into its predefined box? It's as if, overnight, we lose the freedom to dream wildly, to feel deeply, and to be unapologetically ourselves. Instead, we get taught to conform, to meet expectations, to play a role that's no longer ours to choose.

As children, we live with wonder, curiosity, and limitless possibility. The world is full of heroes and fairytales, where we can be anything we want. But as we grow, the stories change. Society tells us how to act, what to think, and who to become. The very things that once fueled our imagination and joy—our passions, our quirks, our feelings—are pushed aside. We begin to operate on autopilot, serving others, doing what is required, and following the script that's been written for us.

The problem is, when we lose touch with that magic, something inside us starts to wither. We forget how to dream, how to believe in ourselves, and how to fight for the life we truly want. Our heroes, the ones who used to inspire us, fade into the background, and the fairies of our childhood seem like distant fantasies. The innocence and wonder of being a child are replaced by the weight of expectations and obligations. And without realizing it, we stop showing up for ourselves.

That's what happened to me. I had to create space for myself in a world that felt overwhelming and dismissive. It was never about me; it was about what I could achieve and how much I could endure. I had to fit into a system that demanded perfection—doing the doing, pushing through the pain, and sacrificing my needs for the sake of others. Emotions were buried under a thick layer of stoicism, and feeling overwhelmed, stressed, or emotionally fragile was simply not allowed. I never learned that being human meant feeling everything—joy, sadness, frustration, vulnerability—and that those feelings didn't make me weak or less than. Instead, I was conditioned to believe that vulnerability was a burden, something to hide and never show.

As a young girl, I was conditioned to believe that my worth was tied to my ability to perform, to succeed, and to achieve—no matter what it cost me emotionally. I didn't have the tools to process my feelings or understand what was happening inside me. And no one around me did either. The idea of emotional regulation, healing, or introspection was foreign. I didn't even know how to begin to address my feelings. They were either ignored or deemed insignificant in the grand scheme of things.

I remember once, in school, when I brought home an A-. I was so proud of myself, but when I showed it to my parents, instead of praise, I was asked, "Why didn't you get an A+?" When I argued that no one in my class had an A+, the response was, "You are not everyone." That moment cemented my belief that nothing I did was ever good enough. I was always striving for perfection, but the bar kept shifting higher. And it wasn't just about grades; it was about everything in life. There was always something more to do, something more to give. The idea that I could simply rest or take a break was foreign, and so, I continued to push myself further and further, never feeling like I was enough as I was.

As I entered my twenties, this mindset began to take its toll on me. I found myself deeply immersed in a cycle of overworking, suppressing my emotions, and avoiding facing what I was truly feeling. I started to feel numb, detached from myself, and overwhelmed by the constant demands of life. I felt like I was carrying a heavy weight that I couldn't shake off. I needed to be strong, but in doing so, I became weaker by the day, mentally and emotionally drained, and disconnected from the very essence of who I was.

Many of us, especially women, have been taught to put everyone else's needs before our own. We're taught that being a "good girl" means sacrificing ourselves to please others, and so we lose ourselves in the process. It's a cycle that seems almost inescapable, especially when we live in a world that celebrates busyness, achievement, and perfection. But in truth, this lifestyle doesn't bring happiness or fulfilment—it leads to burnout, disconnection, and ultimately, a life lived for everyone but yourself. The pressures to "keep going" and "make it work" can keep us trapped in unhealthy cycles for years. I know this first-hand. For me, it manifested in drugs, alcohol, and toxic relationships as my way of coping. There was a moment when I felt so desperate to escape an abusive relationship that I jumped through the window of my own house to rescue my belongings while he was out. It was a moment of sheer survival, trying to break free from the suffocating situation I was trapped in.

After having my heart shattered by another in the most toxic relationship I'd ever experienced, I eventually made the bold decision to leave Brazil and move to New Zealand when I turned 30, following my twin sister and best friend who had moved there a year earlier. I thought a fresh start in a new country would give me the space I needed to heal, but even in this new world, I continued to feel lost and disconnected. The fresh start did little to quell the deep unease that was building inside me. I was still stuck in my old patterns of working hard, pushing my emotions aside, and living with a deep sense of unfulfilled potential. Despite the beauty around me and the new opportunities available, I was still carrying the same baggage I had left behind in Brazil.

It took years of working hard and battling my own internal struggles before I realized that I had been running away from myself. For almost a decade, I kept going, pushing, and striving, but it felt like I was going nowhere. The emotional toll of suppressing my true feelings, my desires, and my needs continued to weigh heavily on me.

One night, after yet another heavy drinking session, something inside me finally snapped. I found myself lying in bed, overwhelmed by the feeling that I was slowly destroying myself. I realized that my bad habits were no longer just a way to cope—they were a slow death sentence. I was terrified. The thought of falling ill or dying from my own actions scared me more than anything else in that moment. I had reached a breaking point. The realization that I was halfway to death, not just physically but emotionally and mentally, was a wake-up call that I couldn't ignore. That was the moment I knew something had to change.

This moment of realization was my turning point, my rock bottom. It was no longer about being tough or pushing through—it was about survival. I was finally ready to confront the uncomfortable truth that I had been running from myself for far too long. I had spent years chasing external success, working hard to fit into a world that demanded perfection, but in doing so, I had lost touch with the very essence of who I was. And if I didn't make a change now, I would continue to live in a state of self-destruction.

The fear of dying prematurely from my own unhealthy habits pushed me into action. I knew I couldn't keep going down this path. I had to choose life over fear, healing over self-destruction. It was time to stop avoiding the pain and to face the emotional wounds I had buried for so long. I made a promise to myself that I would change, no matter how difficult or uncomfortable it felt. The first step was acknowledging that I needed help and that I didn't have to do it alone.

This moment of awakening is something many of us experience. We may reach a point where we realize we can no longer ignore our emotional, physical, and mental well-being. Whether it comes through a crisis or a quiet whisper, we all face moments that force us to confront our own truths. It's never easy, but it is always worth it. Choosing healing, self-love, and authenticity over self-doubt and fear is one of the most powerful decisions we can make for ourselves as women. The journey of reclaiming our worth, letting go of perfectionism, and learning to prioritize our own needs is a lifelong process. But it starts with a choice to be brave, to face our fears, and to say, "I am worthy of healing, of love, and of the life I truly desire." And believe it or not, the smallest step in the right direction can be the biggest step of your life.

I came to the understanding that what I wasn't changing in my life, I was actually choosing and I knew that in order to truly transform, I needed to take action. I had spent so many years trapped in patterns of overworking, suppressing my emotions, and trying to please others. It was exhausting. But the first step towards transformation came when I decided to change my career. After being a chef for over 10 years, the stress and pressure to perform were killing me. The constant demand for perfection, coupled with the intense work hours, had taken a toll on my physical and emotional well-being. I was drained, disconnected, and overwhelmed.

At first, I was so lost in despair that I thought, *Any 9-to-5 will do*—just something to escape the suffocating cycle I was caught in. But deep down, I knew that simply running from one job to another wasn't the solution. I asked myself: *If I choose career x or z, can I imagine myself doing this job for the next 5 or 10 years?* It was a sobering question. It forced me to face the truth that I had no real vision for my life, no clear sense of what I truly wanted or needed. That's when it hit me: I needed to be mindful, intentional, and thoughtful about what I wanted my life to look like—not just on the surface, but at the core.

So, I took a step back and wrote down everything I could think of about how I wanted to live my life, what passions I had, and most importantly, what my non-negotiables were. This process was hard—so much harder than I had anticipated. It revealed just how little I knew about myself. For so long, I had been disconnected from my own desires, my own needs, and my own voice. When it came to choosing what I wanted for my life, I felt completely lost.

But through this deep reflection, I came across hypnotherapy—a tool I had used years earlier to help me quit smoking. I remembered the profound effects it had on me, and how it allowed me to tap into the power of my subconscious to make lasting changes. It was then that I realised it aligned with my non-negotiables: It gave me the freedom of time and location, and it allowed me to help others heal—something I had longed to do. I decided to pursue hypnotherapy as my new career path.

My healing journey began when I chose to study hypnotherapy. But it wasn't just about learning new techniques—it was about diving deep into my own healing journey. I made myself the object of study in every demonstration in class. As I applied each technique, I began to reconnect with parts of myself I had long buried. Through the process, I was able to rewire my mind, heal deep-rooted fears, and break free from limiting beliefs that had been holding me back for years. Hypnotherapy wasn't just a career change for me; it was a life change. It was the space where I found myself again, a space where I could heal, grow, and reconnect with the person I had buried beneath years of stress, emotional numbness, and self-sacrifice.

It's a hard truth to face: When you don't know yourself, making choices can feel impossible. I didn't know what I wanted, what would make me happy, or even what I deserved. I had been living so far outside myself, chasing external approval and success, that I lost touch with my true desires. But this process of getting clear on my non-negotiables and stepping into my own healing helped me find clarity. It showed me that we are allowed to choose. We are allowed to want something different. And we are allowed to build a life based on what feels right for us, not what the world or others think we should do.

It was a painful journey, but it was also a liberating one. And it's one I wouldn't trade for anything. Through this process, I found my true self again, and I made the decision to choose me—something I had never allowed myself to do before.

However, even with all the progress I was making, I still felt stuck in my mind at times. There were so many blind corners I couldn't navigate on my own, and I was struggling to create a clear plan that would give me the clarity and strategy I needed to transform my life. It was at that point I decided to hire my first life coach. The experience was mind-blowing. The clarity and high-level perspective I gained from having an observer with the right mindset was like a breath of fresh air. For the first time, I felt truly listened to, supported, and guided. It was a revelation to realise that I didn't need to carry everything alone. I could ask for help, and I could lean on others to help me see the bigger picture. This was a game-changer.

My coach helped me shift my mindset, reframe my perspective, and set actionable goals that aligned with my true desires. The transformation I experienced was more than just mental clarity; it was a deep, soul-level awakening. It taught me that I didn't have to figure everything out on my own. I didn't have to carry the weight of the world on my shoulders. It was through this process of coaching and healing that I began to understand that I could actually create the life I loved. A life that wasn't defined by others' expectations or by the fear of not measuring up, but one that was based on my own values, passions, and dreams.

This was when everything clicked for me. I realised that my dreams weren't too big or too far out of reach. I had the power to choose how I wanted to live, and I could make it happen. The clarity I gained through working with my life coach gave me the confidence to take bold steps in the direction of my dream life. In fact, it was during this time that my soul-led business idea was born. I wanted to be the inspiring and resourceful person who could guide others—particularly women—on their own journeys of uncovering their full potential. Hypnotherapy would be the tool I used to help dissolve any blocks or limitations standing in the way of their dreams.

This was the turning point. As I started to live in alignment with my true desires, I began to wake up every morning feeling like it was the happiest day of my life. I felt connected to myself, to my purpose, and to the mission of inspiring others to do the same. Everything started to fall into place. My business began to take shape, and the more I walked my talk, the more everything aligned. I was living my dream life, and it felt like every step I took brought me closer to the woman I had always wanted to become.

This transformation was not just about changing my career or learning a new skill; it was about reconnecting with my inner truth, aligning with my authentic self, and stepping into the power I had always carried within me. Stepping into my power had shown me that I was capable of creating a life I loved—and that I had the capacity to inspire others to do the same.

As I reflect on my journey, I am in awe of how far I've come. I'm no longer the woman who felt lost and disconnected from herself.

Today, I am someone who has learned to embrace her emotions, honour her needs, and pursue her dreams with a level of courage and confidence that once seemed impossible. I am living proof that transformation is not just a distant dream but a reality that's within all of us.

When we choose authenticity over fear, when we decide to break free from the limitations that hold us back, we unlock the power to create a life that is truly fulfilling. And while the path to authenticity and transformation isn't easy, it is worth every single step. It's a journey of unlearning, healing, and growth, and it teaches us that we all have the power within us to change our lives. We have the power to break free from the past, rewrite our story, and step into the future we desire.

The key to this transformation is trust. Trusting ourselves. Trusting the process. Trusting the universe. When we trust that we are enough just as we are, everything shifts. The fear starts to fade, and we realise that we can make bold choices. We can step into our greatness, even when the world doesn't fully understand us. We are the authors of our own stories, and each day is an opportunity to choose what we want to create next.

One of the most powerful lessons I've learned on this journey is the importance of surrounding yourself with the right people. No one succeeds alone. Every step I took was supported by those who inspired, encouraged, and believed in me when I struggled to believe in myself. Their energy gave me the strength to keep moving forward, even when the path felt uncertain.

But just as vital as seeking out support was learning to protect myself from negativity. Not everyone understood my decision to change careers and start my own business. When I began sharing my plans, I was met with doubt disguised as concern. "At this age? Are you really going to start over?" "Starting a business is so hard—what if it doesn't work out?" Or my favourite: "You need more balance. Stop taking life so seriously."

At first, these comments shook me. I wanted to explain, to make them understand how much this change meant to me, how deeply I felt called to create a life aligned with my purpose. But no matter how clearly I explained, some people simply couldn't see my vision. And then I realised—it wasn't my job to convince them. Their doubts were not about me; they were about their own fears.

When you decide to take a leap, you will inevitably trigger people. Your willingness to step into the unknown shines a light on their own insecurities. It's not malicious, but it can be discouraging if you're not careful. I had to learn to protect my energy and focus on the people who truly believed in me.

I became intentional about who I shared my plans with. I sought out those who had walked their own paths of transformation, who understood what it meant to take risks and embrace growth. Their belief in me became a lifeline, especially during the moments when my own faith wavered. At the same time, I set boundaries with those who couldn't offer the same support. I didn't cut anyone out of my life, but I stopped allowing their doubts to infiltrate my mind.

Letting go of the need for everyone's approval was freeing. I realised I didn't need the whole world to understand my journey. The only validation I needed was my own. That shift gave me the space to focus on what truly mattered—my "why."

Looking back, I'm even grateful for the criticism. It pushed me to strengthen my belief in myself and my dreams. It taught me to stay grounded in my purpose, regardless of what others thought. If you're on a similar path, remember this: Not everyone will cheer for you, and that's okay. What matters is that you keep moving forward, trusting in your ability to create the life you envision.

The world needs people who are brave enough to grow, even when it's uncomfortable, even when it means letting go of the safety of others' approval. Protect your energy. Seek out those who lift you higher. And when doubt creeps in—whether it's yours or someone else's—remind yourself of why you started. You are building something beautiful, and that's always worth fighting for.

That's the path I've walked. And it's the path I'm helping other women walk today. I've seen first-hand how transformative it can be to embrace your true self. I know that when we decide to step into our authenticity, we unlock the ability to live the life we've always dreamed of. And that's the most beautiful, fulfilling life we can ever create.

Today, I am living my dream life. I trust my decisions, I am grateful for everything that comes my way, and I trust that the universe has my back. My mission is no longer just about my own journey—it's about empowering others to live theirs. I understand now that we are given just one life. It's a precious gift, handed to us on our birthday, and it comes with no guarantees. That's why every day is a gift. Every morning when we wake up, we are given the opportunity to do everything differently. We can stop, start, move, change—it's up to us.

But here's the truth: What you're not changing, you're choosing. If you're reading these words, you're part of a privileged group of people who have access to the tools and knowledge that can make your journey something great. It's within your reach. The power to change, to evolve, and to live a life full of joy and meaning is already within you.

That someone can be you. And when you commit to being the best version of yourself, everyone around you benefits. When you show up for yourself, when you fill your own cup, you can then fill the cups of others without hesitation or depletion. That's when you can be the best mother, partner, coworker, and, most importantly, the best friend to yourself.

When we heal, we break free from the chains of the past and create a new future—not only for ourselves but for everyone we touch. We can choose to be the light. We can choose to live a life full of "yays"— a life that's bold, vibrant, and full of joy. And when we live this way, we show others how to do the same, simply by walking the path ourselves.

This is the ripple effect of transformation. This is the gift we give to the world when we embrace our true selves, when we heal, and when we choose to live authentically. It's not just about our own personal growth; it's about creating a world where healing, empowerment, and authenticity are the norms.

So, do it now. Live your dream life now. Because your life should be like the dreams they said were too big— it should be bold, fearless, and unapologetically authentic. Choose to be the one who breaks the cycles, the one who chooses light over fear, the one who lives a life full of joy and inspiration. When you step into your greatness, you empower everyone around you to do the same.

Because this is it. This is the one life we have. And it's up to us to make it count. Choose to make every day a gift. Choose to be the change. Choose to live a life that is unapologetically, powerfully, and authentically yours. The world is waiting for you to shine, and the time is now.

METH TOXINS

AWARENESS ALLIANCE

Kathi McCarty

Founder

Kathi McCarty is the founder of Meth Toxins Awareness Alliance, dedicated to educating the public about the hidden dangers of methamphetamine contamination from smoking or manufacturing. After discovering her own home had been irreparably damaged by meth toxins, she turned her personal loss into a statewide movement for change.

A passionate advocate and policy champion, Kathi played a key role in driving legislative reform, helping to pass new protections during Colorado's 2023 Legislative Session designed to strengthen disclosure, prevention, and accountability measures in real estate. She continues to work alongside policymakers, industry leaders, and community members to push for stronger safeguards.

A Colorado resident for nearly 30 years, Kathi embraces her state's outdoor lifestyle, enjoying nature and adventure. She enjoys traveling whenever possible. However, her most cherished role is being a proud Grandma and spending time with family and close friends.

She remains committed to creating a safer future for individuals, families and communities by ensuring awareness, education, and prevention remain at the forefront of real estate policy.

https://www.linkedin.com/in/kathi-mccarty
https://www.facebook.com/methtoxinsalliance
https://www.instagram.com/toxinfreezone/
https://methtoxinsalliance.com/

Beyond the Walls

A Story of Home, Betrayal, and Purpose

By Kathi McCarty

"You can plan for everything… and still, life will surprise you in ways you never saw coming."

For thirty years, I built a successful career in mortgage lending and retail banking. It was a world I knew well and thoroughly enjoyed. Contracts, financial strategy, helping people secure properties, both commercial and residential, and guiding them toward financial security and independence.

I was proud of what I had built, appreciative of my stability and the security I created for myself.

Proud that even when I became a single mother, I continued to be proactive about my own financial future. I had done things "right."

Along with my children's father, we had saved for college. Once a single mom, I did the best I could to the best of my ability by them and also contributed to my retirement. I had also purchased a long-term disability plan offered when I started my banking career in 2007, building a foundation to protect my family and my future.

I could be spontaneous in many areas, and also someone who planned not to leave things to chance.

The summer of 2013 marked a milestone. After spending over two years looking for just the right property, I found my dream home in our community of Evergreen, Colorado where I had already lived for almost 2 decades raising a family.

It was everything I had ever wanted, a beautifully restored 1956 log cabin nestled in the pines, perched at the perfect elevation to capture stunning alpenglow sunrises and spectacular fire glowing sunsets over Mount Blue Sky, one of Colorado's majestic 14ers.

Every west-facing window framed a postcard-perfect view, each season unveiling its own unique magic. In the fall, we relished Indian summer days with warm temperatures and crisp, cool nights, as aspen leaves quaked in the wind. Winter blanketed the pine trees in fresh snow, creating a serene and soft white landscape. Spring brought wildflowers bursting to life, painting our landscape with vibrant colors. Throughout the summer, a playground of hiking, biking, and kayaking awaited just beyond our doorstep or a short drive away.

And inside? Love lived here.

This was the home where family and friends gathered for traditional holidays, celebrations, and just because. Our home was open to the boys' friends, and the kitchen and hot tub were always open, where conversations or chill time stretched late into the night.

Months went by into years, and my sons were growing into men. This was our sanctuary, our sacred space. This wasn't just a house. It was also my forever home, the space I envisioned grandchildren growing in, and the legacy I intended to leave to my children and their families.

I had built this life with intention. Overall, I had made smart decisions, thought through the risks, and protected my future.

But no amount of careful planning could prepare me for the one thing I never saw coming, literally.

In early 2016, I began experiencing subtle symptoms, such as dry, itchy eyes. Initially, I attributed these issues to eye strain from too much computer or paperwork. Or possibly extra dry winter air? I managed through the symptoms by using a lot of extra eye drops. Then, one morning, just weeks after these initial signs, I awoke with double vision. Having lost my dad only three days prior, I postponed seeking medical attention, choosing instead to navigate the emotional and logistical challenges that followed his passing, all while keeping one eye closed. Ten days later, I finally consulted a neuro-opthalmologist and was diagnosed with Graves' disease, an autoimmune disorder where the antibodies in the blood attack the thyroid gland. In my case, this led to Thyroid Eye Disease (TED), where the thyroid response targeted the tissues around my eyes, causing inflammation that threatened my vision. Despite monitoring and treatment, within a couple of months, I woke up to find that the color vision in my right eye had vanished, caused by inflammation compressing my optic nerve, leaving everything in various shades of gray.

The next nine months were a series of four surgeries. Surgery one was an orbital decompression to relieve pressure on my optic nerve with bone and tissue removal in my orbital socket. It worked. Color returned to my right eye.

Surgery two was seven weeks later because the color in my left eye too faded. Another emergency surgery to protect my vision, another stretch of recovery, another hopeful wait. This one was successful too. My ability to see color returned.

But my eyes had paid a price. One now pointed inward, the other in and upward, making it impossible to focus. Driving was out of the question. Reading was exhausting with one eye closed. My world had definitely tilted.

Strabismus surgery was number three, with the goal of realigning my eyes forward. This required the expertise of a different specialized doctor over six months later. Unfortunately, the muscle damage around my eyes was significant, and the first attempt failed.

The final attempt to restore eye alignment and vision was 2 weeks later. The strabismus surgeon aligned my eyes as closely as possible, but the damage had been done. The years of pressure, inflammation, and trauma had left me with permanent double vision.

For months, I lived in a haze. I had always been fiercely independent, yet now I couldn't even drive myself to the grocery store, or even all my doctor appointments.

The most challenging aspect wasn't merely the physical limitations; it was the profound fear of the unknown. Yet, amidst this uncertainty, I felt immense gratitude. I had come perilously close to losing my sight in both eyes, and the fact that I could still see was nothing short of miraculous. After five months of post-surgical healing, I discovered a potential solution to my permanent double vision: corrective lenses with built-in prisms. These specialized lenses are designed to align images by bending light before it enters the eye, thereby addressing issues like double vision. When I finally received my prescription glasses, they offered a partial remedy, improving my sight.

My job offered to hold my position open, and they did it for over a year. But deep down, I knew. The life I had built in banking, the one I had excelled in for a decade, was no longer mine.

I had spent my career reading contracts, assessing financials, and guiding others toward security. But I could no longer read the fine print the way I once did. I could no longer trust my eyes to catch the details, to see the numbers clearly, to catch small but important mistakes.

After dedicating decades to my career, I found myself at a crossroads, realizing that my professional path was shifting in unforeseen ways. Embracing this change, I saw an opportunity to explore new avenues that resonated with my evolving passions and values. With gratitude for the experiences that had shaped me, I chose to move forward, eager to discover the possibilities that lay ahead.

I didn't know exactly what was next, but I knew I wanted something meaningful, something expansive, something that wouldn't just sustain me financially but would give me purpose as I entered my sixties.

Then, an opportunity appeared.

A longtime friend and previous work colleague I had known and trusted for thirty-five years had recently opened a holistic wellness center in North Carolina. She invited me to visit, to experience the healing firsthand.

At the time, I was still recovering from my first two surgeries, so I went. While there, she invited me to her annual wellness retreat on the south island, Treasure Beach, Jamaica—a quiet, hidden gem untouched by mass tourism. The moment I arrived, something shifted.

The warm, humid air eased the tension in my body. My eyes, constantly strained in Colorado's dry climate, felt soothed for the first time in years. The island, the people, the pace all felt like a place where I could heal not just physically, but emotionally.

And then, a vision took root. My friend had been looking for a property to host her own retreats instead of renting.

While we were there, a property became available. It was a space perfect for expansion. A vision evolved where people could come for renewal, healing, and transformation.

It felt like fate.

A business that aligned with my values.
An opportunity to create something meaningful.
A way to step into a new chapter on my own terms.

I was all in.

Over the next few months we researched and put into motion purchasing this international property. Once ours, for the next 18 months, I poured my time, money, and energy into our vision. I traveled back and forth, overseeing repairs and new construction, ensuring that everything was done right. I wasn't just a passive investor. I was hands-on, physically working to make this dream a reality.

Jamaica had welcomed me in ways I hadn't expected. My body felt lighter, my spirit stronger, my purpose clearer than ever.

For the first time in years, I felt like I was building something, not just rebuilding from what had been lost, but truly creating something new.

And for a while, it all felt solid.

Until it didn't.

Because I was in Jamaica a lot, I chose to rent out our Colorado home for 1 year to help offset medical deductions on my surgeries and help me save on my mortgage while being away. What seemed like a sensible solution turned out to be my worst nightmare. I had just returned from a long visit to Jamaica, where we finalized construction and furnishing our two new board houses to accommodate guests for retreats we intended to start in early 2019. In October 2018, I got a call from my property management company back in Colorado. That single moment shattered everything.

The company I had entrusted to take care of my home had placed a tenant there just ninety days before. I was told there was a minor maintenance issue at the home, and they had the plumber working on repairs. That was anything but the truth. The maintenance issue was actually the main water line having a break they had chosen to hide, because they had placed a tenant who had turned my home into a meth lab, fully contaminating it beyond repair.

The numbers established by our state health department were staggering, exceeding over two hundred thirty times our state legal limit. My beautiful cabin, my dream home, now was uninhabitable. Condemned. Permanently damaged.

I was drowning in the gravity of it all. My home. My finances. My security. It had all blown up overnight, and in its place was a mountain of civil and criminal legal battles, along with unimaginable grief.

During this challenging period, I noticed a significant change in my friend's behavior. When I needed support the most, she became distant and unresponsive. Demanding, at times, my continued physical and financial involvement regardless of my situation. Reflecting on our relationship, I realized that her engagement had often been self-serving; she was present when benefiting from my contributions that served her.

I had trusted my own judgment, my ability to read people, and my instinct to see the good in others.

And I had been wrong.

That was a bitter pill to swallow.

Some betrayals leave scars. This one certainly did.

But here's what I know now.

True partnership is tested in hardship, not in success.

Integrity doesn't reveal itself when things are easy, it shows up when things get hard.

You don't lose people when you hit hard times. You lose people who were never truly with you, to begin with.

I walked away from Jamaica.

I walked away from the investment.

I walked away from the dream.

Not because I failed.

But because I refused to stay where I wasn't valued.

And, while it was one of the most painful betrayals I had ever faced, it was also one of my greatest teachers.

Because when I look back, I don't just see what I lost.

I see what I gained.

"Some betrayals break you. Others wake you up."

After everything I had been through, the vision loss, the career shift, and the unraveling of my investment in Jamaica, I thought I had experienced the worst of it.

I thought I had already lost everything there was to lose (except my sight). That I was hugely grateful for!

However, life had one more lesson to teach me.

And this time, it wasn't just about loss. It was about seeing the truth: clearly, fully, and without any illusions.

The county had deemed my Evergreen home uninhabitable and condemned after testing positive for meth contamination at over 230 times over the legal limit in the hottest location. Nine of the eleven zones tested between 69-119.5 compared to the state standard of .5 ug/100cm for our Colorado State Health Department guidelines.

My homeowner's insurance denied coverage for methamphetamine contamination, citing standard policy exclusions that exist in all our policies. Similarly, the tenant's insurance refused to cover damages resulting from their criminal activities. Another standard with our home insurance policies. The property management company failed to vet the tenant in any way and neglected to report significant issues, such as necessary water line repairs. After 18 months of legal proceedings, I secured only a partial settlement, covering a fraction of the total loss.

It was over.

So, I did what I had to do. I sold it. It wasn't a financial decision, it was a necessary surrender.

And the realtor who had helped me buy that very home back in 2013, the one I had worked with for decades, the one who knew exactly how much this home had meant to me, was the one who handled the sale.

I trusted her.

She comforted me, acknowledging I was making the right choice for me.

In the end, the house sold for $240,000, about half of what it would have been worth had it still been livable.

It was painful, brutal, but I told myself: *at least it was over.*

Then, just a few months later, my phone rang.

It was my realtor.

Not to check in.
Not to see how I was holding up.
Not to offer a kind word.

She was calling to see if I wanted to buy my home back, and she said, "I know how much you loved that cabin."

I could hardly process what she was saying.

The new buyers had "remediated" the home. Not by removing the meth contamination, as I had been informed by several companies there was no way to remove meth toxins from a log building. The new buyer had the property "cleared" by our state health department by painting it with a product that encapsulates the toxins, sealing them in. A product approved by our state health department to use, but at last check, banned from sale in our state due to its toxicity and VOCs.

On paper, it was **legally** cleared by our state health department!

And because it had been "properly remediated" according to state laws, that meant it could now be resold without any disclosure of its past contamination per our current state regulations in 2018.

The home that had once been condemned and considered unlivable was now a profitable real estate investment.

And somehow, now I was offered the chance to buy back my home, with a level of meth sealed in for an amount around double what they had paid me for it just a few short months ago.

I stood there, phone in hand, feeling a wave of emotions crash over me.

Shock. Disbelief. Anger.

But then, something else rose to the surface.

Clarity.

For the first time in a long time, I saw everything for exactly what it was.

151

I saw how the fine print, the loopholes, and the legal technicalities weren't designed to protect property owners, they were designed to protect profits.

I saw how even the people I had trusted, the ones who had walked beside me for years, had been watching my loss not with sympathy, but with opportunity.

And just like that, I knew what I had to do.

I had to let it go.

There was a brief, fleeting moment where I let myself imagine it.

What if I just took it back? What if I undid the nightmare and tried to reclaim what had been taken from me?

But then reality set in.

That home? It wasn't mine anymore.

The structure might have still been there. The view might have been the same.

But the trust, the safety, the sanctuary?

That was all gone.

And it wasn't just about the money.

It was about knowing, deep in my bones, that I deserved better. My loved ones deserved better!

Because a home is more than walls and windows.

A home is a place where you can breathe, where you feel safe, where you are surrounded by people who have your best interests at heart.

And if a home loses those things?

It's no longer home.

So, I didn't buy it back.

I didn't argue.
I didn't fight.
I didn't waste one more moment holding onto something that had already slipped through my fingers.

Instead, I did the hardest thing I could have done.

I walked away.

And in that moment, I felt something I hadn't felt in a long time.

Relief.

Because for the first time in years, I wasn't clinging to what had been lost.

I was choosing to step into what was next.

There was a time when I thought my home had been stolen from me. That what I had worked so hard to build had been ripped away, piece by piece.

But now?

Now, I see it differently.

I wasn't meant to stay in that house forever.
I wasn't meant to fight battles that had already been lost.
I wasn't meant to pour my energy into chasing what was gone. I was meant to build something new.

And that's exactly what I did.

In letting go?

I finally saw the bigger picture.

This wasn't just about my home, my loss, my fight.

This was about every property owner who didn't know the risk.

This was about every real estate transaction where critical information was being buried.

This was about a system that wasn't designed to protect people similar to me.

So, in 2019, I founded Meth Toxins Awareness Alliance.

At first, it was just me. One woman with a story, a mission, and a refusal to let this happen to someone else.

Then, it became something bigger.

I started speaking out.
I met with lawmakers, real estate professionals, other affiliates who served the real estate industry, and property owners of all types. I fought for, advocated, and championed for disclosure laws, industry-wide testing, and homeowner and tenant protections.

Because this wasn't just about what happened to me.

It was about making sure no one else would have to stand in the wreckage of their life, blindsided, with nowhere to turn.

And as I stepped into this mission, this movement, this fight for awareness and justice, something unexpected happened.

For the first time since losing my home, I felt hope.

Not in a house.

But for my purpose.

"Sometimes what feels like an ending is really an invitation, to rise, to heal, to step into something greater."

For a long time, I carried the weight of everything I had lost.

The home I had built a life in.
The career I had devoted decades to.
The friendships and partnerships I had once trusted.

It was a slow grieving process, one that stretched across years, not days. There were moments when I felt unmoored, drifting between what was and what might be, caught in the in-between space of an identity I was still trying to redefine.

But through it all, one thing became clear: I was still standing.

Despite the losses, despite the betrayals, despite the moments that felt impossible, I was still here.

The more I let go of what I thought my life was supposed to look like, the more I started to see the life that was waiting for me.

Losing has a way of stripping you down to your core.

When there's nothing left to cling to, you have two choices: stay stuck in what's gone, or evaluate and step into what's next.

And once I stopped trying to rebuild what had been lost, I realized something: I didn't want that old life back.

I wanted something new. Something truly aligned with my core values.

Something more expansive.
Something with deeper meaning.
Something that allowed me to turn everything I had been through into something that could help and truly empower others.

I didn't want to just survive my story. I wanted to use it. So, I started speaking out.

At first, it was just small conversations, sharing my experience with people who had no idea that meth contamination could destroy a home overnight.

Then came the meetings with real estate professionals to raise awareness about the prevalence of meth contamination and why it matters, not just for their clients but for their own businesses as well. Gaining their support wasn't easy; I needed more data and more facts to back up my claims. So, I turned to the experts who had guided me through my own experience and, over time, connected with others who had faced similar devastation. I asked detailed questions, dug deeper, and steadily built my expertise, knowing facts that meth usage is still at epidemic levels, manufacturing still is common, and there are no socio-economic or geographical boundaries when it comes to who smokes meth or where. Prevention is my purpose of education, advocacy, and resources.

And slowly, step by step, conversation by conversation, I saw that this wasn't just my fight. This was an issue that needed a voice. And maybe just.

The truth is, I never would have chosen this path.

If you had asked me years ago where I saw myself at this stage in life, I would have told you about the cozy retirement I had planned, the home that was supposed to be my forever sanctuary, the steady career I had built brick by brick.

But life had other plans.

And while I wouldn't have chosen this road, I can stand here today and say—I am grateful for it.

Because out of all the loss, something unexpected was given back to me: a sense of purpose bigger than myself. A mission that lights a fire inside me every day.

A new way to serve, to protect, to advocate, to heal not just for myself, but for the thousands of property owners who deserve to know the risks before it's too late.

For the last several years, I haven't had a permanent address. I have lived in guest rooms, pet sat for friends, stayed with family, and even spent time in my truck camper, choosing to invest every dollar, all my energy, into building this movement.

Some might see that as a sacrifice. But I don't. Because I know now that home is not a place.

Home is the people who show up for you.
Home is the resilience you carry inside you.
Home is the knowing that you are building something that matters.

Home is where my heart is.

I may not have the home I thought I would retire in, but I have something even greater.

I have a mission that fuels me.

I have the love and support of people who truly see me.

I have the unshakable knowing that I am exactly where I am meant to be. And I have so much gratitude! When I think about what could have happened knowing what he was doing in and behind my home, the dangerous equipment, our Stage 2 fire ban while he was there because of our tinder dry conditions, put my neighbors and the whole community at risk of property damage, injury, or worse if my home had a fire.

And if I had to go through every storm, every heartbreak, every hard-earned lesson to get here,

Life doesn't always unfold the way we expect.

Sometimes, the things we hold onto the tightest are the very things we are meant to release.

Sometimes, the roads we never intended to take lead us exactly where we need to be.

And sometimes, when it feels like everything is falling apart, what's actually happening is that something new is being built in its place.

I don't know exactly what comes next.

But I know one thing for certain:

I will keep speaking.
I will keep advocating.
I will keep championing the truth.

Because what happened to me should never happen to someone else.

The life I never planned for.
The mission I never saw coming.
The purpose I was always meant to find goes beyond that four-letter word meth. It is when we lead with integrity today, that we leave a safer legacy for generations to come.

And through these "wonky eyes," I see much clearer.

METABOLIC WISDOM

Elita A'Vard

Metabolic Patient Advocate & Health Coach

Elita is passionate advocate for hope, resilience, and transformation, as a breast cancer thriver, and metabolic patient advocate, she is dedicated to inspiring others to embrace change and take ownership of their health journeys. Elita combines her unique experiences as a mother, and kinesiologist with her expertise in the metabolic approach to cancer care to empower others facing personal and health challenges.

Elita's journey is one of profound transformation. Having overcome a cancer diagnosis and the trials of an emotionally draining relationship, she has emerged as a beacon of hope for those navigating their own adversities. She believes in the power of self-love, flexibility, and courage to spark personal growth and healing.

Elita's mission is to help others discover their own resilience and live with purpose, regardless of the obstacles they face.

Even the toughest battles can lead to empowerment, renewal, and hope.

https://www.linkedin.com/elitaavard
https://www.facebook.com/metabolicwisdom
www.facebook.com/metabolicwisdom
http://www.metabolicwisdom.com.au/

Unbreakable Resilience

A Journey of Strength and Transformation

By Elita A'Vard

Before Cancer

Before cancer, I was many things—a mother, accountant, business owner, and stepmother. And then, there was my role as a wife. That title feels distant and discordant now, a word that barely captures the experience of living under the shadow of a relationship that syphoned my joy, my energy, my self-worth. I was juggling roles like so many women do, determined to keep everything running smoothly for the sake of those around me. My life looked structured on the outside, but there was a side that few saw. I carried a weight, hidden behind the surface of my family, my job, and my life. Inside my marriage, I was trapped, enduring a toxic relationship that drained my soul and left me questioning my worth. I look back at those days now with a mix of sadness and bewilderment—how could I not have seen the corrosive effects of such hidden stress on my mind and body?

For years, I had believed I was living a relatively healthy, active life, dedicated to being the best mother I could be. I stayed strong, even as my husband's words cut deep, spoken with disgust that I masked under the label of "mental illness." It was easier to label it than to face the betrayal of trust, the fractured vows, the erosion of a love that had long since turned toxic. The signs of emotional abuse were subtle at first, creeping in through small criticisms and cold glances, until they grew into harsh words and threats. The person I'd once loved had become my greatest source of pain. Each unkind word felt like a knife's edge, cutting deeper into my spirit. I began to wonder who I was, and what I had become. Every slammed door, every unfulfilled promise, every empty apology—the echoes of these moments built a prison of silence and shame around me. My days became a cycle of endurance, my nights a string of restless hours spent anxiously anticipating the next emotional outburst, and what would be smashed this time.

I was trapped, not by locked doors, but by my own beliefs: that marriage vows were meant to be upheld, that loyalty was a virtue, and that someday, somehow, things would change. But deep down, a part of me knew it was not a question of *if* but *when* my mind and body would cry out for release.

Somehow, I managed to maintain my life on the outside, working as an accountant, showing up at school events, running our business and household, and keeping a brave face. But behind that facade, I felt small and worn down, as if I were a shadow of the person I used to be.

A Glimmer of Hope

Then, a glimmer of hope came when I began studying kinesiology. This wasn't just a course or a career path; it was a lifeline. The fog started to lift! Each treatment with my classmates felt like another small act of liberation, allowing me to glimpse life outside the walls I'd built around myself. Slowly, I began to reclaim pieces of myself, piece by piece, memory by memory. Each moment spent learning the language of energy and healing gave me new strength, feeding an inner courage I didn't know I had. I could feel myself transforming, cocooned in the supportive hands of my classmates, finally strong enough to spread my wings and fly away from a relationship that had cost me too much.

For the first time in years, I felt seen and understood. My classmates became my support network, a circle of healing that I had long been missing. Each session with them gave me a sense of release and a spark of courage that slowly, over time, helped me break free.

Leaving the relationship was not the end but the beginning of a new kind of trial. I entered a state of constant vigilance, waiting for the next shoe to drop, for his inevitable need to "win" to manifest. He was relentless, always finding ways to create fear, with threats so insidious that law enforcement couldn't intervene. I found myself in a precarious situation—financially and emotionally unmoored. I would lie awake, heart racing, wondering if tonight would be the night he broke through my fragile sense of safety. What would he do if he did break in? Would he hurt my son, my innocent boy who was already learning too young about fear and survival? These weren't idle worries; they were my nighttime companions. My ex took control of our finances, the business we had built together, and even the cars we used to get around. I was left stranded in ways that were hard to explain to anyone who hadn't been there. But alongside the struggle, there was a strange, unexpected relief. I felt a glimmer of something I hadn't felt in years: relief. The chokehold of our relationship was loosening, and despite the hardships, a sense of peace began to replace the constant chaos. For the first time, I wasn't fighting to keep my head above water in a sea of insults and accusations. My freedom had come at a high cost, yet it was a cost I was willing to pay.

Time moved in strange, painful cycles as the financial separation dragged on. By the time it reached the final step before court, I was already on a new path, with a loving partner and a new baby. But this sense of rebuilding came crashing down the day my ex returned with a locksmith and the police while I was at home, breastfeeding. It was surreal—a reminder of the lengths he would go to try to keep control, even as our lives had taken on different trajectories.

Diagnosis

The pain of that chapter lingered, compounded by a miscarriage when my daughter was just 11 months old. In those raw, grief-stricken days, I could scarcely imagine facing another trial. I was exhausted—physically, emotionally, and spiritually depleted. I was beginning to find my footing again when I received the news that would shift everything: breast cancer.

It felt surreal, sitting alone in that sterile doctor's office, hearing the diagnosis from a stranger in a mask, his words muffled by COVID restrictions yet piercing all the same. My heart felt like it had stopped, suspended in disbelief. The questions flooded in, one after the other, each one scarier than the last: How would I tell my children? Would I survive this? I was alone at that moment, yet I felt the weight of everyone I loved pressing down on me. I called my family, the words sticking in my throat, struggling to make sense of this diagnosis that felt like the ultimate betrayal. "I have breast cancer." Saying it out loud was like summoning an avalanche. The thought of breaking the news to my parents made me feel incapacitated I actually had to request my brother to do that on my behalf, of course, they called me immediately—answering that phone call was equally as difficult. Somehow, I felt that I had let those closest to me down, yet it was out of my control.

Breaking the news to my son was one of the hardest moments of my life. He was only 12, a boy who had already faced more than most his age. His reaction—full of worry, but tempered by a resilience that made me both proud and heartbroken—tore at me. He asked questions I couldn't answer, questions no mother wants to hear: "Where will I live if you die, Mum?" His voice cracked, and I could see the fear in his eyes, the same fear that haunted me every time I looked in the mirror. But I refused to let him see my weakness. I promised him and myself that I would fight, even though I had no idea how. I saw his innocence dimmed by the weight of adult concerns. My heart still aches for the time we lost to my illness. To protect himself from losing me, he put up walls, what was once such a close mother-and-son bond became strained and distant. We are making up for that now and rediscovering a new kind of relationship that I am excited about, I could not be prouder of the young man that he is becoming.

Fortunately, my daughter was so young that attending doctor appointments with Mummy was all that she knew. However, for me, I felt like my life had taken a sudden turn— one minute, I was really present, enjoying being a new mum with a new life outside of the cloud I once lived under, then the next minute, playdates were replaced with medical appointments.

My partner had already endured the profound losses of both his parents to cancer, and the trauma had left him with a deeply ingrained fear that anyone he loved might one day leave him, too. My diagnosis reawakened his worst fear and sent him into a quiet spiral of anxiety. He grappled with the terrifying possibility of losing me, but rather than allowing us to lean on each other, his fear pulled him inward.

Although he wanted to be there for me, he found himself emotionally paralyzed, struggling with the idea of having to watch someone else he loved go through such a painful journey. He stepped in where he could—taking on the physical tasks, helping with the children, and managing day-to-day needs—but on an emotional level, he felt unreachable. I saw the weight of his worry in his eyes, yet his own pain created a wall that kept us apart just when I needed him most. This left me facing much of the emotional journey on my own, learning to navigate both my pain and his in a way that helped me grow stronger within myself.

The abusive relationship had affected the belief I had in myself to trust my own decisions, as well as my self-worth—and my body was holding the score.

I was feeling so alone and terrified. I remember a vivid moment of sitting on my bedroom floor in tears, and I realised I had two choices: to let this define me in a growth way or to be a victim. That was an easy choice for me; the path wasn't easy, but the choice was.

Cancer became a mirror reflecting back the years of neglect—of my health, my happiness, and my sense of self-worth. I decided to relieve myself of the beliefs that I held for too long, and sought help from a mindset coach to help me stay on track.

The early days were a haze of doctor's appointments, statistics, and well-meaning but often frightening advice. It was only a few weeks from diagnosis until the surgery date, it is such a weird feeling when you can lie in bed feeling this lump, knowing how terrifying it can be and waiting for surgery to get it out. I was still breastfeeding my daughter when diagnosed, so I had to wean her off very quickly to undergo surgery (the surgery notes say copious amounts of blood and milk). Being forced to end this beautiful bonding time with my daughter—not by choice, but because of this disease—left me feeling robbed.

The oncologist talked about survival rates and treatment plans with a detached, clinical tone that made me feel more like a number than a person. I remember sitting in that office, feeling a surge of defiance rise within me. I was more than a statistic; I was a mother, a fighter. How could she use a computer-generated statistic to predict my life with any kind of accuracy, when she had no knowledge about my lifestyle, my genetics, or really anything about me—to her, it appeared as though I was just a number.

I decided I would be more than a statistic; I would fight not only for my survival but for my right to live fully. I wasn't going to let cancer define me.

Making the decision to undergo chemotherapy was one of the most agonising choices I faced. Although my cancer had been surgically removed, chemotherapy was presented as an "insurance policy"— offering only a 7% chance of further reducing my risk, while carrying the possibility of severe side effects and even the chance of inducing another cancer down the line. My family's fear weighed heavily on me, especially when I saw the worry on my loved ones' faces. That fear swayed my decision, and I committed to a course of dose-dense chemotherapy (every two weeks).

But the treatment hit me harder than I'd ever anticipated. I was already underweight after the haemorrhaging from my recent miscarriage, and within three days of starting chemo, I dropped an additional three kilograms. After the first treatment, I experienced such an intense feeling of 'brain fog' I could barely speak. Desperate for relief, I reached out to the medical team for support. One kind nurse reassured me that it didn't have to feel this awful, urging me to call the next day to adjust my medications. However, when I did, a different nurse gave a harsh, unhelpful response: "Bad luck, expect to feel like crap and drink Coca-Cola."

At my next cardiology check, I sought answers for the heart palpitations, shortness of breath, and dizziness I felt. These symptoms had followed me since my mastectomy and miscarriage, and I suspected a blood-related issue. Yet, the cardiologist dismissed me outright, stating—right in front of my partner—that it was "all in my head." Later, a compassionate nurse explained that my symptoms were due to anaemia, but the cardiologist's comment left a lasting impact, shaking my confidence and trust in myself just as I had begun to rebuild it. I couldn't help but feel frustrated at how often women's pain and symptoms are dismissed in medical settings.

I want to note that not everyone has this reaction, in fact, it is quite well tolerated in most people. I was very underweight and depleted already, and my body is often sensitive to medications. This was, of course, compounded by the unfortunate negative experiences I encountered with the medical staff. I acknowledge that these staff are overworked and burnt out, but the responses they gave me could have had a very negative impact on a different person.

That experience pushed me to take charge of my own health and become my own advocate. I knew I could no longer accept feeling unheard. This decision marked the beginning of nearly full-time research, delving into scientifically backed options to find a treatment path that truly felt right for me.

Having a mindset coach really helped me stay true to my new sense of self, instead of being passive about my treatment and healing protocols, I became active in my approach. My initial focus was on healing the wounds from the past relationship and the diagnosis itself, with a big emphasis on getting back to trusting myself and having a newfound self-love. Working on self-love at this time was further complicated by having to face mastectomy scars, and losing my hair and fertility. The day my hair started falling out was one of the most confronting days of my life, but I must say that the day I decided to shave was, conversely, the most empowering day of my life. It was like a path of self-discovery, a newfound sense of freedom I didn't anticipate would come from shaving my head.

Becoming a Beacon of Hope

My journey took a turn when I stumbled upon *The Metabolic Approach to Cancer* by Dr. Nasha Winters. Her words offered more than hope—they gave me a map, a guide to understanding my illness not just as a disease to be fought, but as a sign from my body. I began to see cancer not as an external invader but as something intertwined with my own history, my stress, my choices, and my traumas. Winters' holistic approach to healing resonated with me on a profound level. I decided that, alongside conventional treatment, I would embrace this new perspective, focusing on rebuilding my health from the inside out. This wasn't just a treatment plan; it was a lifeline that allowed me to reclaim my autonomy. In understanding the metabolic roots of cancer, I found a way to make sense of the chaos and to heal from within. I began to rebuild myself—not just physically but emotionally and spiritually. For the first time in years, I was taking control.

For me, this approach wasn't just about battling cancer—it was about reclaiming my life. I started making changes, not just in my diet and lifestyle, but in how I related to myself. I began the journey of self-love, learning to forgive myself for the years spent in pain and silence. I understood that healing meant more than eradicating cancer cells; it meant letting go of the toxic beliefs and relationships that had weighed me down for so long.

I had always considered myself a 'healthy' person, I didn't drink and smoke; I ate healthy, etc… but my eyes were opened so much further after this book and then the advocacy course I did. The Metabolic Approach is about finding the things that contributed to your diagnosis and looking at you from a holistic point of view. It works alongside standard of care and really helps a patient feel empowered about their own journey.

I immersed myself in research, eager to understand every detail. I cut out sugar, overhauled my diet, and committed to a regimen of supplements, meditation, and exercise. I found that the discipline required for this journey was empowering in itself. Every choice, every meal, every breath was a small act of defiance against the disease that had threatened to consume me. The fear that once paralyzed me was slowly replaced by a quiet confidence, a deep trust in my body's ability to heal. It transformed my perspective on life. I see now that my health was never just about the absence of disease. It was about embracing myself fully, flaws and scars and all. I was no longer a passive patient; I became an advocate for my own healing, exploring every avenue, researching, and finding ways to regain my strength. I focused on releasing the toxic remnants of my past, understanding that my body had carried the weight of that relationship for too long, it was a big contributing factor to *why* I got cancer.

Healing meant more than physical recovery; it meant confronting the beliefs I had held about myself for so many years. I realised that everyone in my life, even those who had hurt me, carried their own wounds. Understanding that their actions were a reflection of their pasts, not my worth, was liberating. I let go of old hurts, released the need to carry others' pain, and focused instead on building a life filled with self-love, resilience, and peace.

It was not a linear journey. It came in waves, some days stronger, some days dragging me under. I encountered setbacks and struggled to maintain the discipline of my new routine. But each time I faltered, I thought of my children. My children became my greatest motivators.

I wanted them to see their mother not as a victim but as a woman who rose above her circumstances.

I thought of the life I wanted to build, the life I deserved. Each step forward felt like reclaiming a piece of myself. I was no longer defined by my past, by the abuse, by the cancer. I was creating a new narrative, one rooted in resilience and self-empowerment.

Through it all, I discerned that the journey was not just about surviving—it was about living. Cancer taught me the value of each day, each moment. I had spent years existing in survival mode, but now I was learning to embrace life with gratitude and purpose. I became an advocate, not just for myself but for others. I shared my story, my struggles, and my triumphs, hoping to be a beacon of hope for those facing similar battles. I wanted others to know that healing was possible, that there was light beyond the darkest days.

The metabolic approach not only transformed my health but also reshaped my identity. I learned that healing isn't about returning to who you were before; it's about discovering who you're meant to become. This realisation sparked a sense of purpose I hadn't known I was searching for. I wanted to share this knowledge, to show others that they, too, could take control of their health and their lives.

Becoming an advocate for others was a natural progression. Sharing my story started as an act of vulnerability but quickly became a source of strength. I connected with other women facing similar struggles, offering them the support and understanding I had once longed for. In their stories, I saw pieces of my own journey, and together, we found hope and resilience.

Through this process, I discovered the power of community. No one should have to navigate life's challenges alone, and in sharing my journey, I found a profound sense of connection. Every conversation, every story shared, reminded me that even in our darkest moments, we are never truly alone.

When I look back on my journey, I see how much I've learned about navigating change and facing adversity with resilience and openness. Now, as I connect with others—especially those going through their own health or personal struggles—I feel deeply called to share what's helped me find strength, peace, and empowerment.

I'm passionate about showing others that it's possible to emerge from adversity with gentleness and compassion intact. One of the most essential lessons I share is the power of approaching each challenge with calm, strength, and respect. In my experience, it's easy to let the past weigh us down, but I've learned to draw only on the wisdom it offers without letting it overshadow my present. I encourage others to do the same: to release what no longer serves them and to greet each new obstacle with an open heart, seeing it as an opportunity for growth and self-discovery.

For me, being there for others means sharing both the highs and the lows of my journey so that they can see that change, while daunting, can lead to empowerment. I hope that by sharing my story, I help them find the courage to face their own journeys with strength, flexibility, and a renewed belief in their resilience. In this way, I aim to inspire others to become the strongest, truest versions of themselves, even in the face of life's greatest challenges.

Now, looking back, I see a woman transformed—not just by cancer but by every challenge I had overcome. I am proud of the journey, proud of the scars that tell my story. I have learned that true strength lies not in avoiding pain but in facing it, learning from it, and emerging stronger. Cancer may have changed the course of my life, but it has also given me a new sense of purpose, a deeper connection to myself and those I love. I am not just a survivor; I am a thriver, a woman who has taken her power back and is living her truth.

My past no longer defines me; it fuels my purpose. I am grateful for every challenge, every moment of doubt, because they led me to this place of empowerment.

To anyone reading this who feels trapped by life's circumstances, know this: change is possible. The road may be difficult, but within you lies a strength greater than you realize. Healing is not about perfection; it's about progress. It's about taking one step at a time, even when the path seems unclear.

My journey has taught me that life's greatest challenges can lead to extraordinary transformations. By embracing change, prioritising self-love, and finding the courage to rewrite our stories, we can turn pain into purpose and struggle into strength.

This is my message to you: No matter how dark the journey may seem, there is always light at the end of the tunnel. And sometimes, the most challenging paths lead to the most beautiful destinations.

January Liddell

Financial Strategist

I'm January Liddell, a proud wife of almost 20 years to a retired veteran and a dedicated mom to two amazing kids—an intelligent, handsome son and a care-free beautiful daughter. My life has been a journey of resilience, growth, and passion, all of which I channel into my work as a Retirement Specialist at Ideas By Mike™.

My path into the financial industry was born from a deep desire to protect what matters most—not just for my family but for others striving to secure their future. With four years of experience, I've made it my mission to help individuals achieve tax-free gains and protect their hard-earned assets from market risk and volatility. My passion stems from personal values of stability and peace of mind, values I know are essential for any family planning for a worry-free retirement.

Beyond my professional role, I've embraced life's adventures wholeheartedly. I've written "Alina, The Super Saver," a children's book inspired by my belief in teaching financial literacy early. I also co-host the Sexy Freedom Media Podcast,where I share stories, insights, and inspiration with a mostly female audience. Helen Edwards and I discuss mindset, growth, stepping out of our comfort zones, we have a resident psychiatrist, Dr Gretchen Gavero, and special guests: doctors, authors, publishers, and more.

In my free time, you'll find me riding the waves boogie boarding on the east side, cheering my children who play hockey and who are aspiring actors, making unforgettable memories with my 84 year-old aunty, facilitate a women's connect group, date day/night with my husband, or sharpening my focus at the gun or archery range. I also find solace in the gym, my faith, and the simple joys of family life.

I understand that every family has its own story, challenges, and dreams. That's why I prioritize connection, communication, and trust in every relationship. My clients' success isn't just my goal—it's my passion. I'm here to make sure you feel confident, empowered, and ready to embrace all that life has to offer.

https://www.linkedin.com/in/januaryliddell/
https://www.facebook.com/groups/619316822805111
https://www.instagram.com/alinathehoneymaker
https://www.xtreme1financial.com/
http://www.januaryliddell.com/

From Homemaker to Wealth Maker

Lessons in Growth, Grit, and Grace

By January Liddell

From Homemaker to Wealth Maker: Lessons in Growth, Grit, and Grace

Transitioning from a stay-at-home mom to a successful business owner has been one of the most transformative and challenging journeys of my life. It required courage, perseverance, and an unwavering belief in my ability to rise above obstacles. As a mother to a 16-year-old son and a 9- year-old daughter, and a wife to a soldier deployed seven times, I learned resilience early on. This journey has been about more than building a business; it's about embracing change, growing into my full potential, and setting an example of courage and determination for my family.

This chapter takes you through the highs and lows of my journey. From battling imposter syndrome and balancing the demands of motherhood and entrepreneurship to investing in personal development, I've learned that transformation requires grit and grace. Personal growth, self-care, and adaptability have proven to be essential elements of success.

Learning Independence as a Military Wife

Before starting my business, I built a strong foundation of resilience during my years as a military wife. With my husband deployed seven times, I had to manage all aspects of our home life independently— raising children, paying bills, and handling crises.

One vivid memory stands out: my son was sick, and our car broke down the same day. With my husband away, I prioritized, got my son medical attention, and arranged car repairs. These moments taught me how to manage multiple responsibilities with calmness and clarity.

Over time, I embraced my independence. Each challenge I overcame built my confidence and revealed my inner strength. From navigating bureaucratic paperwork to comforting my children during their father's absence, I approached each situation with determination and grace.

These experiences prepared me for entrepreneurship. Running a business requires the same resilience, adaptability, and problem-solving skills that I honed as a military wife.

Rediscovering My Identity

For years, my identity revolved around being a wife and mother. While raising my children and supporting my husband brought immense joy, a small voice inside me longed for more. I wanted to build something of my own—a legacy reflecting my values, passions, and dreams.

Rediscovering my identity wasn't easy. I had to ask myself difficult questions: Who am I beyond my roles as a mother and wife? What do I want to contribute to the world? Pursuing my dreams didn't mean neglecting my family; it meant showing them the power of resilience and determination.

This phase of rediscovery was liberating yet daunting. Letting go of limiting beliefs, I embraced the idea that my worth wasn't defined by societal expectations but by my willingness to grow and evolve.

Battling Imposter Syndrome

As I began my entrepreneurial journey, I faced imposter syndrome—a persistent voice of self doubt whispering I wasn't qualified or capable.

Social media magnified these insecurities. Seeing others achieve milestones made me question my own potential. However, I realized imposter syndrome affects even the most accomplished individuals. The key was shifting my mindset: instead of focusing on shortcomings, I celebrated small victories—signing a client, completing a project, or consistently showing up for my business. These wins built my confidence over time.

Embracing Personal Development

Investing in personal development was a turning point in my journey. I realized that to become the person I aspired to be, I had to grow myself.

John Maxwell's teachings on leadership became my guiding light. His emphasis on leading with authenticity resonated deeply. Books like Atomic Habits taught me the power of consistent actions, while Crucial Conversations equipped me with tools to navigate difficult discussions.

I also sought guidance from mentors like Ryan Blair. His entrepreneurial insights encouraged me to approach setbacks as opportunities for growth. Therapy was another critical component, allowing me to manage stress, set boundaries, and maintain balance.

Balancing Motherhood, Marriage, and Business

Balancing motherhood, marriage, and entrepreneurship has been one of my greatest challenges. Raising our16-year-old son and 9-year-old daughter while spending quality time with my husband , and building a business required exceptional time management. Early mornings and late nights became my most productive hours, and I developed systems to ensure I could meet my family's needs while dedicating time to my business.

However, I prioritized being present. When I was with my children and husband, I gave them my full attention, whether sitting still watching a movie with my husband, helping my son with schoolwork or listening to my daughter share her stories. Pursuing my dreams wasn't just for me —it was for them, too.

There were moments of guilt, but I reminded myself that I was setting an example. I wanted them to see that it's never too late to chase your dreams and that personal growth is a lifelong journey. By evolving into a better version of me, my relationships with my husband and children became stronger and peace filled our home.

Embracing Change and Transformation

Change is the foundation of growth, though it is often uncomfortable. My transition from stay-at home mom to business owner required stepping out of my comfort zone and embracing transformation—not just external changes but internal ones as well. I leaned heavily on my faith in God. Jeremiah 29:11 became my mantra, "For I know the plans I have for you,"declares the Lord, "Plans to prosper you and not to harm you, plans to give you a hope and a future." With so many changes and transitions, I needed God to be my beacon of light and comfort. It was through Him, I continue to evolve and embrace change and transformation.

Redefining my role within my family was one such change. I worried about losing touch with my children and husband while focusing on my business, but I found ways to involve them in my journey. My son asked questions about entrepreneurship, while my daughter loved to "help Mommy with her big ideas." My husband helped me prepare and set up my in person meetings. These moments reminded me that change can bring us closer together.

I also had to adapt to the unpredictability of entrepreneurship. Running a business brought unexpected setbacks, demanding deadlines, and fluctuating income. These challenges pushed me to grow emotionally and mentally, teaching me to trust my instincts and approach problems creatively.

Expanding My Comfort Zone

Building a business required stepping far beyond my comfort zone. Networking, marketing myself, and taking on leadership roles initially felt intimidating. However, I understood that growth only happens when we challenge ourselves.

Small, intentional steps helped me expand my comfort zone. I practiced public speaking, joined networking events, and sought mentors who could guide me. One pivotal moment came when I organized an event in Phoenix, Arizona. Overwhelmed with anxiety, I almost gave my speaking moment to one of my friends and colleagues. However, I pushed through, and the experience was transformative, reminding me of the power of authenticity and connection.

Leadership and Self-Leadership

Leadership has been an ongoing lesson for me. As a stay-at-home mom, I learned through hands on experience how to lead by being mom to my children. Moms have to navigate through our days by delegating chores, having "board meetings" with my family about our systems at home: laundry, washing dishes, sweeping and mopping, and any aspect pertaining to how we run our home, and by showing up as the parent and wife, who may not always be sunshine and rainbows. Through John Maxwell's teachings, I learned leadership wasn't about control but empowerment. Leading myself—setting goals, staying disciplined, and holding myself accountable—was just as important as leading others.

Facing Financial Challenges

Starting a business came with financial challenges. With a limited budget, I had to prioritize investments that would yield long-term growth, such as personal development and quality tools. There were months of fluctuating income, but these challenges taught me financial discipline and resourcefulness.

Prioritizing Mental Health and Self-Care

Success means little without mental and emotional well-being. In the early days, I neglected self care, leading to stress and burnout. Over time, I realized self-care was non-negotiable. Exercise, journaling, and moments of stillness became part of my routine. Therapy also helped me unpack emotional challenges and build resilience. Praying and being present with God is my other non negotiable.

The Power of Mentorship

Mentorship was invaluable on my journey. Ryan Blair's insights pushed me to think bigger and view setbacks as opportunities. Other women who had navigated similar transitions inspired me with their stories of resilience and triumph.

Embracing Lifelong Growth

One empowering realization is that growth is a lifelong journey. There is no final destination— only continuous learning and striving to become the best version of yourself. I approach challenges as opportunities to learn, reflect, and adapt.

This mindset extends beyond my professional life. As a mother, I'm learning how to better support my children. As a wife, I nurture my marriage and appreciate my husband's sacrifices. And as a business owner, I'm dedicated to refining my skills and serving my clients with excellence.

A Legacy of Transformation

Reflecting on my journey, I'm filled with gratitude for how far I've come. The transition from homemaker to wealth maker is more than a story of professional success—it's a story of personal transformation.

Through challenges and triumphs, I've become more confident, resilient, and compassionate. I'm proud to set an example for my children, showing them that it's never too late to pursue your dreams and embrace the person you're meant to become.

JUN INTERNATIONAL COACHING

Ozzin Jun

Founder & CEO, Business Mentor, Keynote Speaker

Ozzin Jun, The Wealth Queen, is a Forbes-featured award-winning business mentor, keynote speaker, and host of The Inspiration Science Podcast, ranked among the Top 50 Mental Health Podcasts. Featured in

Yahoo, US Times, and over 210 global publications, Ozzin is recognized for her transformative impact.

After surviving a traumatic kidnap and rape in 2019, she overcame chronic illness and six-figure debt, building a thriving business rooted in purpose and faith. Ozzin has empowered over 15,000 lives, helping coaches and entrepreneurs scale to multi 6-7 figures by mastering brand messaging and leadership. Her clients include Hollywood directors and billionaires.

When not serving as a business mentor, Ozzin is a UN Peace Ambassador and a co-pilot with her partner, traveling the world.

To learn how Ozzin can help you build a wildly profitable online business aligned with your purpose, visit her Instagram @ozzinjun..

https://www.linkedin.com/in/ozzinjun/
https://www.facebook.com/ozzin.jun/
https://www.instagram.com/ozzinjun/
https://linktr.ee/ozzinjun

Marry Yourself

Chaos as Your Guide to Purpose

By Ozzin Jun

Introduction

In 2019, I found myself trapped in the dead of night, kidnapped by a man I once trusted. My screams were swallowed by the silence of isolation as I sat in a car, helpless and afraid, the world as I knew it crumbling around me. Months of stalking, harassment, and threats had culminated in this horrifying event. I had tried to set boundaries, to let go of the toxic relationship that had consumed me, but his refusal to accept the breakup led to unimaginable chaos. In a desperate moment, I managed to send a single text: "I'm kidnapped, help me." That text became my lifeline. But by the grace of God, I got out of this and created not just a life to survive but to truly thrive. This chaos changed my life forever.

However, the healing process was a messy process and often very frustrating. Returning to life after such trauma wasn't easy. It was the beginning of a battle for my mind, body, and soul. I walked the halls of school as a shadow of myself, carrying emotional wounds that ran far deeper than anyone could see. Sleepless nights, anxiety, panic attacks, PTSD, and chronic illness plagued me. My body screamed for rest while my mind tried to push forward with positivity to build my dreams. Maybe you've felt that, too, when your ambition clashes with a body that refuses to cooperate.

But let me ask you this: Have you ever stopped to wonder if your pain might hold a message for you? What if the chaos you're experiencing is a guide, not a barrier? For years, I believed I could outrun the effects of my trauma. I threw myself into art, music, therapy, and positivity. It helped me to a certain degree, but the weight of unresolved pain lingered. It wasn't until I embraced what I now call "Marrying Yourself" that I began to heal. Marrying yourself is about more than self-love, it's about giving your life to Jesus, making a commitment to yourself, surrendering to your purpose, and living free from societal labels or expectations.

Healing often feels like two steps forward and one step back. We don't know if we truly healed until we get tested in a new relationship or situation where we could get triggered but choose to respond differently. When I entered a new and loving relationship in 2021 after this horrible trauma, old wounds started to come up. Certain parts of me felt triggered. But it was also transformative, because it gave me an opportunity to heal parts in me where I was giving my power away. By leaning into my chaos instead of resisting it, I found more clarity and a purpose greater than myself.

In 2020, I dropped out of university in Switzerland to build a business that aligned with my purpose. In just eight months, I earned my first six figures. I've since impacted over 15,000 lives and created a million-dollar movement. My purpose evolved into empowering holistic healing in people. I'm obsessed with showing women how they can have it all: thriving relationships, great health, and daily big purposeful bank.

According to a study, nearly 70% of people feel trapped in jobs that lack fulfillment. Maybe you're chasing the "right" job or relationship, waiting for the perfect moment to launch your business, hoping for happiness. But what if the answer isn't outside you? What if the chaos you're running from is actually your mirror, showing you your true purpose? Your mess can become your greatest message. Your pain can be turned into a transformational movement. The moment you commit to yourself, everything changes. I know this because that's how I changed my life and the lives of many other people. Let me show you how to embrace your chaos by marrying yourself, and live the life you've always deserved. My Marry Yourself framework is mainly built on 3 steps.

1. Divorce Your Old Identity: Clear the Path for Purpose

Expansion and growth are framed very glamorously when we speak about it. But often, we don't address how true expansion can be very painful. It takes us to sit in discomfort to rise. It's not necessarily about adding a lot of new things but letting go of things that drain you mentally, emotionally, or financially. I've invested in many programs, mentors, and courses over the past years. While strategies, frameworks, and blueprints were certainly valuable, the most impactful training wasn't about those. Nothing could surpass the power of developing self-awareness and leadership skills. That's why I see so many women I work with achieving major breakthroughs through leadership and identity training.

The reason why most affirmations are not effectively working for most people, is because they don't truly feel it and make it part of their identity. For example, if you never made a million, it's hard to feel like you have a million. It's easier to tune into the feeling of wins you already had, e.g., tuning into the emotion when you celebrated a $10K cash month. Another thing is that people separate the thing they want to change about themselves too much from their identity, e.g., "I want to lose weight and eat healthier." A better way is to make it deeply part of your identity. For example, "I eat healthy daily to feel healthy and more energetic, and I work out because it's just who I am." Your words have power, especially the ones you say to yourself. If you constantly tell yourself, "I'm anxious," or "I'm not good at this," you reinforce those beliefs. Instead, try this: Separate your circumstances from your identity. Instead of saying, "I'm an anxious person," say, "I'm feeling anxious in x moments because of x." These small shifts in language create big shifts in mindset. You're not defined by your struggles, they're just part of your journey.

To marry yourself, you must first let go of who you used to be and what you subconsciously or consciously accepted as your identity. It's about stepping into your future self, the version of you who embodies the life you want, who speaks with confidence, who acts with purpose. Stop holding onto old beliefs, habits, and stories that keep you trapped and no longer serve you. Ask yourself: Who are you right now? And who is the person you're meant to become? Imagine the version of you that has already achieved your dreams. What does she think? How does she show up? How does she navigate challenges? What does she wear? How does she feel? Where is she? To marry yourself, you must start living like that version today.

Let's try this together. Take a piece of paper and draw two columns. On the left, write "Old Me" (or give it a name that resonates, like "Broke Version"), and on the right, write "Future Me" (maybe "Million-Dollar Me" or something inspiring). Start listing the beliefs, thoughts, and habits that belong to your old identity. Then, on the right, write the thoughts, actions, and values of your future self.

For example, my "Broke Version" used to think:

- "I don't have money for this."
- "I'll do it all myself."
- "I don't have time."
- "It's too hard."

But my "Awake Version" says:

- "How can I afford this?"
- "I invest in myself because I'm worthy."
- "I make time for what matters."
- "I choose collaboration over competition."

Do you see the shift? Now, it's your turn. What's holding you back, and how does your future self approach these same challenges differently? Stop waiting to be this new version of yourself one day. Just be her right now. How's your awake version showing up? What is her identity, and what thoughts, habits, behaviors, and new standards does she normalize? Start small. Write down the beliefs, habits, and stories you're ready to let go of. You don't need to have it all figured out or change everything at once. It's about observing your own decisions more day-to-day and making decisions that align with your vision and values. Have self-compassion in the process of your transformation. This is your time. The version of you who's bold, confident, and unstoppable is already within you. It's time to let her shine.

From External Validation to Internal Fulfillment

Many of us live according to the labels and expectations placed on us by others. Society tells you how you should act, what you should prioritize, and even how much you're allowed to dream. Maybe your family labeled you as "bad with money," and now you shy away from financial goals. Perhaps someone told you that your dreams were "too big," so you scaled them down. Ask yourself this: Whose voice is holding you back? Don't accept the labels and roles that society puts on you. Re-create your own self-image. You were not put on this earth to fit into someone else's expectations. Research by Bronnie Ware, a palliative care nurse, revealed that the number one regret of the dying is, "I wish I had the courage to live a life true to myself, not the life others expected of me." Don't wait until it's too late. Your goals are possible. But first, you must let go of the mental prison built from other people's "shoulds." Build an unshakable sense of self-worth that isn't tied to external circumstances. Your self-worth isn't defined by your bank account, your job title, or your relationship status.

Romans 12:2 (NIV)—"Do not conform to the pattern of this world, but be transformed by the renewing of your mind. Then you will be able to test and approve what God's will is—his good, pleasing, and perfect will." This verse speaks to breaking free from the constraints of worldly expectations, encouraging transformation by renewing your mind, and aligning yourself with God's plan.

Galatians 1:10 (NIV)—"Am I now trying to win the approval of human beings, or of God? Or am I trying to please people? If I were still trying to please people, I would not be a servant of Christ." Paul challenges us to question whose approval we seek. True freedom comes from seeking God's approval, not the approval of others.

Breaking Free from Limiting Beliefs

The process of letting go starts with awareness. Pay attention to your triggers. What beliefs or situations make you feel small, insecure, or stuck? Instead of judging yourself for these feelings, lean into them with curiosity. For example, if you've always believed you're "bad with finances," ask yourself: Where did this belief come from? Is it actually true? Often, these beliefs stem from past experiences or comments that we internalize as truth. Recognize that they're not your reality, they're just a story you've been telling yourself. You must differentiate facts and stories. Most of the problems you deal with are most likely stories, not facts. Shifting your identity isn't about faking it until you make it. It's about making it until you make it. Move powerfully from a place as if your vision is already done.

2. Date Yourself: Courageously Craft Your New Reality

There is only one thing worse than having to deal with temporary disappointment, and that is to realize that in the avoidance of potential failure, you created a disappointing life. The reason why most people don't do things is because they are scared to be disappointed. So, they usually move in two ways: They either avoid it completely, or they play it small so that they don't get disappointed. But here's the thing: By avoiding risks or shrinking your dreams, you risk living a life full of regrets. If you truly believe you can be, do, and have whatever you desire in this lifetime, then there's only one skill you need to master: learning how to navigate the temporary feeling of not having what you want *yet*. What if you could appreciate the space between your desire and the fulfillment of it? What if you could find magic in that in-between moment? It's not about settling, it's about balancing gratitude for what you already have while staying focused on your vision. You can't have "more" without truly appreciating what's already good in your life. While you're busy fantasizing about the future, you might unknowingly lose sight of the present. Own your genius unapologetically and recognize how incredible you already are. Stop creating from a place of distant hope and start creating from a place of unshakable power that you already possess. The question is not whether you are influential or not, but it is, what will you create with the influence you have? Embody leadership that makes it impossible for you to go backward. This is extraordinary identity work. It's not just about what you're building, it's about who you are while you're building it.

On tough days, instead of dwelling on what's missing, shift your focus to what's already good. Sometimes, being productive means giving yourself permission to rest fully. Especially as a woman, it's important to honor your body's unique cycles and rhythms. Your health is your foundation. What if you gave yourself permission to feel the full range of emotions, allowing yourself to be sad when you're sad or angry when you're angry? It's okay to feel disappointed. It's okay not to have everything you want *yet*. You're not behind. You're exactly where you need to be. In those moments when you feel frustrated because growth isn't happening as fast as you'd like, trust that these are the moments when God is sculpting your character the most. Trust His timing while taking bold action. Bless your waiting times because they're preparing you for your calling in life.

When your vision excites you but also scares you, and when you find yourself thinking, *"Am I crazy for doing this?"* that's when you know your vision is big enough. If your purpose doesn't make you cry, it often isn't strong enough. Build a deeper relationship by exploring yourself with curiosity.

In life, as we let go of things, people, or environments that no longer serve us, it's time to take the next essential step: dating yourself. Dating yourself means building a relationship of trust and investment. It involves taking the time to explore your values and desires, and having honest conversations with yourself. It is about showing up for you in a deep, intentional way. Think of the five love languages by Gary Chapman: physical touch, acts of service, gifts, words of affirmation, and quality time. Reflect on:

- How often do I spend quality time with myself?
- Do I treat myself with kindness and affirm my worth?
- Am I doing acts of service for myself, like preparing nourishing meals or creating peaceful spaces?
- What do I truly value?

- How can I show up for myself today?
- What small win can I celebrate right now?

For example, if you've ever struggled with your finances, you might relate to this. Maybe money feels unreliable to you, sometimes it's there, and sometimes it's not. Do you avoid checking your bank account because it triggers feelings of shame or lack? What if you started treating money like a relationship? Imagine money is your partner. When you stop viewing money as a thing but treat it as an actual healthy relationship, things can change. Would you ignore it for weeks at a time? Would you avoid spending quality time together? The way you relate to money is a reflection of the way you treat yourself. Ask yourself these questions and answer them without self-judgment or shame. We are our own triggers. Whenever you get triggered, know that there's potential for a new opportunity and more growth. In such moments, say: "Interesting that I feel this. Why is that?" When you're curious about yourself, you'll be able to create a life that you love more easily. Dating yourself means exploring your own needs, values, and desires with curiosity and care.

Explore and Reassess Your Values

When was the last time you allowed yourself to try something new simply to see if you would enjoy it? This kind of exploration is a form of self-love, acting on your ideas and learning from the experience. Reflect regularly on what matters most to you and allow your values to serve as a compass for decision-making. You might find that your values and priorities shift over time. That's okay, life is all about evolution. Take some time to reflect on what matters most to you right now. Your values are your compass, and they'll help you make decisions that feel aligned. My own values have evolved significantly over the past few years. Four years ago, I used to prioritize mastery over health. Now, they have shifted to God, Love, Health, Integrity, and Mastery. Although these changes were subtle, they had a profound impact on my life. For example, I used to tolerate sacrificing my health for the sake of my work and personal growth. I'd stay up late, neglecting my own needs for the sake of mastery. Today, while still deeply committed to growth and mastery, I prioritize my faith and health. I begin my days with prayer and approach each "yes" with more intention, recognizing that every "yes" is a "no" to something else. This shift has led to clearer boundaries and new standards for my business, such as being unavailable on certain days for client calls or support. Define your personal and business values.

There will be moments when your boundaries are tested, especially when others try to step over them or ask to be the exception. You might feel guilty for standing firm, but in honoring your boundaries, you're not just protecting your own well-being, you're positioning yourself to serve the world more effectively. What would it look like to realign your actions with your current values? Don't confuse having boundaries with being mean. By setting clear boundaries, you also show others how to set their own.

Lead with Courage, Not Confidence

Great things have happened in my life not because I was confident, but because I leaned into courage despite fear. Don't wait until you feel confident to take action. Instead, lean into courage and choose it repeatedly. Some women start out something with courage, and then, they plug out from it because they lack self-trust or don't see results yet. Confidence is built by constantly doing something that puts you in discomfort. Small wins create momentum to create compounded success. I call it success stacking. Celebrate your micro successes, and exponential success will come from those. It's not about becoming fearless but putting fear into your passenger seat while you are the driver. Be bold and audacious in what you do and how you do it. Courage to stand firm in your own beliefs creates magnetism.

What do I need, want, and expect in the key areas of my life: relationships, business, health, or personal growth? Get clear about the kind of experience you desire in each area. What holds you back isn't your capabilities, it's a lack of courage. Fear, perfectionism, and self-doubt act as "pain-avoiders" that keep you stuck in a cycle of waiting. These feelings might seem like valid reasons to hold back, but they're actually excuses. The longer you wait for your ducks to line up, the longer you delay the life you desire. Stop waiting for permission. Start before you feel ready. Maybe you've told yourself, I'll do it when I have more time, more money, or more qualifications. These "ducks" you think need to be in a row are holding you back. Let's work through this with a simple exercise:

The Duck Exercise to Get Into Action

1. **What's something you've always wanted but put off because you didn't feel ready?** For example, starting your own business, committing to a fitness journey, or pursuing a dream relationship.
2. **What ducks have you told yourself need to be in a row first?** Write them down. Maybe Duck 1 says: *You're not qualified enough.* Duck 2 says: *It's not the right time.* Duck 3 says: *You don't have enough money.*
3. **How do these ducks make you feel?** Notice the fear, doubt, or hesitation they create.
4. **If you had no limitations and couldn't fail, what would you pursue right now?** Imagine the freedom of taking action without fear holding you back.

Take the first courageous step toward your goal, no matter how small. Stop waiting for everything to be perfect. Ditch the ducks and start today.

3. Marry Yourself: Commit to Living with Integrity & Purpose

Now, it's time to make a vow. Just as marriage is a commitment, this is about dedicating yourself to living by the values you've uncovered. This is your "vow" phase, where you hold yourself accountable and honor yourself in all areas of life. Treat your health, wealth, and relationships as sacred commitments. Set up routines that allow you to honor these vows, such as a weekly "Money Date" to check in on your financial health or intentional time to reconnect with loved ones. Imagine building an inner support team where you're your own life coach, doctor, and friend. This is the process of integrating your dates and your values into your lifestyle. Confidence is built by sticking to your own vows that you declare to yourself. You build inner credibility toward yourself, more self-trust, and more boldness. You also build external credibility and set the tone for how others treat you. Move with integrity in your words, actions, and behavior.

More Gifts Come with Greater Responsibility

One of the biggest blessings you can receive after experiencing traumas, toxic relationships, chaos, or rock-bottom moments is the ability to reclaim stronger self-worth. Anchored self-worth leads to better health, deeper loving relationships, and the ability to make the income you desire. I observed many survivors of abuse or rape feeling often "not enough" in various ways. There's a pattern of being a people-pleaser, having difficulty saying "no," and feeling that we deserve the suffering, even though we don't want it. But I've also witnessed the surprising flipside in my own life and the lives of many other women. If you've been incredibly hurt and experienced trauma, you also have the ability to rise much higher in life and achieve bigger success. The way you lead your lows shows how you lead your highs. Because of pain, you may have gained many more gifts, such as empathy to understand others who have gone through similar experiences. You've built stronger resilience. You might have less tolerance for certain things than many other people would accept because you've been in the past that version, who tolerated a lot of the BS. You know how it affected you. Because you walked through hell, you appreciate and hold your standards to walk in heaven. Many people I've met who've gone through traumatic experiences struggle with their health, healing process, making the desired income, and feel they're falling behind. But in reality, what if all those experiences actually put you ahead in life? Because they blessed you with more wisdom, gifts, insights, perspectives, and so many other things. Turn everything that happened in your life into a stepping stone for greater success.

Write Your Own Vows and Sign the Contract

I want you to write your own wedding contract with 3-5 vows to yourself. Choose commitments that align with your values in health, wealth, and relationships. If there's a specific area of your life you want to transform, you can focus on that part and break your vows into more specific commitments.

For example, I committed to regular "Money Dates," where I sat down once a week to learn more about finances and my own money habits. Within eight months, I went from managing debt to achieving six-figure months. I learned to pay attention to my finances, understand my numbers, and detach my self-worth from my bank account. When you hold yourself accountable, you transform from within.

Another example is when I dropped out of university. I wrote down the exact reasons why I made that decision and outlined how I would use my time differently instead of sitting in lectures. I created business and career-focused vows, promising myself that I would build a purposeful business with specific goals and never quit, no matter the level of frustration I faced. I signed it and placed it in my office as a constant reminder. Today, that contract has become my reality.

Remember: You are not married to your wedding contract. In my book, I discuss the difference between a covenant (lifelong commitments) and contracts (commitments for a specific season of life). It's essential to reevaluate your vows, take consistent action, and adapt them as you evolve.

My current wedding contract includes five areas of vows I made to myself:

- Spiritual Health
- Physical Health
- Relationships
- Wealth & Business
- Mental Health

For each category, I wrote down one non-negotiable commitment that I uphold daily—no excuses. Over time, I realized how essential it is to work on multiple areas simultaneously to achieve success. For example, the better your health, the easier it becomes to perform at your best and pour into others.

Now it's your turn: Write down your own vows, digitally or handwritten, sign it, and place them somewhere visible. Read them daily, take action (discipline over motivation), and use them as a tool to build your vision.

Next Steps

When you heal yourself, you create a ripple effect. When you share your story, you speak on behalf of millions, empowering others to use their voices. When you vulnerably share the most shameful parts of your story and boldly celebrate your wins, you create the greatest impact. When you marry yourself, you become your own best partner, showing up for yourself with the love, care, and devotion you deserve. To marry yourself is to declare that your worth is not determined by anyone else but by the love you give to yourself and the standards you uphold. When you marry yourself, you stop seeking validation from others. You begin living from the truth of who you are, and everything else falls into place. To marry yourself means letting go of your old version and anchoring yourself in your new version through Christ. You use your chaos as a mirror to discover your God-given purpose by surrendering to Him. God doesn't want you to be stuck in chaos, but he will lead you to put order in your life. Your chaos can be your catalyst. What will you do today to honor this commitment to yourself? What small step will you take toward a meaningful, purposeful life? I'm here to help you break free from future regrets before they break you.

In my *Marry Yourself* book, I guide you through a transformative journey that goes beyond the common three steps of divorcing your past identity, dating yourself, and marrying yourself. It also includes the engagement, the honeymoon, and the symbolic dance of rebuilding your life. This process is built on the foundations of self-worth and faith in God. Whether you've experienced trauma, abuse, or rock-bottom moments, or you aspire to go from good to delusionally great, my book helps you reclaim your life by honoring your core values in health, wealth, and relationships.

Picture this: standing at the altar of your own life, fully ready to say "I do" to your most authentic self. You'll learn how to heal your past wounds, embrace your true worth, and prioritize your dreams over the limiting beliefs that have kept you stagnant. It's a battle-tested, soul-shifting process that combines wisdom through Jesus, self-help tools, and creative strategies that changed my life. It's time to stop waiting for the world to validate your worth and start saying "I do" to the life you deserve, one that aligns with your purpose, health, wealth, and thriving relationships.

If you're ready to stop living someone else's dream and start living the one you were born to create, order my book, Marry Yourself, via my Instagram @ozzinjun or LinkedIn Ozzin Jun.

When you order my book Marry Yourself, you'll receive a template of the Self-Marriage contract along with other resources to help you turn your dreams into reality. I'd love to hear about your breakthroughs and realizations from this chapter, and connect with you!

Brenda Sepulveda

Brenda Sepulveda is a powerful voice for women who have faced life's challenges and emerged stronger through their faith. In a society that often replaces true love with fleeting substitutes like sex, money, and fame, Brenda's story offers a reminder that real love comes from the one true source—Jesus Christ. A woman who has thrived, survived, and been deeply humbled by her experiences, she has found her strength in God's purpose for her life.

Brenda's journey has been shaped by adversity, but it is her unwavering faith that has kept her standing, rising higher with each step. Her story is one of empowerment, resilience, and a call to women who feel they need someone else to get them through tough times. Brenda's message is clear: they are never alone. Through her words, she hopes to inspire, motivate, and encourage women who are struggling, showing them that they, too, can stand strong in their identity and rise with God's guidance.

Brenda is excited to share her testimony, knowing that it will touch the hearts of many and encourage them to embrace their purpose with confidence and faith.

https://www.linkedin.com/in/brenda-sepulveda-445932160
https://www.facebook.com/brenda.sepulveda.12/
https://www.instagram.com/bluebrenda77/

A New Beginning

When Lost, Look Deep Inside Of You.

By Brenda Sepulveda

"Be reminded on this day that throughout your life: Emotions will always be "A Part of You," was what I learned first (during this beginning journey of mine). It was taught to me by my Great Friend & Coach Martina Joy, as she mentioned this fact was in the *Inside Out* movie. So, what exactly does this mean when starting in the early stages? How does one project better decisions based on such a statement, considering that emotions play a crucial role in the daily tasks in this corporate world we live in? How do you even begin to look for the main resources? Where do you resort to? In the beginning, it can feel incredibly overwhelming to think through so many thoughts, and it might even keep you distracted and feeling like you're stuck. Do not be dismayed, because it is never as bad as it seems at first. Beware, it takes changes and sacrifices that you must make in order to see results. Remember these three.

1) Commitment,

2) Goal

3) Persistency

"My name is Brenda Sepulveda," I replied to Martina Joy, when I first met her during the business seminar of her good friend, Brendon Burchard. The first keynotes of shared information that was being given in this seminar were all signaling that I needed to make some changes in my current lifestyle, and in order to do that, I would have to create a whole different person than the one I currently was. My biggest strength (as well as it is my current weakness) has always been my heart. I choose to trust and move into things a bit too soon, without really thinking things through. By trial and error, this has indeed cost me a lot of losses that have been hard to endure and recover from.

In this event, my whole perspective on all things has indeed taken a whole turn for the betterment of my current established future circumstances. As it turns out, many questions were indeed answered through the testimonials of those who were on stage, sharing their life stories with us who were eager to learn more and more about them. While changing your mindset plays a crucial role, it is only part of the whole sacrifice that comes afterward: vis-à-vis, starting off with recognizing that you deserve more, and this means that you should never settle for the bare minimum because those around you will treat you like that if you let them. I will never forget in what circumstances I started writing my story in my own personalized journal throughout the many different changes that arose in my life. One of the biggest things that changed was understanding that the world doesn't owe you anything. Alongside this journey of emotions, understanding this phrase plays the crucial role of reminding you that "You" are the only one who can change your future. No one else will do it for you. Oh my… Get excited, my friend, because great things are within your "Immediate Future" starting right now.

Learning to understand that I will always have emotions has helped me to understand not to beat myself up too much when I do not always succeed in a certain mission or task. Failures are all part of what makes you succeed eventually in the greater goal. Everything happens for the betterment of the future you are seeking to achieve.

As long as you always continue forward, your goals are always within your grasp.

I like to classify myself as a "Branding Ambassador," who is currently constantly seeking to expand more and more amongst the higher brands of companies worldwide. I create content, artistic photos, and creative arts, for both, companies and localized events where creativity is a must. My abilities, like so much else, were not something that just came to me. Tony Robbins mentioned to me in person, "Concentrate on your Higher Strengths," and use that to project your "Higher goals," and indeed, he was right. Success is within reach. I now run my Postmark store, alongside that of my own clientele, outside of social media. I am always open to continuing & expanding My talents, seeing that in this line of work, you always have room for much greater growth opportunities. Keep in mind that while the answers do not always come to you at the exact time that you seek, there is always a resource that you can always turn to, in order to achieve your goal.

Beware that these 5 following things are also things to keep in mind when researching options for resources.

1.) Understand that "People that ARE successful are "Not always eager to share their secrets with you: (Yet, ;understanding the reasons as to why they are like this will help you to understand "The Key to their success". It is NOT about them being greedy or prideful, but rather a way to help you to see the "Key Pointer Steps" needed in order to get ahead in (In their Business) including the need to protect their ideas and sources, and assure themselves that "You Are a Trusted Person whom can be relied on. (I learned this from My great Female Friend & Sister, Mishelle Chavez.) as well as a few others who also showed me this.

2.) When you have officially discussed resources and key points regarding your goals, remember to "Keep an "NDA" agreement to completely protect your ideas and sources and assure yourself that whatever you discuss, with any one said person, will be completely safeguarded. (Note: Be open enough to explain why your reasons to request an "NDA Agreement",) and never be afraid to openly discuss and explain it. They are your Ideas. Protect them with your life.

3.) You are the only version of yourself in this dimension. No one else can do what you can because you have your own talents, gifts, as well as "God Given Talents" that most likely others have not even begun to hear about. Funny story here, but I will tell it just because it is now a "A great New Technique" for trimming your eyebrows. Check this out: What is now called "Eyebrow Threading", generally speaking is "what I and another young female learned", (who's name I can not recall), when I was in "Juvenile Hall" @ the age of 13. Except that: in this place, we were not allowed to have any sharp objects, so the only way we created to take care of our "eyebrows" was to use the threads of our socks. Imagine that! And, here is the kicker: I can not lie about this because I can indeed show a "Live Demonstration" that "Eyebrow Threading" was created by someone who knew they had a "Bright Idea", and decided to move on and "Blow it up" to what it is now. "This Person" did not just leave it at "Idea" and that's it. No: He or she took "Action".

4.) Never ever: "Let yourself be overthrown" or bombarded with nothing but "Positive, Motivational, and Consistent" Words that will progress you forwards, not keep you stuck in a "Negative ambiance" that makes you end up in a "Stuck Loop", leaving you with no solutions. Remember also, "that friends who are only your friends so long as you pay for everything, and are always available", are not your "True Friends". They are just people taking advantage of you. Let them go, (If you must), because in the end, when you continue being stuck, and they succeed, they will not take you with them, (when and If) they succeed at all.

5.) And last but not least: Always remember the value on the "The things that you have to Offer", because the world may not always see the "Potential In You", and (even then, you may very well encounter people) that will see a certain of potential in you, (except that they will focus more on the negative effects) of what you lack expertise in, rather than to focus on "what makes you A great option" for an even higher (Collaboration).

From Point 5). I need to give credits to "Rhonda Renee Swan, Brian Swan and Hanalei Swan: (Also known as the "Unstoppable Family".) They are key examples of "People Who have Believed in Me" and have done many of the things that no other "Entrepreneurial Person" has done for me. I greatly appreciate them for all their great teachings, and their ample "Opportunities" that I am always seeking to learn more and more of. I have come a long way ever since meeting them. One of them: being this here. Writing this chapter is only : 1 of many more upcoming projects that I will be doing this year. Never forget: That believing in yourself : may sound easy, but it is definitely not easy at all. "Whoopi Goldberg" said it in "Sister Act" regarding the book called "Letters to a Young Poet", who always kept saying that he wanted to be a writer. Except "He always doubted his potential", Until he finally decided to "Stop the doubts, and Action" on all his Poems in order to share them with the world. Which is how we can all search up his great book of "Poems" that are more than inspirational.

Someone once told me "No one said it would be easy, but It is Simple". This has a few points of "grey areas" to it, but in the end, it is true. I am living witness of this like so many other writers out there. Yet overall, It really does not get any simpler than this. With the right set of people, the right mindset, the right resources, and with "A can do Attitude" willing to be open-minded to expand into infinite "Growth", the possibilities really become endless. I know you have probably heard this be4, but just know, not everyone is the same. I am one of those willing to share what I have learned since I started this journey. So please, Rejoice and continue the journey here, be4 you can soon become "An Author" yourself.

In conclusion, use the resources closest to you, like Fiverr, Facebook, Instagram, and Linkedin, to name a few and remember the biggest lesson of all. Many people will say they will willingly help you, but that is not always so. Remember, you are the one seeking to succeed, and you ARE the only ONE who will achieve it. Eventually, like-minded folks will cross paths with you, and the opportunities will expand. These are all my experiences as I continue moving forward in my ongoing journey. I enjoy meeting new females who constantly have the newest life stories to share. I want all to know that I am an open-minded female, 36 years of age, willing to cooperate in any future collaborations that present themselves. The future is within our grasp, so never ever give up, regardless of the obstacles.

Last but not least, concentrate on your goal and never, ever give in to negative remarks from outer circles. Remember always, "They are not where you are now, which means, they can not think like you until they discipline themselves like you have." This one was from my good friend Cole Hatter. I will never forget the chance I missed out on because of his expensive $2,500 workshop, but I now see why he does what he does. Keep it up, my good friend. As for us ladies, let us keep moving past all our fears, traumas, etc. To continue growing around all of those around us, and even those that are not close to us, to grow from them as well. Each journey is unique, and I am eager to learn about your story. Email my team @ BrendaMars0715@gmail.com and we will surely reply back ASAP.

For business inquiries, my email is BrendaMars0715@gmail.com. Let's make the future much brighter because Time is short lived, so make the most of it, and be ready to share your "Journey" with others while also increasing your "Opportunities" in the current present day. God Bless you all.

RACHAEL VENEMA
PHOTOGRAPHY

Rachael Venema
Fine Art Portrait Photographer

Rachael Venema is a fine art photographer with over nine years of experience creating timeless, heirloom-quality portraits.

As the owner of Rachael Venema Photography, she specializes in capturing authentic emotions and crafting stunning artwork for families, professionals, and brands. Her luxury, full-service experience ensures each session is uniquely tailored to her clients' style and vision.

Beyond photography, Rachael is a wife to her husband, Joe, and a mom to three amazing children. Together, they love going on adventures and embracing new experiences. Having moved seven times across the U.S., she understands the power of change, community, and preserving life's most meaningful moments.

In From Fear to Flourish: Embracing Change, Community, and Purpose, Rachael shares her journey of overcoming fear, embracing transformation, and finding purpose. Her story will inspire you to step out of your comfort zone, embrace new opportunities, and build a life filled with passion and connection.

https://www.linkedin.com/in/rachael-venema-cpp-0a931433/
https://www.facebook.com/rachaelvphotography1/
https://www.instagram.com/rachaelvenemaphotography/
https://www.rachaelvenema.com
https://www.rachaelvenema.com/storytelling-sessions

From Fear to Flourish

Embracing Change, Community, and Purpose

By Rachael Venema

Rachael lay on the mat, her chest rising and falling with the rhythm of her breath. The room was quiet, except for the occasional sniffle or sigh from others in the circle. However, within her, a storm raged. Memories she hadn't touched in years rose to the surface—moments of doubt, fear, and the overwhelming burden of always needing to be "enough."

And then, like a crack in a dam, it broke. The tears came first, hot and unrelenting, followed by a deep, guttural sob. It wasn't just pain leaving her body; it was years of limiting beliefs and self-doubt. As the tears flowed, Rachael realized how much she had been carrying. Years of trying to prove her worth, of seeking validation in places that could never truly fill her. But in that moment, as she let go, she could feel God whispering to me: 'You are enough. Just as you are.'

This transformative moment in 2023 was guided by Bridgette Simmonds during a breathwork session at The Radiance Retreat, hosted by Rachael's life coach, Jennifer Kremer. It was not just a release—it was a rebirth. As the session ended, a wave of clarity washed over her. She was ready to accept her story, her gifts, and her purpose with an openness she had never known before.

Rachael's journey has always been defined by transformation and a willingness to step into the unknown. For the past 10 years, she has run a successful photography business, now in its fourth location. Her business goes beyond capturing images—it's about connecting with her clients, creating stories through her art, and inspiring others to embrace their own beauty and purpose.

Rachael was born and raised in South Holland, Illinois, where she lived her entire childhood in the same house her parents still call home. Her life of change began after she married Joe. Having never moved before, she vividly remembers the day they packed up their lives and drove to Washington State, where Joe had accepted his first teaching job. She recalls driving on the highway through the Skagit Valley, marveling at the beauty around her, and thinking, *How crazy it is that God brought us here.*

Those three years in Washington were filled with incredible experiences of growth and some of the most painful challenges. Rachael worked for a bookkeeping service with two locations, which meant that every spring, she drove through the breathtaking tulip fields from one office to the other. "It was magical," she recalls.

She and Joe also became part of a church plant during their time there, forming connections with some of the most incredible Christians they had ever met. Every Sunday, they worshipped together, creating a strong sense of community. Many of the members commuted from up to an hour away, often staying afterward to share meals and fellowship. One woman, an older Dutch lady, became like a surrogate family member, regularly checking in on them and inviting them over. "She knew what it was like to leave family behind," Rachael says, "and she shared stories of her own journey, immigrating and being apart from her mother for years."

When they decided to move to Indiana to be closer to family again, it was hard to say goodbye to these people who had walked alongside them in their first few years of marriage. Goodbyes are the hardest thing about moving. "I didn't understand why we were being called to Indiana at first, but looking back, I see how those years gave us our first home, the births of our boys, and friendships that walked with us through our hardest moments. God's hand was steady, even when I couldn't see the path ahead."

In Indiana, Rachael and Joe bought their first home and had their first two children. After their first child, Isaac, was born, Rachael faced unexpected health challenges. Blood pressure issues required her to see a heart doctor for six weeks. "I was a mess," she remembers. But the kindness of others left a lasting impact. One day, a friend came by and simply vacuumed her house and tidied up. "It was such a simple yet kind gesture, and I'll never forget it," Rachael says.

Another moment of grace came when she thought she had miscarried their second child, Seth. A dear friend came over, sat with her, and prayed until Joe could arrive to take her to the doctor. Miraculously, Seth was okay—it was just a placenta bleed—but not being left alone to worry and wonder was a gift Rachael would always treasure.

When the family later moved to the Chattanooga area, Rachael and Joe arrived with their two young boys, ages 2 years and 3 months. They were waiting for their home in Indiana to sell, and a kind family generously let them stay in their condo in a 55+ community until the sale went through. With only one car, Rachael often found herself at home with her two boys—potty training a toddler while managing sleepless nights with a fussy baby.

After visiting a local church, one woman who became a dear friend extended simple yet life-changing kindnesses. She would invite Rachael to go to the aquarium or the park, offering her an escape from the monotony of being home alone with two little ones. "Those small things that might seem insignificant to some were a lifeline to me," Rachael recalls. "Just having someone to call when you needed to get out of the house, or a resource to find a good doctor or mechanic, meant everything."

As they settled in Chattanooga, Rachael found more connections that became deeply meaningful. She joined a women's book club, where the ladies enjoyed discussing books and offering each other life advice. The camaraderie and shared wisdom created bonds that Rachael still treasures. Two other friends began inviting her for Friday morning coffee, where they'd stay in their pajamas while their little ones played. "It was such a gift," Rachael says. "We could be real and authentic, supporting one another in a way that made not having family nearby a little easier to bear."

Rachael also became the secretary for a local church. Though her family didn't attend the church, the community embraced her as one of their own. During a year filled with health challenges for both her and her children, the church family stepped in to help. They cleaned her home, brought meals, and sent her notes of comfort that carried her through some of her darkest days.

One friend even slept on her couch when Rachael had to be rushed to the ER due to a miscarriage. Another friend took her children when Joe had a medical emergency, allowing Rachael to focus on her husband without worrying about her boys. "It was overwhelming in the best way," Rachael says. "Their love and care made such a difference in that season of life."

In life, many of us—if not all—have experienced pain or moments of darkness that leave us questioning and searching for answers. For Rachael, one of the darkest moments came when she miscarried her baby at 13 weeks. The loss was devastating on its own, but it was made even more traumatic by the treatment she received at the hospital. She vividly remembers how they handled her baby, discarding the tiny life as if it were meaningless, as though it was just a piece of trash.

"There are things in life that we just won't understand on this side of heaven," Rachael reflects. "And this is one of them. Why at 13 weeks, there was no heartbeat. Why did our baby have to go to heaven so soon?"

Even in the midst of the pain and unanswered questions, Rachael finds comfort in her faith. "All I know is that my baby is in heaven with Jesus, worshipping our Lord and Savior," she says. "That thought brings me peace, even when the ache in my heart remains."

Through this experience and many others, Rachael has come to believe that our pain and hardships are not meant to be carried alone. Instead, they are opportunities to connect, grow, and support one another. "Our painful and hard life experiences shape us," she explains. "And by sharing them with others, we can help them through their difficult times, too."

Rachael believes deeply in the power of shared experiences. When we open up about our struggles, we allow others to lean on us and find strength in knowing they're not alone. And in turn, we grow stronger ourselves. "Life isn't meant to be lived in isolation," Rachael says. "We are here to share our burdens, lift each other up, and grow together—even through the darkest of times."

This belief has shaped how Rachael approaches her relationships, her work, and her purpose. Whether through her photography, her community work, or the groups she's created, she's made it her mission to create spaces where people feel seen, heard, and supported.

"Each chapter of our lives has brought new challenges but also new opportunities for growth, connection, and impact. Looking back, I can see how each experience was a stepping stone to where I am now."

When their family lived in Oskaloosa, Iowa, for just two years, Rachael was given an incredible opportunity that shaped her perspective on her business and her own potential. A local dental office was remodeling its historic building, and the owners, Eric and Amy, invited Rachael to create custom artwork to reflect the town's heritage and the beauty of its community. This became one of the largest and most meaningful projects Rachael has ever worked on for a company.

Each art piece was carefully crafted from a portrait Rachael took of a scene or event. She captured moments that celebrated the charm and spirit of Oskaloosa, from the owner's favorite view of his drive home in the fall at sunrise, to local 4-H events at the Southern Iowa Fair featuring the poultry show and bottle bucket calf show. She documented the vibrancy of Sweet Corn Serenade and the energy of a high school football game played against the backdrop of a stunning sunset.

Rachael also collaborated with the local historical society to uncover old images of the dental office's building and its street, which were prominently displayed in the lobby. She even created artwork featuring antique dental tools that adorned the office hallway. These pieces, seamlessly blending the past and present, reflected the historic features preserved during the remodel.

This project became more than just a creative endeavor—it was a turning point. Working alongside the interior designer, Janel, and the owners, Eric and Amy, Rachael saw how her work could be valued in a professional setting. The three of them formed a special bond as they brought the vision for the dental office to life, creating a space that honored history while embracing a fresh start.

"Amy believed in me and gave me an opportunity that showed me I was capable and talented enough to pursue my business full-time," Rachael says. "She saw potential in people and helped them see it in themselves."

Amy's impact on Rachael's life was profound. Tragically, Amy passed away on Christmas morning, December 25, 2024, after battling a tumor in her brain stem. At her funeral, someone described Amy as a "facilitator of dreams," and Rachael couldn't agree more.

"She was exactly that—someone who saw the best in people and encouraged them to chase their dreams. Amy had incredible vision, not just for herself and her family but for everyone she encountered," Rachael recalls.

Amy's belief in Rachael's talent was a gift that shaped her path forward. But beyond that, Amy's friendship left an indelible mark. She was the kind of person who made everyone she met feel special, from the cashier at the grocery store to strangers she encountered in daily life. Her positivity, her kindness, and the way she radiated the light of Jesus left an undeniable impact on the world around her. Amy didn't just give Rachael an opportunity; she saw something in her that she hadn't fully seen in herself yet. Her belief was like a mirror, reflecting back to Rachael, the dreams she had been too afraid to step into.

"Amy truly made this world a better place," Rachael reflects. "She was a gift to everyone who knew her, and her encouragement continues to inspire me every day."

Looking back, Rachael marvels at how God's hand has been woven through their lives, guiding them in ways she couldn't have imagined. She often tells people that one of the greatest blessings of moving so often has been the incredible people they've met along the way. "Each place we've lived, God has placed us in the lives of others— sometimes to help them through a difficult time, and other times so they could help us through ours," she says.

From the tulip fields of Washington to the church family in Indiana and the close-knit friendships in Chattanooga, each chapter of their journey has been marked by God's provision. "The goodbyes are always hard," Rachael admits, "but the connections we've made and the ways we've seen God work through those relationships make it all worthwhile."

One of the most significant lessons Rachael learned through these moves was how to create community. So often, she heard from others how hard it is to be the new person in a town. "It *is* hard," Rachael admits, "but you also get to choose what you make of it." Sitting at home and complaining about not having friends wasn't going to change anything. Talking about how others weren't including her wasn't helpful, either. Instead, she began to look at the situation from a different perspective.

"I realized that people who've grown up in one place, surrounded by family and lifelong friends, often don't have room for more friendships. Their cups are full," Rachael explains. "It's not that they're purposely excluding anyone—they just aren't aware of the need."

With this understanding, Rachael began seeking out others who were new or looking for connection. She got involved in her children's schools, volunteered at the local community garden, joined a Pilates group, and found other ways to bring people together. These intentional efforts helped her build authentic friendships and create a sense of belonging in each new place.

Rachael has always had a heart for serving, which was evident during her time in Ripon, California. She was deeply involved in her community, serving on the Chamber Board of Directors, Rotary, Love Ripon, Garden Joy, a local magazine, and even helping with the local Ripon Farmers Market. "I loved being part of the community and seeing everyone come together," Rachael reflects.

Through these avenues of service, Rachael connected with countless people in the community. She used these opportunities not only to contribute but also to help others grow. Whether she was brainstorming with a local business owner or sharing insights on marketing, her goal was always to give back and uplift those around her.

One of her most impactful contributions was founding *Women Empowering Women*, a group where a different woman shared her story each month. The gatherings were transformative. "It was amazing to see how hearing someone's story and learning about their journey inspired and encouraged the women who attended," Rachael says.

The stories shared in the group often sparked something profound in those who heard them. Women walked away feeling seen, understood, and motivated to take the next step toward their own dreams. For Rachael, these gatherings were more than just events— they were a testament to the power of connection and shared experiences. "I've always loved hearing people's stories," she says. "There's so much strength and wisdom in each person's journey, and often, it's the encouragement someone else needs to move forward."

One particularly moving story came from a woman who shared her painful childhood of abuse. She spoke about how the trauma left her feeling unvalued and worthless, a belief she carried with her into adulthood and even into her marriage. Recently divorced, she was stepping into her own power and rediscovering who she was meant to be. She had become a leader both professionally in her career and personally among her family and friends. "I've learned that I am valued and that I have so much to give to this world," she said. "And I want to help others rise alongside me." Her transformation inspired everyone in the room, reminding them that even the darkest chapters of life can give way to incredible growth and strength.

Another woman shared her story of loss and resilience. She spoke about losing her brother, enduring multiple miscarriages, and going through the grueling process of IVF. Despite the immense pain, she took the steps necessary to create the life she wanted and to become the woman she aspired to be. Her journey taught her to care deeply for others and to persevere through life's challenges. "So often, we don't know someone's past, and we judge them based on where they are today," Rachael reflects. "What we don't realize is what it took for them to get to where they are now."

These stories served as powerful reminders: no one else has walked in your shoes. No one else can truly understand the pain, the perseverance, and the strength it takes to rise above life's challenges. "Forget the critics," Rachael says. "Forget those who judge you or assume you have it easy. They don't know what it took to get you here. They've never walked your path. So rise above the judgment, and keep taking steps toward your dreams."

She encourages women not to settle or feel stuck. "We've only been given this one life," Rachael says. "We have the power to take the steps needed to get to where we want to be. And as we climb, we must remember those who helped us along the way."

For Rachael, lifting others up isn't just an act of kindness—it's a way to build community and a life filled with purpose. "As we help others rise, it's a tremendous blessing," she reflects. "And when we finally reach the place we've been working toward, it's a lot less lonely because we've built a community along the way."

Through *Women Empowering Women*, Rachael saw firsthand how storytelling has the power to inspire, heal, and connect. She continues to carry that vision forward, reminding women everywhere that their stories matter, their dreams are valid, and they have the strength to rise above any challenge.

In Ripon, California, one friend in particular left a lasting impression. This woman had a remarkable heart and a gift for seeing those who needed community. She would intentionally invite women—those who might otherwise feel overlooked—to lunches, park playdates with their kids, or other gatherings. "Not many people have that gift of creating connections for others, but she did," Rachael recalls. "She will always have a special place in my heart for the way she brought people together."

Through these experiences, Rachael learned that meaningful connections don't happen by accident—they happen when we show up, reach out, and create space for others.

One thing Rachael would love to see more of is mutual support among people in the same industry. She's noticed that, particularly in local settings, there's often an unspoken barrier between those who are seen as "competitors." Whether it's photographers or other small business owners, insecurities can prevent people from reaching out or supporting one another. "Instead of thriving together, we often knock each other down or stay away because we assume they won't talk to us," Rachael reflects.

This mindset can hold everyone back, but Rachael has always approached her work differently. She believes in lifting others up, even those in the same industry. "I've been where the photographer just starting out is," she says. "I know how overwhelming it is to try to figure out everything on your own. That's why I've always been willing to give advice or help others in their journey. It's not just about competition—it's about community."

Rachael understands that insecurities can make it hard to ask for or accept help. But she encourages others to move past those fears and seek connection. "We all have something to learn from each other," she says. "By supporting and mentoring others, we can grow together instead of tearing each other down."

This mindset was a guiding principle in how Rachael ran her business, especially during her time in Ripon, California. Whether she was brainstorming ideas with a fellow business owner or encouraging a new photographer to step out of their comfort zone, her goal was always the same: to help others rise. "There's enough room for all of us," she says. "When we work together, we don't just build businesses—we build a stronger community."

Rachael has been able to build a network of photographer connections across the country, and for that, she is so grateful. Over the years, she's learned how important it is to have support from others who truly understand the unique challenges of running a business in the same industry.

One year, Rachael fell and broke her wrist during what was supposed to be one of her busiest weeks. She didn't know how she would manage her packed schedule, especially a full day of headshot sessions. In that moment of crisis, she reached out to another photographer in her network, who stepped in to help her with the session. "I couldn't have done it without them," Rachael says. "It reminded me of how much we need each other and how powerful it is to have people you can rely on."

This experience strengthened her belief that there's no need to fear or avoid connecting with others in the same industry. "If you're nervous about your competition, don't be," she advises. "There are clients out there for everyone, and the ones who are meant for you will find you."

By building connections and supporting one another, everyone can thrive. "We can accomplish so much more together," Rachael says. "Whether it's advice, encouragement, or stepping in during an emergency, having a network of people in your corner makes all the difference."

Rachael loves working with every photography client she has the privilege of photographing. While each session is unique, the ones that touch her heart the most are those that capture the essence of a family, the love between a couple, the tender bond between a mother and child, or the story of an individual. These sessions aren't just about creating beautiful images—they're about preserving stories that matter.

One session that will forever hold a special place in Rachael's heart was when she decided to offer *Storytelling Portrait Sessions*. These sessions are designed to capture not just a person's image but their essence and story, creating a legacy that they and their loved ones can cherish for years to come.

Rachael had the privilege of photographing Jayne, who was 17 at the time, along with her beloved horse, Mexico. Jayne had struggled with anxiety and depression for years, and her horse became a lifeline for her. "He's the reason I get up in the morning," Jayne shared during her session. "It's him, and my relationship with God, that keeps me going."

The session was magical from start to finish. Everything came together beautifully—from Jayne's flowing dress to her perfectly styled hair and makeup, to the stunning natural location they chose. Rachael remembers how the light filtered through the trees as Jayne and Mexico moved together, their bond evident in every moment. The way Jayne's face lit up when she looked at her horse, the trust Mexico had in her, and the peaceful connection between them were breathtaking to witness.

It wasn't just a photo session; it was a moment of healing and celebration. Rachael created not only stunning portraits but also a video of Jayne telling her story. The video, paired with printed artwork and an album, became a tangible reminder of Jayne's strength, her resilience, and the unshakable value she brings to the world.

"Jayne's session was so much more than capturing a beautiful girl and her horse," Rachael says. "It was about documenting her story—her struggles, her faith, and the love that gave her hope. Now she has this legacy to remind her of her worth, her bond with Mexico, and how God is always with her, in both the good times and the bad."

It's sessions like this that fuel Rachael's passion for her work. They remind her why she does what she does—helping people see their own value and preserving the moments that make life meaningful. Storytelling Portrait Sessions have become one of Rachael's favorite offerings, allowing her to not only create art but also help clients reflect on the beauty and strength within their own stories.

"Moments like these remind me why I picked up the camera in the first place—not just to capture beauty but to preserve the essence of someone's story, to give them something to hold on to when life feels heavy." At the heart of her vision is her passion for *storytelling portrait sessions*. These sessions combine photos and video to capture an individual's story, creating a legacy that inspires others and reminds people of their unique purpose. "We all have a story worth sharing," she says. "I want my work to show people the beauty of their journey and the impact they have on the world."

Since relocating to Ankeny, Iowa, in June 2024, Rachael has continued to grow and evolve. She still flies back to California for portrait sessions while building her business in Iowa. She is exploring new possibilities, from writing a solo book to starting a podcast to coaching other business owners.

Rachael's journey of transformation hasn't just been about her business—it's been deeply personal. A pivotal shift came when she began to value and love herself. At first, the idea felt foreign and uncomfortable, but she now sees it as essential. "When we value ourselves, we teach others to do the same," she explains. "If we don't recognize our own gifts and what we bring to the world, how can we expect others to see it?"

This lesson resonates deeply with women, who often devalue their talents or give too much of themselves away, leading to burnout and lost joy. "We need to stop apologizing for our dreams and start owning our worth," Rachael says. "When we do, we create space for success and fulfillment." For so long, Rachael struggled to accept her value. It felt foreign—almost selfish—to believe that what she had to offer mattered. But the truth is, when we *don't* value ourselves, we unconsciously teach others to do the same. Now, Rachael lives differently. She walks into rooms knowing she belongs. She charges her worth without guilt. And she teaches other women to do the same because she knows how much it changes everything.

Rachael's story isn't just her own; it's an invitation to accept change, transformation, and the power of community.

"God gives us nudges for a reason," she says. "When we listen to those whispers in our hearts, we're listening to His calling. He has given each of us a purpose to impact the world in a way only we can."

Her advice is simple: Don't let fear hold you back. Don't worry about what others might say or whether they'll judge you. "No one knows your story, and no one knows your heart. By following your heart and trusting God's plan, big things happen."

Rachael challenges every woman reading this to take one step today toward her dream. "Whatever step you feel called to take—whether it's starting a new chapter in your career, pursuing a dream, or finding your voice—know that it's okay to start small. You don't need to see the whole path to take the first step. Trust the nudges. Surround yourself with people who will cheer you on, and be willing to embrace the unknown. It's in those spaces of discomfort where transformation truly happens."

The radiant queen inside you is waiting. Step into your calling, and watch your story transform into something extraordinary. Rachael knows what it's like to doubt yourself. She knows what it's like to let fear keep you stuck. But she also knows what happens when you step forward anyway—when you trust that small voice inside telling you that you were made for more. So here's her challenge to you: Take one step today. Just one. Write down your dream. Send the email. Have the conversation. Take the first step, and watch what happens when you trust the journey God has for you.

REGENERATIVE LAW
INSTITUTE

Helen Holden Slottje

Regenerative Wholeness Alchemist

Helen Holden Slottje, a former 'Big Law' Harvard educated lawyer, transforms seemingly impossible challenges into pathways for profound transformative change. As founder of the Regenerative Law Institute, she guides visionaries and changemakers in reimagining systems built on 'command and control' to embody the wisdom of living wholeness.

Her alchemical approach emerged from her groundbreaking environmental advocacy work, where she conceived and manifested what many deemed impossible: the successful grassroots movement that banned fracking in New York State, earning her the Goldman Environmental Prize (the 'Green Nobel'). This victory revealed a profound truth that now guides her work: transformation becomes possible when we maintain coherence rather than fragment under ever increasing pressure. Helen helps clients navigate complexity during collapse of meaning structures, aligning with regenerative principles that naturally transform systems to inherent health. Her work bridges consciousness evolution with the emergence of new societal structures beyond predatory paradigms. .

https://www.linkedin.com/in/helenslottje/

https://www.facebook.com/p/Helen-Holden-Slottje-100045362995968/

https://www.instagram.com/hslottje/

https://www.regenerativelaw.com

https://www.imaginethenerve.com/

No Fracking Way

Regenerative Transformation

By Helen Holden Slottje

An oversized man in the crowd heckled me as I stood on stage in a Broome County theater, next to the mayor of Dish, Texas. As a lawyer, I was educating the audience about "home rule" and community sovereignty. Just across the New York state line in Dimock, Pennsylvania, water was coming out of faucets brown and flammable after nearby gas drilling. Yet, as I stood there, trying to decide how to respond to the heckler, I felt something far deeper than the immediate tension of the moment. It was as if the fractures beneath our feet—the very fault lines being brought to maximum pressure by the fracking industry—were mirrored in our communities, our systems, and our own consciousness.

The compression I felt that night wasn't just external; it was internal, societal, and existential.

This is the *'Dark Fire'* of our time: a compression so intense that it feels like annihilation, yet within it lies the potential for *Regenerative Divergence*[SM]. But first, we must confront the myths that distort our understanding of transformation and prevent us from navigating to *Regenerative Divergence*. The path of *Regenerative Divergence* can be described as the narrow gate, a space in the heart, the eye of the needle, and a quantum tunnel. The alchemical path is difficult and requires facing challenges and opposition.

You don't have to be fighting fracking to know what it's like to feel trapped—suffocating under pressure, pushing against systems and circumstances that seem too big, too rigged, too out of our control.

Like me, you've likely tried to work harder—only to be dogged by stereotypes that call for your smiling subordination, leaving you exhausted and disillusioned, or perhaps even labeled the problem when you stop smiling when you are treated like a second-class citizen. No matter where you search, you can't quite find what you are looking for. Maybe you've been told to compromise. To play the game. To make the best of what's already broken.

And maybe, deep down, you're starting to sense that an ability to adapt to increasingly toxic environments in a predator/prey dynamic is not a skill you want to hone and pass on to future generations as your legacy.

When you start to see the bigger picture, it becomes increasingly clear that we aren't just dealing with a bad apple here and there. And we aren't just up against a few particularly greedy or ill-intentioned corporations. Nor is what we face limited to dysfunctional bureaucracies that seek to buffer those benefiting from predator/prey relationships from the "disruption" by those "prey" that resist their subordination.

I've seen fracking up close. It holds a dark mirror to a fundamental flaw, a flaw in how we think, act, and relate—a fragmentation so fundamental it keeps us trapped in patterns of harm, even when we're trying to do good.

Here's the truth: You can't fix a broken system using the same thinking that created the breakdown.

Domination as Power

Our hierarchical mindset fragments both systems and consciousness, perpetuating cycles of extraction and control. We accept the myth that power flows from domination—that certain individuals and groups are entitled to control systems, people, outcomes, and resources.

Once in place, the predator/prey dominator system maintains its power by creating deep "gravity wells" that pull resources toward artificial centers of control. This isn't just a metaphor—it's the same principle as how mass curves spacetime, and how concentrated power warps the social field.

Think of how water naturally flows toward the deepest point. Similarly, in these artificially deepened spaces:

- Resources get pulled toward centers of control
- Attention gets trapped in immediate survival needs
- Energy gets consumed maintaining basic stability
- Natural patterns of connection break down

In fact, when we are under pressure, our nervous system defaults to survival mode. This distorts our field of vision in three ways:

- o **Amplification of threats**: We focus on what's collapsing, losing sight of what's emerging. We lose our ability to hear the higher-pitched human voice and instead focus our attention on tuning into the lower-pitched predator frequency.
- o **Our peripheral vision narrows**: filtering out the subtleties of our broader context. As we fixate on immediate threats, we lose sight of the higher-frequency, emergent possibilities that flicker at the margins. This contraction of vision not only reinforces our tendency to see reality in rigid, false

        binaries but also severs our connection to the rich, interconnected whole.

    o **Our cognitive system defaults to (false) binaries**: "Fight or flight," "win or lose," "fix it or give up." Nuance and a field beyond the opposites are entirely unavailable. Compression pulls apart what is naturally whole. Instead of experiencing reality as a coherent, interconnected system, we see fragments of ourselves, separate from the whole.

This creates a self-reinforcing cycle—the deeper the attentional gravity well gets, the more energy it takes just to maintain position, let alone climb out. This is precisely how black holes form in space, and how systemic oppression maintains itself.

This myth blocks *Regenerative Divergence* by staving off evolutionary pressure and prolonging life inside the chrysalis through repair of the chrysalis rather than allowing the evolutionary pressure to flow and bring forth a higher order of organization.

Gradual Evolution

Another myth locking us in the predator/prey dominator system and buffering *Regenerative Divergence* is believing that transformation happens incrementally, through small steps and gradual reforms. This misunderstands the nature of phase transitions. Just as water doesn't gradually become steam, systems under maximum compression don't evolve linearly. They either collapse or reorganize entirely.

Plasma—the fourth state of matter—offers a powerful metaphor here. When gas is subjected to intense energy, it doesn't evolve into plasma step by step; it undergoes a quantum leap into a state of coherence, where individual particles shed their rigid boundaries and operate as part of a unified, dynamic field. This is the essence of the

Dark Fire transformation: a total reorganization into a higher order while retaining individual essence.

When a system reaches maximum compression, something extraordinary happens. Like water molecules under intense pressure that must either maintain their current state or transform completely into steam, consciousness faces a quantum choice point. This isn't a gradual decision—it's a fundamental bifurcation where the old pattern becomes impossible to maintain.

Think of being in that moment of unbearable pressure, when everything in you wants to contract, to protect, to maintain rigid boundaries. This is the precise point where the revolutionary truth reveals itself: the very intensity that seems to be crushing us creates the exact conditions required for a breakthrough. The pressure isn't just stress to be endured—it's the catalyst for transformation.

What makes this moment so crucial is that there's no middle ground. Just as water can't partially become steam, systems under maximum compression face a binary choice: If they try to maintain rigid boundaries and individual control, they exhaust themselves, fighting against overwhelming pressure. Like a fist clenching tighter and tighter, this path leads to either collapse or brittleness. The very attempt to maintain separation becomes a form of self-imprisonment.

Belief in incremental change, prolongs the inevitable and makes it increasingly more difficult for transformation to emerge as the increasingly toxic environment is absorbed in the background.

Certainty as Competency and Merit

Also locking us in the dominator predator/prey system is the belief that certainty signals competency and merit. In times of intense pressure, narrow vision, and false certainty become seductive. They offer the illusion of control and stability, but they are signals of distortion, not clarity. Compression narrows our field of vision, making us blind to the larger geometric and relational patterns that connect us to the whole.

Certainty locks us into old paradigms, preventing the very openness and fluidity needed for transformation. It is only by surrendering certainty and embracing the creative tension of the unknown that we can move through the quantum tunnel. Trying to "fix" what's broken while trapped inside this distortion is like trying to escape a maze without being able to see the map. The compression limits our ability to imagine alternatives, and every effort to "repair" ends up reinforcing the very patterns we're trying to escape.

For example:

- When the dominator system (paradoxically) creates shortages through its efforts to control, the system demands more control, more force, and more extraction to "solve" the shortage "problem."
- When we feel fear, we cling harder to comfort, unable to see that the path forward lies through radical courage, not collapse into compromise.

Compression tricks us into mistaking the *cocoon* for the butterfly, the *seed* for the tree. It keeps us patching together what's falling apart, rather than trusting the transformation that requires letting go.

This fragmentation reinforces a sense of helplessness: the system feels too big, the problems too complex, and we feel too small to make a difference.

Repairing the Seed: Fix, Fight, or Force

The final myth that we will discuss is that transformation is about repair and a "return" or a going back— fixing what's broken, including through force. This belief keeps us glued to the fragments of old, outdated systems that no longer serve, trying to patch cracks and restore what was. But just as a seed must crack open for the tree to emerge, true transformation cannot happen through repair. Repair is anti-life when applied to systems at an evolutionary point—it is akin to forcing the chrysalis back together instead of letting the butterfly emerge.

We cannot see that letting go of the shell is the pathway to what comes next.

What this myth misses is that the seed's purpose isn't to last forever; it's to create the conditions for something entirely new. Repairing the seed is not only futile but also counterproductive and anti-evolutionary—it delays the inevitable and obstructs the regenerative cycle.

The Hidden Potential in Maximum Pressure

Yet, as it turns out, this intense compression is not all bad news. Just as matter under extreme pressure must either maintain its current state or undergo a complete phase transition (like water becoming steam), consciousness under peak compression faces a quantum bifurcation choice point:

- Complete collapse into fragmentation
- Breakthrough into expanded possibilities and realities

This isn't poetic—it's a precise description of how phase transitions work, whether in matter or consciousness. The very intensity that seems to trap us also creates the potential for dramatic transformation that transcends the limitations of the fragmented system.

This reveals a profound truth: Liberation comes not from separation but from deeper participation in the collective field. Power in a regenerative system isn't about control; it's about resonance and alignment with the whole.

The Dimensions of Transformation

To transcend these limiting myths and move through the *Dark Fire*, we must align with the deeper dimensions of transformation. These dimensions form a three-dimensional triangle, a tetrahedral model— a coherent framework for navigating the quantum tunnel and emerging into a state of regenerative coherence.

The four dimensions of *Regenerative Divergence*—pattern recognition, phase alignment, uncertainty navigation, and field generation—aren't separate techniques but facets of a single transformative movement, like the four faces of a tetrahedron creating a complete form. When we understand how the four faces work together, we discover something revolutionary: Breakthrough doesn't require fighting against overwhelming forces—it involves learning to sense and align with the natural dynamics already in motion.

Think of a sailor learning to read waves. The power of the ocean isn't something to fight against—it's the very force that enables movement. But this requires developing an entirely different kind of literacy. Instead of seeing waves as threats to be conquered, the sailor learns to feel how they move, where they gather force, and how to align with their momentum. This isn't just a metaphor—it's precisely how breakthrough happens in any complex system approaching transformation.

1. **Pattern Recognition: Awareness**

    The first dimension, pattern recognition, is like learning to read the ocean's movements. It requires developing sensitivity to how systems actually function—not just their surface features but their deeper dynamics. When we face that heckler in a community meeting, for instance, we're not just encountering an individual's resistance. We're seeing how systems maintain themselves by exhausting challenges through a kind of immune response. Understanding this pattern transforms how we engage—instead of exhausting ourselves fighting surface manifestations, we learn to sense where systems are actually vulnerable to change.

    Part of pattern recognition is recognizing the patterns of distortion. We must see how compression narrows our vision, fragments our awareness, and distorts our perception of reality. This is a facet of awareness, where we hold space for honest reflection without collapsing into blame or despair.

    We recognize the compression for what it is—not a permanent reality, but a transitional state. Like a birth canal, its purpose isn't to crush us but to pressure us into transformation.

To see clearly again, we must shift:

*   From **fragmented focus** to **field awareness**: Expanding our vision beyond the immediate pressure to sense the larger wave patterns of life at play.

- From **rigid control** to **natural alignment**: Letting go of the need to force outcomes and learning to move with the currents.
- From **fear-based reaction** to **coherent response**: Cultivating the ability to hold uncertainty while riding the wave without collapsing back into old patterns.

Regenerative Reflection:

Identify where you're holding on—where you're trying to fix, fight, or force. Ask:

- What am I clinging to that no longer serves?
- Where am I resisting riding the waves?

2. **Realignment: Trusting the Patterns of Life**

This leads naturally to the second dimension: learning to recognize and align with phase transitions. Just as a sailor learns to feel when a wave is building momentum, we can develop literacy in sensing when systems are approaching transformation points. The increasing rigidity of control structures, the spontaneous emergence of new forms of organization, and the growing instability of artificial boundaries—these aren't separate problems to solve but coherent indicators that old patterns are reaching their limits while new possibilities are gathering force.

This requires trusting in life's inherent coherence and allowing the pressure of compression to catalyze reorganization rather than resisting it.

Regenerative Reflection:

Shift from "fixing" to aligning. Let go of the belief that control equals safety. Ask:

- What would happen if I stopped forcing outcomes?
- How can I align with patterns that feel more alive, natural, and true?

3. **Resonance: Navigating Uncertainty**

The third dimension, navigating uncertainty, is perhaps the most challenging because it requires unlearning our addiction to control. We've been conditioned to see uncertainty as a problem to solve rather than a field of possibility to explore. But just as a sailor learns to trust the dynamic balance of riding the wave—neither rigid nor passive but responsively engaged—we can develop the capacity to move with rather than against the emergent intelligence of living systems. This isn't about becoming passive or surrendering to chaos—it's about discovering how supporting natural movement is more powerful than forcing artificial control.

Resonance is the field where transformation happens. By aligning with the natural patterns of coherence, we create conditions for quantum emergence. This is not about forcing outcomes but about cultivating relationships and systems that amplify alignment and allow new possibilities to unfold.

Regenerative Reflection:

Transformation happens through resonance, not force. Ask:

- What relationships, environments, or ideas amplify alignment and flow?
- Where can I create spaces of coherence that allow new possibilities to emerge?

4. **Regeneration: Field Generation**

The fourth dimension, field generation, is what makes breakthroughs regenerative rather than temporary. Like learning how ongoing ocean currents affect individual waves, we discover how to create and maintain the conditions that enable new patterns to stabilize and spread. This involves developing literacy in how fields of relationship and resonance work—how coherent connections enable change to propagate through systems in ways that force never could.

This is the dimension where new patterns stabilize and evolve. This is the phase where the unnecessary dissolves, leaving only the essence to emerge and thrive. It is not a return to what was but the creation of something entirely new—a state of coherence that mirrors the plasma field, where individual essence is enhanced through dynamic interconnection.

When David Bohm studied electrons in metals, he discovered something revolutionary: the more fully an electron participated in the collective plasma state, the more freedom it gained. This seems paradoxical from our usual perspective, where we associate freedom with separation and independence. But Bohm found that electrons actually became more liberated through deeper participation in the collective field.

This reveals a profound principle about the relationship between individual freedom and collective coherence. In a plasma state:

- The very act of participating in the collective field liberates individual particles from local constraints.

- Deeper engagement with the whole actually increases rather than restricts freedom of movement.
- Individual identity isn't lost but enhanced through resonant relationship with the field.
- Power emerges through coherent relationship rather than domination.

Think of how this transforms our understanding of breakthrough at maximum compression. Just as electrons gain freedom through full participation in the plasma state, consciousness under intense pressure faces a similar choice point:

- Maintain rigid boundaries and stay trapped in limited movement.
- Or "let go" into fuller participation in the collective field and gain new degrees of freedom. This isn't surrendering or giving up—it's a revolutionary shift into a higher order of coherent relationship. The very pressure that seemed to trap us becomes the force that enables a breakthrough.
- This transforms how we understand the intense pressure of our current moment. The increasing compression we feel—whether personal, social, or systemic—isn't just stress to be endured. It's creating the precise conditions where quantum breakthrough becomes possible. The choice isn't between fighting harder or giving up. It's whether we'll trust the transformation that becomes possible when we allow pressure to catalyze our evolution into a higher state of coherent relationship.

This isn't just theoretical physics—it's a precise description of how transformation actually works in any system approaching a phase transition. The path to freedom isn't through fighting against the pressure but through allowing it to catalyze a shift into a higher state of coherent relationship.

When these dimensions work together, something remarkable becomes possible. Instead of exhausting ourselves when fighting against overwhelming systems, we learn to sense and align with the transformative dynamics already in motion. The very forces that seemed to trap us become the leverage points for change. The pressure that felt crushing becomes the catalyst for a breakthrough.

This isn't abstract theory—it's how transformation actually works, whether in physical systems, living organisms, or social structures. When water reaches its phase transition point, for instance, it doesn't gradually become steam. The very pressure that seems to trap it in liquid form eventually creates the precise conditions required for phase transition. Similarly, systems under maximum compression don't gradually evolve—they either maintain their current state or undergo revolutionary transformation.

Regenerative Reflection:

Build systems that nourish life rather than extract from it. Ask:

- How can I create structures that support growth, evolution, and wholeness?
- What seeds of possibility am I planting for the future?

Signs of Approaching Breakthrough

Like water approaching its phase transition point, consciousness shows specific markers when nearing a breakthrough:

1. **System Indicators**
   - Increasing rigidity in old patterns
   - Growing instability in artificial structures
   - Spontaneous coherence in new forms

        o   Natural reorganization emerging
2. **Field Effects**
        o   Stronger resonance between aligned elements
        o   Increased synchronicity and connection
        o   Emergence of new pattern possibilities
        o   Growth of coherent relationship networks
3. **Consciousness Markers**
        o   Expanded perception beyond compression
        o   Recognition of larger patterns
        o   Access to new geometric possibilities
        o   Trust in natural intelligence

The Path of Regenerative Divergence

True transformation isn't comfortable. It's not about patching over problems, holding onto what's familiar, or managing the status quo. It's about surrendering to the *Dark Fire* of evolution—trusting that the collapse of old forms creates the space for something new to emerge.

The implications are profound. Our current convergence of crises—environmental, social, political—isn't just a series of problems to solve. It's a coherent pattern indicating that multiple systems are approaching phase transitions simultaneously. The increasing intensity of backlash against change, the spontaneous emergence of new forms of organization, the growing instability of artificial boundaries—are signs that transformation isn't just possible but imminent.

This is both a challenge and an unprecedented opportunity. The challenge is learning to navigate intense uncertainty as multiple systems approach transformation points simultaneously. The opportunity is that a breakthrough in one area can catalyze and support transformation across interconnected systems.

The choice we face isn't between fighting harder or giving up. It's whether we'll develop the literacy required to sense and align with the transformative dynamics already in motion. The pressure we feel isn't just resistance to change—it's the very force that makes breakthrough possible. The question is whether we'll learn to work with rather than against these deeper patterns.

This understanding offers both hope and direction. Hope because breakthrough doesn't require overcoming impossible odds through force—it involves aligning with and supporting natural transformation processes. Direction because we can learn to sense and work with these dynamics rather than exhausting ourselves to fight against them.

The path forward isn't about fixing what's broken. It's about midwifing the birth of what's already trying to emerge. Like scouts learning to read trails or sailors learning to work with wind patterns, we can develop literacy in sensing and aligning with the deeper currents of change. The future isn't something we force our way into—it's something we learn to sense and support into being.

This is the promise hidden within our current crisis: not the restoration of what was, but a breakthrough into what's possible. The pressure we feel isn't punishment—it's the catalyst for transformation. The choice is whether we'll learn to read and work with these deeper patterns or continue burnout trying to fight them. The narrow gate awaits. The wisdom to pass through it lies in learning to trust and align with the very forces that seem to oppose us.

The Promise of Transformation

Beyond the Fracking Point

The revolutionary truth is that maximum compression itself generates the conditions for a breakthrough. When systems reach peak rigidity, they create the precise circumstances required for consciousness to make quantum leaps into new possibilities.

This understanding transforms how we approach change:

- Instead of fighting compression, we use its energy for transformation
- Rather than forcing solutions, we enable natural evolution
- Instead of maintaining fragmentation, we support coherent emergence

The Geometry of Liberation

True liberation comes not through:

- Fighting old patterns (which reinforces them)
- Seeking incremental reform (which maintains basic geometry)
- Forcing change through will (which creates new compression)

But through:

- Recognition of natural patterns
- Alignment with geometric intelligence
- Support for coherent evolution
- Trust in life's wisdom

Conclusion: The Eye of the Needle

We stand at a profound threshold. The very intensity of systemic compression creates the conditions for evolutionary breakthrough. The choice is not between:

- Fighting harder within broken systems
- Accepting limitations and control
- Finding better ways to cope with fragmentation

But whether we will:

- Trust the intelligence emerging through crisis
- Support natural evolution beyond compression
- Allow quantum breakthrough into new possibilities

The path forward isn't about fixing what's broken—it's about allowing the emergence of what's already trying to be born. Through the geometry of transformation, we can move beyond fragmentation into the coherent fields of a new way of being.

This is the promise hidden within maximum compression: not the restoration of what was, but a breakthrough into what's possible.

The compression we feel is not the end; it is the beginning of a profound transformation. The *Dark Fire* of our time is forging a new coherence, one that cannot be reached through repair, certainty, or domination. It requires us to move through the quantum tunnel—the narrow gate where everything unnecessary falls away, and only the essence remains.

The question is not whether we will face the fire—it is already here. The question is whether we will collapse under its weight or allow it to liberate us into a higher order of being. The path forward is not about fighting harder or fixing faster; it is about surrendering to the deeper intelligence of life itself and emerging on the other side as co-creators of a coherent, regenerative world.

MS.OCEANSIDE REAL ESTATE

Melissa Huk

Founder & CEO

Your story begins somewhere, but its starting point does not define its destination. For over three decades, as a proud San Diego native, I have devoted my career in real estate to advocating for those who feel unheard, proving that circumstances do not dictate potential. No matter where you come from, there is always room to rise, achieve more, and rewrite your future.

Success is not determined by where you begin—it is forged through resilience, tenacity, and the courage to push beyond limitations. As a fierce negotiator and trusted advisor, I have spent my career helping people find more than just homes—I help them discover new opportunities, security, and a foundation for a better future. Whether guiding military families through transitions, assisting buyers and sellers, or supporting those facing life's toughest moments, my mission remains the same: to uplift, empower, and create lasting impact.

Beyond real estate, I am a devoted wife, proud mother, and loving grandmother. Today, I share my journey because I believe stories have power—the power to inspire, to motivate, and to remind us that no past can hold us back from the future we are meant to embrace. Your next chapter is waiting. Step into it with confidence.

Yours in success,
Melissa Huk

https://www.linkedin.com/in/imsellingsandiego/
https://www.facebook.com/msoceansiderealestate/
https://www.instagram.com/ms.oceansiderealestate/
https://imsellingsandiego.com/
https://www.msoceansiderealestate.com/

From Darkness To Dawn

A Journey of Resilience And Transformation

By Melissa Huk

The darkness of the early mornings mirrored the bleakness of my life back then. The sky would be a deep, inky black, slowly giving way to the gray dawn, much like my own life at that time—filled with despair, desperation, and fear but inching toward a glimmer of hope. I was a child of two alcoholic parents, bullied as a kid and teenager, married young, and became a divorced mother of three, trapped in a cycle of abusive and degrading marriages, left with nothing but my fierce desire to create a better life for my children and myself. I knew the cycle must be broken.

The Abyss: A Journey Through Survival and Strength

When my last marriage collapsed, it wasn't just the loss of a relationship—it was the unraveling of the fragile stability I had fought so hard to maintain. The weight of failure pressed on my chest like an anchor, suffocating and relentless. My finances were in ruins, my credit cards maxed out just to keep the lights on, and my car—a battered relic held together by sheer will—was a daily reminder of how far I had fallen. Every morning, I woke up to a battlefield where survival meant working two jobs, raising my children alone, and caring for a child with special challenges and nothing but grit and prayer to carry me through.

There were nights I lay awake, staring at the ceiling, drowning in anxiety over overdue bills, wondering how I was going to pay for the next meal . Swallowing my pride, I stood in church lines asking for help, feeling the sting of shame tighten around me like a noose. Every job rejection, every door slammed in my face, whispered the same cruel message: You're not enough. You'll never break free.

But somewhere in the wreckage of my life, I found something I never expected—unyielding resilience. It didn't arrive in grand gestures or moments of clarity. It crept in through exhaustion, through the relentless push to wake up and fight another day, through the unwavering love I had for my children. I didn't have a clear roadmap, no guarantees of success. All I had was a decision—to refuse to let my circumstances define my future. And so, I kept moving forward. Because survival wasn't enough. I was going to rise.

The Spark of Change

A single conversation ignited a shift in my mindset. An old friend—once a struggling single mother like me—had built a thriving career in real estate. Her journey wasn't just inspiring; it was proof that reinvention was possible. For the first time in a long time, I saw a way out—a glimmer of hope beyond survival.

With nothing to lose and everything to gain, I took a leap of faith. I enrolled in a real estate course, financing it with yet another credit card, despite having no savings and an already overwhelming schedule. The weight of responsibility never eased, but neither did my determination. Learning had never come easy for me, but I refused to let that stop me. Every spare moment became an opportunity to study—late into the night after my children were asleep, in between jobs, and whenever doubt tried to creep in.

This was more than a career move. It was my way forward. My way up. My way out.

The First Steps

Earning my real estate license was more than just an accomplishment—it was a breakthrough. Passing the exam on my first attempt felt like a victory over every doubt, every hardship, every voice that had told me I wasn't enough. But the journey was far from over.

The industry was ruthless, an unforgiving world where experience and connections reigned. I had neither. Each rejection felt like a door slamming shut, a reminder of how far I still had to go. But I refused to let failure define my future.

I took every opportunity, no matter how small. I listed homes in overlooked neighborhoods, knocked on doors that had never been opened to me, made cold calls despite the sting of rejection, and showed up—again and again—at networking events where I felt invisible. Slowly, persistence turned into progress. My first sale wasn't extravagant, but it was proof that I belonged here. That I was capable. That this new chapter was mine to write.

Overcoming Obstacles

The road ahead was anything but easy. Balancing a demanding new career while raising my children alone felt like an uphill battle. There were days when exhaustion consumed me, moments when I questioned if I was failing at everything. My car—an ever-present reminder of my struggles—broke down so often it felt like a test of my endurance. Every costly repair was another financial setback, yet I refused to stop moving forward.

One of my greatest challenges was mastering time. My clients needed my full attention, my children deserved my presence, and I was stretched impossibly thin. The weight of responsibility never lessened, but I learned to navigate it. The constant demands forced me to sharpen my focus, teaching me resilience, discipline, and the true meaning of perseverance.

A Breakthrough

My turning point came with a listing that no one wanted—a home that had sat untouched on the market for over a year. Every other agent had walked away, leaving the owners feeling hopeless. But where others saw failure, I saw possibility.

I threw myself into the challenge, pouring in time, energy, and strategy. I advised on key renovations, meticulously staged the home, crafted a compelling marketing plan, and reached out to every contact I had built. I refused to let this property be forgotten.

Within two months—back in the mid-90s, when this was no small feat—the home sold. It was more than just a financial win; it was proof that my perseverance meant something. That my hard work and sacrifices weren't in vain. More importantly, it cemented my reputation. The referrals started trickling in, and for the first time, I wasn't just surviving in real estate—I was building something real.importantly, it established me as a competent and reliable agent. Referrals began to trickle in, and my business started to grow.

Achieving Success

As my real estate career gained momentum, my financial struggles slowly loosened their grip. The mountain of debt that once felt impossible to climb was gradually erased. I bought a reliable car, no longer fearing every unexpected breakdown, and most importantly, I secured a home my children could take pride in—a place that symbolized stability, safety, and a future built on resilience.

Owning multiple properties had once felt like an unattainable dream, a fantasy reserved for others. But as my income grew, I refused to let fear hold me back. I invested with intention, first purchasing a rental property, then another. Each acquisition was more than just financial growth—it was proof of perseverance, a tangible reminder of the journey from struggle to strength.

Balancing Life and Career

Even as my career flourished, breaking free from the cycles of my past remained an uphill battle. I was still unlearning the family dynamics that had shaped me, still struggling against the patterns that threatened to pull me back. My children were my greatest priority, yet the weight of providing for them often kept me from the very moments I longed to share. I showed up when I could—school events, milestones, stolen pockets of time—but I couldn't ignore the quiet loneliness they sometimes felt, the unspoken longing for more of me.

Resentment lingered—not toward them, but toward the reality that my role as a provider sometimes overshadowed my role as a mother. The exhaustion was relentless, and doubt whispered that I was failing them in ways I couldn't fix. But despite the gaps, despite the struggles, I held onto one truth: I was giving them stability, a home, a foundation stronger than the one I had known. And in that, every sacrifice held meaning.

Empowerment and Independence

Achieving financial stability ignited a profound sense of liberation. No longer shackled by circumstance, I shed the need to rely on anyone else for survival. I held the reins of my own destiny, finally able to provide for my family in ways that once felt unattainable. My journey from struggle to success was never just about money—it was about reclaiming my power, my identity, and my self-worth.

With that strength came a calling. I became a mentor to women who stood where I once had, trapped by fear and uncertainty. Sharing my story, offering guidance, and reminding them of their own untapped resilience became my greatest fulfillment. I needed them to see that no hardship was final, no setback permanent. The very obstacles they believed would break them were, in truth, the stepping stones to a life they had yet to claim.

Looking Forward

Today, my life stands as proof that resilience and determination can carve a path through even the fiercest storms. I continue to chase new goals, both personally and professionally, knowing that growth never ends. Challenges will come, but so will opportunities. The foundation I've built is unshakable, and I step into the future with unwavering confidence and a heart full of purpose.

Looking back, I am overwhelmed with gratitude. Every hardship, every trial, shaped me into the woman I am today. They forged my perseverance, deepened my self-belief, and revealed the boundless strength of the human spirit. My story is not just about survival—it is about transformation, a declaration that no matter how dark the present may feel, the future remains unwritten. A brighter tomorrow is not just possible—it is yours to claim.

Final Thoughts

To anyone standing in the depths of their own struggle, I leave you with this:

Never surrender. No matter how impossible the road ahead may seem, you hold within you the strength to rise. Trust yourself, lean on those who uplift you, and take that first, courageous step toward change. The path will not be easy—it will test you, break you, and demand more than you ever thought you could give. But every step forward, no matter how small, is a victory.

Remember this: The darkest nights birth the most brilliant dawns. Your story is not over. Your future is waiting. Claim it with everything you have.

Much love and boundless success to you.

Melissa Huk

Ms. Oceanside

Natalie Jade Pinnell

Business Strategist & Operations Expert

Natalie Jade is a Business Strategist, Operations Consultant, Best-Selling Author, Speaker and Advocate. With a unique and out of the box thinking approach, she helps coaches and entrepreneurs do business with more clarity, ease and impact.

Featured in major international publications, Natalie has decades of experience running operations and building large brands, providing a bridge between big vision and tangible real-world results.

As an integrator for powerful visionaries, Natalie is not only able to just see your vision, but she is able to transform it, making it happen, and turn high-stress growth into aligned success, joy and fulfilment.

In her spare time you'll find her being a fierce advocate in the neurodiversity space, spearheading change and reform, and taking care of her own little humans in the highlands of Scotland.

To learn more about Natalie and how she can help you take your business to the next level, visit www.nataliejade.com.

https://www.linkedin.com/in/natalie-jade
https://www.facebook.com/natspinnell
https://www.instagram.com/nataliejadepinnell/
https://www.nataliejade.com/l

F The Formula

By Natalie Jade Pinnell

What if I told you that my wealthiest moment didn't come from hitting consistent multi-six-figure income, scaling my thriving business management and digital marketing agency, or even achieving those first coveted "$10k months" that everyone in the solopreneur space seems to chase?

What if instead I told you that it came on an ordinary Tuesday afternoon, sitting cross-legged on my living room floor with my daughter?

The same daughter whose autism diagnosis had once seemed like it would shatter all our carefully laid plans for life and "success". A diagnosis that, at the time, filled me with dread for her and brought so many questions as to what would be possible for both our family, and for her future. The same daughter who would ultimately teach me more about "wealth" (and actually myself) than any business mentor or coach ever could.

In that moment, watching her fully engaged and present, her joy radiating through the room, I realized something profound: I was rich beyond measure.

More than that... as a family, we are rich beyond measure.

Not in the way that society measures wealth – with bank balances and business metrics – nor in terms of what societal expectations tell us what life "should" look like. We were living our TRUTH.

Fully, happily and without constraint, doubt or limitation.

We have something far more precious. Something that so many of us are missing in our day-to-day lives.

Connection. Peace. Purpose.

She gave me the biggest gift. The things that truly matter.

The moment that we received her diagnosis, I knew that our life was likely going to look "different" to what we had expected. But, with curious and open minds, our journey led us down a path to ultimate freedom. It forced us as parents to let go of all those 'shoulds', and instead embrace what is true for us and live that fully.

With no shame, no blame, and absolute pure LOVE.

I know that all sounds simple, but I would be lying if I didn't say that for me it was a painful process. It required burning down, and letting go. Of dreams, goals, expectations and self. To truly see what mattered, and to embrace, with love, a very different path. To find and meet our truth with acceptance and understanding. But the reality is that when I was able to do that, a whole new world of possibility opened up.

As I sat there, on that Tuesday afternoon, I realised that we had everything we needed. I realised there was nothing more important, than being exactly where we were, and I knew that the impact of moments like this were going to have ripple effects that neither of us could truly understand. I let go of the to do list, I let go of the "shoulds" and I surrendered to living our unconventional truth boldly. And in doing so helped her feel seen, heard, honoured and most importantly fully loved and respected. I embraced the unknown.

Here is the thing though… So many of us are living a lie.

Pretending to be someone we are not, trying to be just like the person that we put up on a pedestal. Wanting what other people have. Fearful of others judgements, deciding to stay small, and prioritise fitting in. Doing things that we intuitively know don't feel right, or blindly following the masses without taking a moment to tune in to ourselves and our truth.

Because… the truth is…it takes work to live in authenticity. It is the less easy path in some ways. But actually the easiest path in the long run.

My daughter taught me to embrace our whole truth, fearlessly and fiercely. Something I will forever be grateful for.

You see, when my daughter received her autism diagnosis, I did what any driven, successful and solution orientated person would do: I tried to "fix" the situation. I researched, I planned, I strategized – applying all the skills and experience that I had, to try and support my child. These methods had served me so well in building my agency. But they didn't work so well in this situation. Life had other plans for me and my family, and my daughter had other lessons to teach me.

The thing is, we had done all the things we were told to do when she was born. We followed the prescribed path that was expected of us as parents. And it cost us everything. We suddenly realised that the prescribed path really was no longer serving our family. Which led us to sync deep into our hearts to uncover OUR (and most importantly her) real truth.

And that Truth led us to our ultimate liberation. A decision to unwaveringly choice to do things differently.

We are told that our daughter's diagnosis is "limiting" but we feel far from it. In fact, it broke us out of the rat race, out of the "system" that oppressed us, and ultimately let us embrace life and love in the fullest of capacities. But… this was a journey. It didn't happen overnight. And in fact, I lost my way along the journey.

When we first received the diagnosis I spent every waking minute trying to find the "fix". As an enneagram 6, I work hard to create security. To make things safe, reliable, to problem solve. I explored all the therapies, pouring my heart and soul and every waking minute into finding ways and means to support her.

All the while, continuing to try and "fit in" and be involved in things that were debilitating and destroying her.

The thing is… I needed her to show me. I needed her to break down the box I didn't even realise I was living in. I needed her to force me to break down those barriers and choose a different reality.

I couldn't have ever have done it without her. Break free from conformity, and realise how it was suffocating us.

Like many entrepreneurs, I had spent a decade building what looked like success from the outside. To many, I had it "all". In my mind, it was in the name of creating lifestyle and financial freedom for my family.

The agency, the income, the accolades and the achievements that should have made me feel successful. Yet with each milestone, each celebrated revenue goal, I felt increasingly hollow. I had somehow lost my way in the pursuit of "success", going against the very thing I stand for, and that she taught me,… doing things differently. I ultimately lost the freedom I had been striving for.

It wasn't until life circumstances forced me to question everything I thought I knew about success, that I found my true path and calling – or rather, my true light.

You see, sometimes we're called to be lighthouses. To stand firm in the storm, steady and a beacon of light no matter what storms we are facing. To free ourselves from others' expectations, judgments, and well-meaning advice. To shine our light not just for ourselves, but for others who might be searching for permission to choose a different path.

But my personal path to this understanding wasn't straightforward. I had to go through my own journey, release the subconscious beliefs and behaviours that were limiting me, and choose to face the shadows and the fears that I spent a long time avoiding.

My success had come from hard work, determination, resilience and a deep desire to provide for my family. But I wasn't being honest with myself, and some of this effort was coming from a place of avoidance and trauma. Overworking rather than facing my own demons.

In fact, it took my daughter's own breakdown to show me what true success and wealth really means.

She showed me what TRULY mattered.

You see when I took a step back, for a moment, and looked at our reality. I found that i was still falling into the trap of searching for what others deem to be "successful". As a driven, and solution oriented person, I could spent every moment researching, planning, strategising, creating, but the point is you have to stop and most importantly LISTEN.

Listen to my daughter, even without verbal language. Listen to the nudges and the intuition. Listen to what your heart wants.

Life has lessons in every experience.

While I was busy trying to make everything fit into society's box of what success should look like, my daughter was showing me, with unwavering authenticity, that there is profound strength in being exactly who you are. Even when – especially when – that means not fitting in, being brave and releasing the "shoulds" that we all carry with us daily.

I finally realised that I had been trapped in the cycle, that I help others to avoid in business, by following formulas that don't fit our souls, nor our real goals.

It's a pattern I see constantly in the business world now -- talented, passionate, and experienced entrepreneurs losing their way in a sea of identical formulas and one-size-fits-all solutions. Trying to find the quick fix, shiny squirrel syndrome distracting them from what really matters.

More often than not, they come to me exhausted and disheartened, and ready to give up on their passion, having invested thousands in programs that promised success but delivered only templates. Templates that worked perfectly... for someone else. Templates that did not consider their individual personalities, goals nor clients.

Templates that destroyed their business. And more importantly their passion.

You see, life isn't supposed to be a template. Nor is business.

True freedom lies when you think outside the box and you refuse to be constrained by one.

My most miserable month in business was my first $10k month. It was something I was conditioned to strive for, but that month brought me distress and distraction. But I ignored that emotion, and thought I was just doing it wrong.

So many of my clients are (or have been) in the same situation. They "did everything right" but their voices are heavy, confused and filled with self doubt. "I followed the Formula but it isn't working for me".

Let me let you into a secret....

There is no secret formula.

In fact, if you are looking for a formula, it's likely that you've lost your way. It's likely that you need to take a step back and reassess rather than looking for answers outside of yourself.

That's what my daughter teaches me, I can spend hours researching, educating myself, and looking for the quick fix, or I can stop, take a moment, be present, listen, and connect, both with myself and with her.

What are we embodying, and crucially what are we teaching (our clients or our children).

The truth is, so many of these entrepreneurs aren't failing because they are doing something wrong. They have just lost their way with the weight of the noise and societal expectations. Instagram is full of the picture perfect coaches, with gorgeous branding, sunning themselves in exotic locations. And while this is true for some, what you don't see is the behind the scenes reality.

What you don't see is that this might not work for you and your business model, and what you certainly don't see are many of the real numbers. Having worked behind the scenes for many 6-7 figure business owners, there are so many just struggling to even pay themselves.

The truth is, these entrepreneurs are struggling because they are trying to do someone elses version of "right".

When my child received her diagnosis, I won't deny it, I went into a place of mournning. Mourning all the things I thought our lives would look like. Mourning a reality that was never mine to claim in the first place.

Trying to force her to fit into environments that weren't right for her, only added to the distress and her struggles.

When ships follow a compass that isn't calibrated to their own true north. They get lost. And that can happen in both life and business, finding yourself further and further away from your intended destination.

What is the answer? Wayfinding.

You see, these struggles that I witnessed across the board, with one-size-fits-all formulas weren't just observations, they became my calling. A calling to find a different path, from my own journey of breaking free, I found my true purpose as a business strategist that helps others chart their own unique course to success. A course that leaves them free, fulfilled and financially abundant.

The problem with formulas, is they fail to see you as an individual. How you want to show up, how many hours you want to work, in what spaces you want to engage, and how your clients best receive your magic. They strip away the essence, leaving something unrecognisable, and most importantly, something you begin to resent and abandon.

Formula's don't account for your individual needs, maybe you are a single parent who needs flexibility above all else, or an introvert whose genius emerges in one on one settings rather than massive webinars. Maybe you are a creative who works in inspirational bursts rather than rigid schedules. Maybe the formula and "system" that is supposed to save you, actually boxes you in, and burns you out.

Trust me, i know, I fell in to the same trap!!! Even knowing what I know, and doing what I do.

It took that moment of presence, and of realisation to see that there was only one thing that truly mattered, and to embrace all of what that means for us in life and business.

For me that looked like burning down the business model that I built for over a decade. It meant reassessing my priorities, and it meant TRULY walking my talk.

When you become clear on your dreams, and I mean really crystal clear, and commit to them with unwavering trust, you experience what true freedom really is.

I've always had the ability to hear my clients vision, see the potential and opportunities, and break it down into actionable steps, and a clear path of how we are going to get there. Helping entrepreneurs to translate their vision into reality - on their terms.

I always say, I'm glad my daughter chose me to be her Mama. She has communication challenges, and I'm able to translate things in a non traditional way. She inspires me every day with how she chooses to bravely, and fearlessly show up and show us who she is. And I want more of that for all of us. Just as I learned to translate my daughters unique way of seeing the world into something others can understand, I also help entrepreneurs to translate their vision into tangible reality, and even better, on their own terms.

But creating a custom path isnt just about strategy. It requires something far more fundamental. The courage to be authentically yourself in a world that pressures us to conform.

The bravest thing you can do in business – and in life – is to stop performing and start BEing. But here's what they don't tell you about authenticity: it's not just about being yourself. It's about being yourself when everything and everyone around you suggests you should be something else.

THIS IS TRULY WHERE THE MAGIC LIES.

The past 6 years I've been learning these lessons, whether it is seeing my clients be pulled off path and guiding them back to their true north, through the constant battles and advocacy that is required to support my unwaveringly authentic daughter to survive in systems and constructs that not only aren't designed for her, but actually do her harm, to finally dismantling my "successful" agency to build something fully alignment with my own personal truth (and no one elses).

Authenticity is such a buzz word.

So much so that it's almost lost it's impact and meaning. How many of us today can hold our hands up and say we operate from a place of TRUE authenticity. But the truth is, authenticity isn't just something to shove in your copy to make you sound more trustworthy, nor is it just a nice idea to have, it's a true and practical path to liberation.

Often times, when you are operating from a place of true authenticity, it requires a letting go of many things you thought, knew and loved. Things you had taken on over the years as being "yours' but in reality were just conditioning and expectations. When you are being truly authentic, it can mean making hard decisions. That's why it is rare to see in today's society. We are built to consume, for convenience, and for compliance.

It takes courage and bravery to choose another path.

Bravery isn't about being fearless – it's about feeling the fear and choosing trust anyway. When we talk about breaking out of society's boxes, we're really talking about a series of small, brave choices that add up to transformation.

Here's what I've learned about choosing your own path:

Trust Over Terror

That voice telling you "this is crazy" or "what will people think?" – it's just fear dressed up as logic. The braver choice is to listen to that quieter voice, the one that whispers "what if?" and "why not?"

When we talk about breaking free, it's natural to focus on what we might lose. But what I've witnessed, both in my own journey and my clients' transformations, is that what we think we're losing often pales in comparison to what we stand to gain.

The minute I chose a different path for me and my daughter, our world EXPANDED. Almost instantly. I had been so stuck in the grind that I had failed to see so much opportunity outside of that.

Sometimes having "nothing to lose" is actually having everything to gain. When we strip away all the "shoulds" and expectations, when we're willing to question everything we've built, that's when true liberation becomes possible.

I see it in my clients' stories, and on my own personal journey – these moments of beautiful demolition and rebuild. The corporate executive who walked away from her six-figure salary to build a lifestyle business that not only matched her income but gave her back her life. The successful coach who dared to burn down her "profitable" but soul-crushing business model to create something truly aligned with her gifts, tripling her income while working half the hours. And for me, stepping fully into my calling, no longer hiding behind a brand, and shining a beacon of light for those that really need to see it.

For me, this isn't about isolated success stories, I'm seeing more and more of them. They're part of a larger revolution in terms of how we both define and pursue success. A revolution I'm embracing and proud to be part of, both as a business strategist and as an advocate for those who dare to do things differently.

You don't get to where you want to be by playing small. It's those scary decisions that usually result in the biggest impact.

What if you redefine wealth, the ripples of profitability grow far and wide the moment I made that decision. In letting go, I found both freedom and success.

I remember my mother telling me when I was younger, that a clairvoyant had told her that her eldest child would choose and operate from a place of love. That's been my journey, choosing love over conventional models of success, has actually been my biggest evolution and growth edge.

In 2024, I was faced with my biggest challenge. National media got hold of a story involving my daughter, and I was thrown into the world of advocacy on a level I never knew existed. Forced to let go of my "should's" I was receiving countless messages thanking me for being a voice for those that struggle to be seen and heard.

Of course, this came with its own challenges. Having to be courageous, take a stand, and face the trolls and the hatred, from people that love to tear people down. I had to stand strong, shine a light, and weather the storm. And I did it alone.

No one, should ever have to face that alone.

And nor should you.

"F the formula" isn't just a catchy phrase – it's a revolution in how to approach success. Because you didn't get here by playing small or following someone else's blueprint. In fact you were born on this planet with your own, and designed to forge your own path. You got here by daring to believe there could be a different way. Surely that's one of the reasons you started your own business anyway?

If you're ready to:

- Stop doing business by someone else's rules
- Create success that feels like coming home to yourself
- Make the impact you know you're capable of
- Build something truly aligned with your soul

Then consider this your lighthouse moment. Your invitation to trust that the path that feels right to your soul – even if it looks different from everyone else's – is exactly the path you should be on.

Because you don't need another formula. You need support in creating your own way. You need someone who can see your vision, translate it into strategy, and help you build it with confidence and ease.

Let me be that steady light guiding you home to yourself. Let me help you create the kind of success that feels like freedom, the kind of impact that changes lives, the kind of business you actually love showing up to every day.

It's time to shine your light, without apology or permission. Because the world doesn't need another copy – it needs your unique magic.

Are you ready to break free?

1000 RIPPLE EFFECTS

Stacey Huish

Founder

Stacey Huish
A Strong Powerful Game Changer!
A Speaker, Educator, Author and Lover of Life!

A freespirit who is affectionately known as the Game Changer. I am an earth healer, a heart healer, a lover of life, raising the vibration of love to help as many people as possible to live passionate, purpose filled lives, awaken the planet and enable the divine purpose of the universe to unfold.

That is My Life!

That is my purpose for being here!

I am a Social Entrepreneur, 1 Million Women Ambassador and a Change Maker. A woman who puts her heart and soul into everything she does. A woman who loves people and loves life.

https://www.facebook.com/1000rippleeffects.com

http://www.1000rippleeffects.com/

Will It Happen?

By Stacey Huish

Success starts at the end of the finish line. ~ Stacey Huish
Seeing things through to completion is what changes the world. ~ Stacey Huish

I spent a lot of time listening to kids. Their dreams, their struggles, their challenges. These kids are the ones who have no support. They live life on their own. They figure it out along the way. They make child decisions with adult consequences. There is nobody guiding them, teaching them, showing them what to do. Nobody helps these kids. They are left to their own devices to work it out. They have the hardest lessons. Life is their teacher. The university of hard knocks. I can't let these kids keep living like this. They need help, they need support, they need guidance.

"Supported kids are successful kids." ~ Stacey Huish

The question I had to answer was: How do I reach all the kids out there in the world and give them the knowledge and the information they need to succeed?

Walking through the supermarket, the answer came to me. I will write a book, *1000 Ripple Effects*. There will be stories from people all over the world. I personally don't have all the answers, but we, as a collective, do. The community are the ones who have the knowledge and the wisdom to help these kids become healthy, functioning adults. It takes a village to raise a child.

I set out on the journey and invited 1000 people to write a story. They each had to answer the question:
What advice would you give 15–21 year olds becoming an adult?

I reminded each author to write their stories, remembering:

This is a very important and very significant transition in their life. This is the time they break away from the family unit and become the Man/Woman they are going to be. This is when they work out what they stand for in life, what they value, and what they are going to do. This is also when they start to live their life purpose.

As the stories came in, I read them. Their words moved me to tears. The emotion in each story touched my heart and my soul deeply. Every child reading these words will be able to make the transition from Boy to Man, Girl to Woman very easily. There is so much knowledge and wisdom being shared. There is true genuine care in each story.

One afternoon I received a letter. This letter is what made my decision final. I must get the stories out to the kids all around the world.

Let me read this letter to you. It is from a woman who shares her story from when she was a little girl. I actually know this woman personally. I've watched her grow up, and I've watched her transform into a beautiful woman. I know the life that she has lived and the struggles that she has overcome. She has a really important message for everyone out there, so here it goes.

"From my heart to your heart, this is so much more than just a story. No one knows this, but everyone needs to know. No one truly understands just how important these stories actually are and what these stories do. How they make a difference in the lives of people just like me. So, I'm going to tell you how important they are.

Everyone seems to think that this is just a story, but I'm here to tell you that it is not. It is so much more than just a story. I grew up an orphan, not knowing whom to ask, when everyone else turned to their parents or the people around them. I turned to your story, I read your words, I listened to your voice, I took your advice. You were there for me when no one else was. In my hour of Darkness, your story is all I had. You spoke to my heart, and you whispered in my ear. It was you who provided comfort in my hour of need. You reached out across the oceans, and you held my hand. I know because I felt it. You sat with me for hours and days on end until the last tear was shed. Your words were my blanket that wrapped me up so warmly you were my hug at the end of my day. Because of you, I was able to keep going and take another step. I knew what to do. You told me, you wrote it down for me to read. You gave me the greatest gift of all, your words, your wisdom, your knowledge, your love. Every time I read another story, I unwrapped another gift. Another precious jewel, a gem that I kept inside me, inside my heart. This is just like having access to the world's most precious key, unlocking my mind, unlocking my soul, unlocking my life. You were my golden compass, guiding me, directing me, and showing me where to go and what to do. My voice got stronger, my love grew deeper, and I stepped into my purpose. You kissed my wounds all better. You mended my broken heart, and you kissed me goodnight. You opened up and shared your truth. I was inspired by your courage and your willingness to be yourself, and because of you, I opened up to a truth inside of me. I danced into my freedom. You were the spark to my light, and because you were brave enough to ignite your own, you taught me how to solve problems. You taught me how to be kind to people. You taught me to love myself and to care for others. Your story did all of that! Because of you, I succeeded. I took your knowledge and your wisdom and now teach others what you taught me. I want the mums to know that you are my mum. I want the dads to know that you were my dad. I want you to know how I feel about you. I have only met you through your story, and I may never meet you in person. I may never laugh with you or cry with you or even get to give you that hug that you gave me, but I want you to know that I love you with all my heart because you were the one who made a difference in my life and that is why your story is that important."

That is one very powerful story and it touched me very deeply in the core of my heart. To think there's a child out there in this world who only has stories as their mum and dad breaks my heart. This is the whole reason why I have put this book project together. This is the whole reason because there are so many kids out there, exactly like this little girl who never had a mum or a dad and only ever relied on the stories they read through a book.

It is important to finish this book. I have to get the money to get this book published.

I stand firm in making this dream happen.

No matter what, I will get my *1000 Ripple Effects* book published.
I had already gathered stories from 1000 people from around the globe.
Put all the stories into a series of six books. Made the book covers, got the publisher's contract and set up book distribution gigs for next year.
Over the past few years, I have tried to raise funds by selling a financial product. I also made an online business and tried selling things. However, these methods did not work.

Why did I start this online business? To get the money needed to get my book published.

Why did I try to sell the financial product? To get the money needed to get my book published.

Every time, I asked myself, "Why did I try _____?" The answer was always the same. To get the money needed to publish my book.

Now I have brought my focus back to the book. I started looking for grants to get my book published. I found a grant. I spent time writing the grant. Answering all the questions. The day before the grant was due, I was putting in the final words, adding the support documents, and submitting the grant to publish the book.

The waiting game begins. It is 12 weeks before I get an answer about the success of this grant. Will I be successful in winning the grant, or won't I?

In a cruel, cold, and heartless world, this book will be the lighthouse, the shining light at the end of the tunnel, the one resource everyone can go to to get answers. *1000 Ripple Effects* is creating a ripple effect for the people reading it. The stories in this book will be read by many people. The stories are designed to uplift, restore faith in humanity, and touch the hearts of many. Can you see how we are creating 1000 ripple effects right across the world? And how those ripple effects are creating more ripple effects?

If you have a dream, make it happen!

You and Me

We Cast a Pebble

We Make a Wave!

We Create 1000 Ripple Effects Today!

This story is due before I find out the results of the grant.
To know what happened, did I get the grant?

Did the book get published?

You will need to visit the website
www.1000RippleEffects.com/grant.html

JOURNEY TO BUSINESS SUCCESS

Andrea C Russell

Business Implementation & Financial Accountability Coach

Andrea Russell is a business coach dedicated to helping Christian female entrepreneurs find clarity, grow profitable businesses, and live with purpose.

With over 12 years of experience in financial accountability and strategy, Andrea knows the struggles of juggling faith, family, and finances while running a business.

She created the Sweet Spot Client Profiler and other tools to help women identify their best clients, simplify their operations, and scale their businesses with confidence.

Andrea believes every business should honor God, create meaningful impact, and provide the freedom to live abundantly.

When she's not coaching, Andrea enjoys connecting with her community, inspiring others through her faith, and equipping women to overcome challenges.

Her mission is simple: to empower Christian women to achieve success without sacrificing their values.

https://www.linkedin.com/in/andrearussell1875/
https://www.facebook.com/acrbookkeepingplus
https://www.instagram.com/christianwomenpreneur/
https://www.journeytobusinesssuccess.com
https://resources.andrearussellcoach.com/home

Rising Above

Transforming Pain Into Purpose and Learning to
S.O.A.R

By Andrea C Russell

The Smell of Pastries and the Seeds of Purpose

Waking up to the smell of freshly baked pastries was one of the best parts of my childhood. Every morning, I would rush into the kitchen to find my mother covered in flour, sweat on her brow, working tirelessly to fill customer orders. Her hands moved quickly, rolling dough and checking the oven as she wiped her face with a hand towel. She had been awake since dawn, preparing bread, pies, cookies— whatever her customers needed.

As I stood there watching her work, I was amazed. My mother wasn't just baking; she was building something special. Cars would pull up one after the other, and customers would exchange cash for the delicious goods she had worked so hard to create. All the money went into a cigar box tucked away in the kitchen, and to my young mind, it seemed like magic. I couldn't believe how much money she was making!

Despite the hard work, my mother always found a way to enjoy herself. A small TV sat in the corner of the kitchen, and as she worked, she'd watch *All My Children*. Erica Kane was her favorite, and she'd laugh as she kneaded dough. Watching her joy and determination left a lasting impression on me.

It was in those early moments that I decided I wanted to be just like her. My mother embodied the verse:
"Whatever you do, work at it with all your heart, as working for the Lord, not for human masters." – Colossians 3:23.

Her dedication inspired me to dream big. I wanted to try my hand at making money, just like she did. My plan? Sneak some extra pastries into my school bag and sell them during lunch. At just eight years old, I became a little entrepreneur. I'd exchange pastries for coins and use the money to buy chicken and fries. I was thrilled with my success, but of course, I kept it a secret from my mother.

Selling pastries at school was more than just fun; it lit a fire inside me. I felt the thrill of earning money and the satisfaction of doing something on my own. This small beginning sparked my passion for entrepreneurship and set me on a path to learn more. I started craving books about business, eager to understand how I could grow and succeed.

My mother's example taught me that hard work and the courage to keep going are key to achieving all that God has planned for us. Her story was remarkable. She hadn't finished elementary school—she often went to school barefoot and had to stay home to care for her father, who struggled with alcoholism. But she never let those hardships define her. Instead, they gave her strength.

Seeing her wake up before dawn, pouring her heart into her work, and putting smiles on her customers' faces planted something powerful in me. I realized that, like her, I could use the gifts God gave me to create something meaningful. My mother's resilience and faith showed me that no challenge is too big to overcome.

Her life reflected the truth of the verse:
"Start children off on the way they should go, and even when they are old, they will not turn from it." – Proverbs 22:6.

The lessons she taught me—resilience, independence, and faith—became the foundation for everything I would do. Watching her build a better life for our family through hard work and joy taught me to dream bigger, work harder, and trust God's plan.

Building Strength from Simple Beginnings

Our home wasn't just a place to eat, sleep, and live—it was a hub of ideas, hard work, and dreams. My stepdad, a painting contractor, never finished school, but he was one of the best on the island. I still remember watching him work on massive projects, like painting an 18-story hotel while hanging from a scaffold. It looked terrifying, but he tackled it with confidence and skill.

Both my stepdad and my mother managed their businesses by relying on their God-given talents. Watching them use their gifts to create opportunities inspired me deeply. My mother's bakery and, later, our clothing store weren't just businesses—they were classrooms where I learned the value of strategy and intuition.

As a child, I was at the top of my class, especially in math, and my mother encouraged me to use my abilities. She trusted me to price the merchandise for her store, and that simple act built my confidence. I felt proud knowing that I could contribute in a way she couldn't because of her limited education. Helping her make decisions about what to buy for the store and how to price items gave me a sense of responsibility and purpose. Even as a teenager, I believed I could accomplish anything I set my mind to.

Helping my mother with the store and typing up painting proposals for my stepdad laid the foundation for my future. They taught me the importance of work ethic, resilience, and problem-solving. My stepdad often told me, "If something doesn't work the first time, don't give up. Keep trying until you find what works." Those words stuck with me and became a guiding principle in my life.

While my parents worked hard, my mother made sure my sister and I attended church, even though she didn't join us in those early years. Going to that small church became a critical part of my upbringing. Singing duets with my sister and being involved in the church community planted seeds of faith in my heart.

I started reading my Bible, intrigued by its stories and characters, even if I didn't fully understand them at the time. As I grew older, I began reading business books alongside the Bible. It was then I realized that entrepreneurship wasn't just about making money—it was about solving problems and serving others. This revelation shaped how I viewed success and built a strong foundation for my life.

These early lessons—faith, resilience, and a commitment to serving others—laid the groundwork for what would later become the S.O.A.R. system. Those moments taught me how to **Strategize**, **Optimize**, **Achieve**, and **Reflect**—skills that would carry me through challenges and successes.

But nothing could prepare me for what was about to happen next…

Shattered Truths, Unbreakable Spirit

One morning, as I was walking to the bus stop with my cousin, everything changed. It was an ordinary day—until she blurted out something that stopped me in my tracks. "I saw a picture of your real dad at Momma's house," she said casually.

Confused, I asked, "What do you mean, my real dad?" She looked at me like I should already know and said, "There's a picture of him in a coffin. Momma told me your dad is dead."

Her words hit me like a ton of bricks. My heart started pounding, my eyes filled with tears, and my day was ruined. I was only 15, and suddenly, my entire world felt like it had been turned upside down. There was no cell phone to call home and no one to talk to. I spent the whole day crying, trying to make sense of this new reality.

When I finally got home, I was filled with sadness and a deep sense of betrayal. I just wanted to talk to my mother, hoping my cousin had gotten it wrong. When I told her what my cousin said, she looked at me and confirmed my worst fear.

Instead of comforting me, her words made it worse. She said my stepdad was the one who had cared for me and that my biological father was "no good." She accused me of being ungrateful for crying over him. Her response stung deeply, and I felt like the blame for her pain was being placed on me. The conversation ended abruptly and was never brought up again.

That day shattered everything I thought I knew. It wasn't just my family that felt broken—it was my understanding of who I was. I held on to her words like shards of glass, each one cutting deeper. But even in that pain, something shifted in me.

I decided I wouldn't let this moment define me. Instead, I would use it as fuel to succeed. I threw myself into learning, growing, and becoming the best I could be. It was my way of coping with the pain and creating a way out of the deception I felt surrounded by.

Looking back now, I can see how God was working through it all. The verse *"And we know that in all things God works for the good of those who love him, who have been called according to his purpose"* (Romans 8:28) reminds me that even in heartbreak, God is shaping us for His purpose. That experience gave me resilience and taught me to use my pain as a driving force.

I also made a promise to myself that day: I would never let my children feel the way I did. I would be honest with them, no matter how hard the truth might be.

Heartbreak is one of life's hardest trials, but it's also one of the greatest teachers. It's through these challenges that we mature and become the people God wants us to be. As James 1:2-4 says, *"Consider it pure joy, my brothers and sisters, whenever you face trials of many kinds, because you know that the testing of your faith produces perseverance. Let perseverance finish its work so that you may be mature and complete, not lacking anything."*

The pain of that day left a shadow over my relationship with my mother for years. It wasn't that I didn't love her—I did—but resentment lingered. Even so, I continued excelling in school, singing at church, and pursuing my dreams. In those dark moments, the Lord became real to me. His hand was guiding me, even when I couldn't see it.

That wasn't the last challenge I faced. Years later, I bought a home that turned into a financial disaster, forcing me to file for bankruptcy in 2008. I fought hard to avoid it, praying constantly for guidance. But when it became clear that I had no other choice, I trusted God and moved forward. That experience taught me humility and the strength to rebuild.

Now, I use those lessons to help other Christian female entrepreneurs succeed. I show them how to align their businesses with their God-given talents and overcome their own challenges.

It's through these painful experiences that I've learned to S.O.A.R.— to **Strategize**, **Optimize**, **Achieve**, and **Reflect**. These trials didn't break me; they shaped me into the person God always intended me to be."

Learning to "S.O.A.R Rising Above Life's Challenges"

It's my life experiences—both the triumphs and the challenges—that taught me to focus on S.O.A.R., just like an eagle rising above the storm. S.O.A.R. isn't just a framework; it's a way to live, guided by faith and resilience. Let me break it down for you:

S: Strategize

Watching my mother in those early years taught me the importance of having a plan. Without a strategy, even the best intentions can fail. Strategies aren't just about setting goals; they're about having the courage to start, even when the path ahead isn't clear.

Whether it was helping my mother price items in her store or later creating detailed plans for multimillion-dollar businesses, I learned that strategy is the foundation for success. Proverbs 16:3 reminds us, *"Commit to the Lord whatever you do, and He will establish your plans."* By giving my plans to God, I found the clarity and strength to move forward, no matter how daunting the challenge.

"O: Optimize"

As I grew older, I realized that balancing work, faith, and daily life wasn't optional—it was essential. Pain taught me to value every resource I had, from time and finances to the lessons I'd learned and the wisdom of the Bible. Optimization became a way to survive, and, eventually, a way to thrive.

Through each challenge, I learned how to maximize what was in front of me, whether it was stretching a small budget, leaning on my faith, or managing my time wisely. Psalm 90:12 says, *"Teach us to number our days, that we may gain a heart of wisdom."* This wisdom became my strength, showing me how to turn hardships into opportunities.

A: Achieve

Each small win felt like a triumph over the past, a testament to God's faithfulness in my life. Whether it was teaching myself Lotus 1-2-3, pursuing my master's degree in Accounting, or helping businesses achieve over $15 million in profits through implementation, I learned that success isn't about one big moment—it's about the steps you take every day.

Philippians 4:13 reminds us, *"I can do all this through Him who gives me strength."* Every achievement, no matter how small, is proof of God's hand in my life. Each victory brought me closer to the person He created me to be.

R: Reflect

Reflection has been my anchor. It keeps me grounded and reminds me of God's goodness. Looking back on where I've come from, I see how He has guided my path and given me the strength to keep going. Every struggle has matured me and made me stronger.

Psalm 139:23 says, *"Search me, God, and know my heart; test me and know my anxious thoughts."* Reflection allows me to see the lessons in my challenges and to give thanks for God's provision at every step of my journey.

I constantly take time to reflect on what God has done, thanking Him for where He has brought me and staying excited about where He's taking me next. His hand has been on my life every step of the way, and I trust Him to guide me as I continue to S.O.A.R.

Through S.O.A.R.—**Strategize, Optimize, Achieve, Reflect**—I've learned to rise above challenges, align my efforts with God's purpose, and use my experiences to help others do the same. It's not just a system; it's a testimony of what God can do when we trust Him fully.

From Brokenness to Beauty: The Power to S.O.A.R

As I wrap up my story, you might be wondering, "Did you ever have that conversation with your mother?" Yes, I did. It was one of the most necessary conversations of my life. For us to move forward, we had to address the pain and misunderstanding from all those years ago.

She explained that my biological father had died in a car crash before I was even a year old. Pretending it didn't happen felt easier for her at the time, but we both realized that even the best intentions don't always lead to the right choices. Through that conversation, I finally understood the depth of her pain. It brought us closer, and I can confidently say we now share the most beautiful mother-daughter relationship. Even more, she eventually gave her life to Christ, which meant the world to me.

Looking back on everything, I have no regrets—only gratitude. Every trial, every challenge, and every heartbreak has shaped me into the person I am today. I am the founder of an accounting firm, a business implementation and financial accountability coach, and someone who has helped countless business owners achieve success through financial freedom. But most importantly, I am a woman transformed by God's grace and a living testament to His faithfulness.

Each experience, no matter how difficult, has been a stepping stone toward my purpose. Today, I guide others to embrace their own transformation through the **S.O.A.R.** system. And the best part? You can do the same.

Here's how you can start applying **S.O.A.R.** in your own life today:

- **Strategize**: Take time to create strategies that will move your business and personal life forward. Think about what steps you need to take to reach your goals.
- **Optimize**: Look at your resources—time, finances, skills—and make them count. Don't let anything go to waste.
- **Achieve**: Celebrate every win, no matter how small. Each success is a testament to God's faithfulness in your life.
- **Reflect**: Take time to reflect on the goodness of God. Look back at how He's brought you through and give Him thanks.

Transformation isn't easy—it requires faith, perseverance, and a willingness to grow. But let me leave you with this: *"Transformation is never easy, but it's always worth it. God's grace turns brokenness into beauty, and through Him, we can all S.O.A.R."*

So, start today. Begin your journey of transformation, trusting that God is with you every step of the way. You were made to S.O.A.R.

PRIMERIDGE CONSULTING LLC

Rita Uchenna Ohia - Iheanacho

Vice President of Operations

Rita Uchenna Ohia - Iheanacho is a devoted wife and a loving mother to her special boys and amazing girls. With a heart full of compassion and a passion for service, she has built a career as a dedicated healthcare professional (Registered Nurse) for over 16 years and a strong advocate for those who cannot speak for themselves.

Beyond her work in healthcare, Rita is a fierce entrepreneur, leader and business coach in the insurance industry, thriving as a licensed financial professional. She is deeply committed to empowering individuals, particularly women, to take control of their financial futures and secure their lives with confidence. Through her expertise and unwavering dedication, she continues to make a lasting impact, ensuring that financial literacy and security become accessible to all.

https://www.linkedin.com/in/rita-ohia-iheanacho-7ab252140/
https://www.facebook.com/rita.ohia
https://www.instagram.com/ritaohia/
https://www.primeridgeconsulting.com/

My Journey To Accountability

By Rita Uchenna Ohia – Iheanacho

Chapter 1: The Beginning of Self-Discovery

I had always known what it felt like to exist   but never truly to *be*. For most of my life, I floated in the space between what I was and what I could become. There was an overwhelming sense of something missing, a void that gnawed at me. I lived, but I didn't understand myself. I hadn't learned what it meant to be fully accountable for my thoughts, actions, and, ultimately, my growth.

It wasn't that I didn't care. In fact, I cared deeply. But I was caught in the comfort of my circumstances, blaming the world around me for the lack of progress in my life. I would point fingers—at my job, at others, at fate. "If only," I would think, "I had this, or I hadn't experienced that,   everything would be different." My growth was stunted because I believed everything outside of me was responsible for my happiness, my success, and my failures.

Then came the day when I faced an undeniable truth that shook me to my core.

Chapter 2: The Moment of Reckoning

It happened on an ordinary day—one of those gray afternoons where the sky seemed to reflect the mood I had been carrying for weeks. I was l   ying down in my bed after working for 20 hours at the hospital as a registered nurse. It was still the pandemic, and after experiencing the numbness of bagging so many bodies that passed on due to complications from COVID-19,   i   t put things in perspective for me. I could be the one who is being bagged, and if that were   the case, what would my legacy be?   I worked so hard and   have had a good career, yet I was still BROKE.

I was making enough not to qualify for any free government aid but not enough to afford anything without working overtime. I realized it was not about how much I made but it was about how much of that money worked for me. The more I thought about it, the more I realized how much I had been avoiding personal responsibility in my own life. I kept relying on my government, my job, and my husband to take control of my finances. Maybe get overtime and   work more hours; that was just a pacifier to the problem but not the solution. I have been doing that since I was 16 years of age, yet I had enough to get by but not enough to be financially independent. I was lost in a sea of uncertainty, and I realized that I had no clear direction. I had failed to communicate expectations, failed to lead by example, and, worst of all,   failed to be honest with myself about my own limitations, which was that I needed to open my mind to knowledge and step outside my comfort zone.

It was at that moment I felt the weight of accountability settling   in. I couldn't blame anybody for   my situation if I was not willing to change it; "What you are not changing, you are choosing."   I was the one who hadn't taken charge. I was the one who hadn't prepared myself for success by not being open-minded to change and knowledge. I was the one who wanted to stay in my comfort zone.

This was my wake-up call: If I wanted to create change, I had to be the change.

Chapter 3: The Shifting Perspective

Taking accountability is not just about accepting responsibility for mistakes, it's about looking inward, being honest with yourself, and choosing to grow from those experiences. It meant no longer accepting the victim mentality and instead empowering myself to take control.

I started small. I began by acknowledging my role in situations where I had previously blamed others. Instead of criticizing, I asked myself, *What could I have done differently?* " Slowly, my thinking began to shift from "I can't" to "I will." The world didn't need to change for me to grow. I just needed to take ownership of my actions and reactions.

It wasn't always easy. I learned that accountability required humility. There were times I had to admit I was wrong, not just to others but also to myself. Yet, with each acknowledgment, a new sense of clarity emerged. I was beginning to see that my future was not dictated by anyone else's decisions. It was my responsibility, and that realization was both liberating and daunting.

Chapter 4: Embracing Ownership

As I continued to walk this path of accountability, I noticed how my relationships began to shift. I stopped waiting for others to change. Instead, I started adjusting my responses. I apologized more often, not because I was wrong all the time, but because I had come to understand how my actions impacted others. I took ownership of my decisions—small and large—and slowly, the way I interacted with people transformed.

I began to see the world differently. I was no longer a passive observer. I was an active participant in creating my reality. I started holding myself accountable not just for my mistakes   but for my successes, too. I celebrated my victories with the same sense of ownership that I applied to my shortcomings. I was learning to love both sides of the coin—the triumphs and the failures—because both were part of the journey.

Chapter 5: The Power of Consistency

Accountability isn't a one-time thing. It's practice, a daily commitment to yourself. I realized that transformation doesn't happen overnight   but through consistent effort and conscious choices. I started developing habits that nurtured accountability: journaling to reflect on my decisions, setting clear intentions for my actions, and holding myself to the highest standard of integrity.

I began to see how small, consistent actions could lead to profound changes. I no longer sought shortcuts or quick fixes. The journey was not about perfection   but about progress. Every day became a new opportunity to better myself, to learn from my mistakes, and to build trust with myself and others.

Chapter 6: The Ripple Effect

As I grew more accountable for my life, I noticed the ripple effects on the world around me. The people in my life noticed changes. My colleagues respected me more, as I had learned to take responsibility not just for my actions but for the way I led others. My personal relationships deepened because I was no longer relying on others to make me feel whole. I had discovered my own strength, and I was able to share that energy with those around me.

The ripple effect of personal accountability reached beyond my professional and personal life. It reached into the way I viewed the world, the way I interacted with strangers, and even the way I perceived challenges. Accountability had given me a new lens through which to view my reality. It allowed me to embrace the fullness of who I was and the potential of who I could become.

Chapter 7: Life Transformed

In the end, it wasn't just my external circumstances that changed, it was my internal landscape. I became more self-assured, more resilient, and more at peace with my imperfections. I learned that accountability is not about perfection   but about the willingness to learn, grow, and take responsibility for the life you're creating.

It was a journey that began with the simple act of accepting responsibility. But that simple act led me to a profound transformation: a life that is actively lived, fully owned, and unapologetically mine.

Epilogue: A New Beginning

As I reflect on the path I've walked, I understand that transformation is an ongoing process. Accountability is not a destination   but a lifelong practice that shapes who I am and who I am becoming. The power of this journey lies not in reaching a final goal   but in the commitment to evolve every day. By taking accountability, I found my true self—no longer a passive observer   but an empowered creator of my own reality. And the journey continues.

THE FEMMEPRENEUR PATHFINDER

Tina Kapp-Kailea

Founder, Author, Speaker & Wild Executive

Tina Kapp-Kailea is an award-winning embodiment coach, bestselling author, and international speaker dedicated to helping high-achieving women reconnect with their true selves and lead lives of authenticity, balance, and purpose. She empowers corporate women and entrepreneurs to break free from burnout, self-doubt, and overgiving. With her unique approach, Tina blends intuitive mentorship and deep personal transformation, guiding women to tap into their feminine power and step into leadership without sacrificing their well-being. Having navigated the demanding corporate world, Tina intimately understands the struggle of feeling disconnected, exhausted, and "not enough." Her journey from corporate burnout to living as a wild, unapologetic woman has become the foundation of her work, inspiring others to reclaim their energy, set boundaries, and lead from a place of authenticity and joy. Tina's bestselling book CORPORATE REWILDING – A Wild Woman's Guide to Reclaiming Your Feminine Power won the Global Bronze Book Award and is a must-read.

https://www.linkedin.com/in/tinakkailea/
https://www.facebook.com/tinakkailea
https://www.instagram.com/the_femmepreneur/
http://www.femmepeneurpathfinder.com/
https://www.femmepreneurpathfinder.com/instagram

The R.E.A.L.I.G.N. Reset
– From Hustle to Harmony

Break the Burnout Cycle, Recode the Hustle, and
Create a Life That Feels Good Again

By Tina Kapp-Kailea

When Success Isn't Enough

When was the last time you felt truly alive?

Not just busy, not just fine, but deeply, vibrantly alive, buzzing with purpose and joy? If you're like many of the accomplished yet quietly crumbling women I meet, it might feel like a distant memory.

That was me. I had the corner office, the big salary, a packed schedule, and the polished façade rushing from meeting to meeting with a coffee in my hand. On paper, my life was a dream. In reality? It felt more like a beautifully curated nightmare. Here's the thing — success looks great on paper. For years, I thought I had it all and checked every box society handed me, yet I found myself standing in the middle of my so-called perfect life, and every morning I woke up every day to a life that felt utterly empty.

Success is seductive. It promises happiness but often leaves a void. I followed every rule, living the 'dream life' — independent, accomplished, and in a country that most people have on their bucket list. But beneath the glossy surface, I was losing myself. I grew up a wild child in Europe, spirited with dreams bigger than the conventional paths laid before me. My hero wasn't a princess; it was Pippi Longstocking, with her fearless, defying antics and rebellion against the rules that tried to box her in.

Fast forward to adulthood, and I found myself suffocating under the weight of societal expectations. "Be nice, be quiet, succeed," they said. And I listened, dimming my light to fit in until my vibrant essence was buried under layers of "should" and "must."

At 25, a golden job opportunity whisked me away to New Zealand — my shot at freedom and adventure. But instead of finding liberation, I lost myself in the relentless pursuit of approval and found myself climbing a career ladder that drained me. The ambitious, vibrant woman who once dreamed boldly became a hollow shell in a sea of expectations and personal heartbreak. There's a dangerous trap hidden in ambition. The higher you climb, the harder it becomes to admit that you might be on the wrong ladder. I ignored that quiet voice inside me for years, convincing myself that more achievements would silence it. Spoiler alert — they didn't.

Success has a way of masking the cracks and the façade was hiding the cracks for a while, but they were spreading — missed workouts, sleepless nights, a constant state of deep-rooted panic. My body screamed for a break, but I pushed it aside, trying to stay ahead of the competition and maintain the illusion of a perfect life. Success, after all, was about thriving, or so I thought.

The breaking point? Permanent fatigue, five miscarriages, a crumbling marriage, and a soul so starved for joy that every day felt like a battle. My body was trying to tell me something, but I ignored it. I was too busy being 'successful.' My body was breaking down, and my spirit was crushed. It was either make changes or break completely.

One of the hardest truths I faced was that I had built my entire existence on proving my worth to everyone but myself. Success, I realized, wasn't about the accolades or the income; it was about alignment. Misaligned success is an empty achievement. I lived that lie, believing more accomplishments would fill the void. But that was not true.

So, what do you do when success isn't enough? When you wake up one day and realize you're merely existing, not living? I had traded my dreams for a title, my passion for productivity, and my joy for a paycheck. That realization was terrifying but also liberating. It forced me to confront the truth: I was living someone else's dream. It also gave me the freedom to reimagine my life differently.

My journey back to alignment wasn't easy, but it was transformative. Realizing you're out of alignment is one thing; doing something about it is quite another. Admitting I wasn't okay was the hardest part. Allowing yourself to feel the pain, the disappointment, the grief, and deciding to change was the path to true change.

Success isn't the problem. Misaligned success is.

This isn't about walking away from your goals or achievements. It's about ensuring they truly resonate with your deepest values and desires. We often climb ladders without asking where they lead. It's time to check your compass.

If any of this resonates with you, know this: You are not broken, and you are not stuck.

What you feel is a signal — not of failure, but of misalignment. It's your soul's call to reassess, to stop proving, and to start living on your terms.

Are you ready to recalibrate? To build a life that doesn't just look good but feels good? To find the freedom on the other side of fear and alignment on the other side of change?

If so, this chapter is for you. This journey is for you.

And this moment — right here — is your starting line for something extraordinary.

The Moment It All Changed

"She didn't take as much time off the last time it happened! Not sure why she is now…"

Those words whispered just outside my glass-walled office where I sat, hollow and raw, still echoing in my mind. They weren't just talking about any mundane task at the office; they were talking about my life — my private pain aired like office gossip. The *last time* they were referring to was my fourth miscarriage in two years, and my pain was so deep it felt physical.

My workplace, with its trendy open-plan layout and buzzing creativity, didn't shield me from the sting of that comment, which pierced right through me and made me gasp.

At that moment, life seemed to slow down, and a voice inside me screamed, "Why do you keep up with this? For what? Why don't you just leave?" How much more was I willing to endure? How much of myself was I willing to sacrifice? How much of myself was I willing to lose?

I remember staring blankly at my computer screen, the spreadsheets and emails blurring into one meaningless stream. The weight of my grief felt like a freight train bearing down on me.

My body felt heavy, sinking into my office chair, and my chest tightened with a pressure I couldn't name. It was grief — layered, deep, and heavy with years of silenced pain. I had become so good at pushing through the emotional torment that I forgot what it felt like to actually feel.

Tears welled up in my eyes, but I didn't dare let them fall. I couldn't let them see me break, let anyone see me so 'weak.' Not here. Vulnerability seemed like a luxury I couldn't afford in a workplace that valued toxic positivity and performance over humanity. So, I swallowed the lump in my throat, took a deep breath, and fixed the mask of composure I wore so well. But inside? Inside, I was falling apart.

I couldn't stop replaying the sonographer's cold words at my last ultrasound appointment in my head, "I'm so sorry, but there is no heartbeat." After four miscarriages, I was having weekly scans to check the progress, and I had clung to hope each week, leaving the clinic with a smile — until everything crumbled in week eleven. It wasn't another devastating loss of another baby; it was the loss of future possibilities, of having control over my own body, and a harsh awakening to the reality that perhaps my relentless drive had come at an unbearable cost I could no longer ignore.

My miscarriages weren't isolated incidents; it was the culmination of years spent ignoring the desperate pleas from my body. The sleepless nights, the skipped meals, the relentless, caffeine-fuelled workdays — it all added up. My body had been trying to tell me for years that I was out of alignment, but I had been too busy proving my worth to listen.

Sitting in my glass office, I felt detached, like a spectator in my own life, mechanically moving through my tasks — answering emails, nodding in meetings, managing a team. Inside, I was unravelling. The disconnect between who I was and who I pretended to be had grown so vast that I no longer recognized myself.

I wasn't just physically exhausted; I was existentially depleted. I had crafted a life that looked perfect on the outside but was hollow on the inside. I had traded my joy for achievements, my intuition for logic, and my true self for a title. Now, everything was crumbling around me.

Finally, I had enough. I walked out of the office, the cool air slapping me awake as I passed reception on autopilot. I drove aimlessly, ending up at a local park. There, on a bench under the rustling leaves with the sun shining on my face, I allowed myself to really break down and let the tears flow. I cried for everything lost — my babies, for the marriage that was hanging by a thread, and for the woman I used to be before life ground her down. I cried because I didn't know how to fix it, how to climb out of the hole I had dug myself into.

But here's the thing about hitting rock bottom — it forces you to pause and reflect. And in that profound stillness, a quiet voice whispered inside me, "Enough." Enough pretending, enough pushing through the pain. It was time for a change.

That wasn't the end of my struggles, but it marked a new beginning. It was the first time I truly confronted the unsustainable life I had been leading — one built on other people's expectations and societal notions of success. And it was killing me.

I didn't have all the answers that day, but I made a promise to myself to find my way back to authenticity. To reconnect with the young girl full of dreams before the world told her who to be and rediscover what truly mattered — rebuilding a life filled with genuine joy and fulfillment.

It wasn't a dramatic decision or a bold declaration that changed everything instantly, no, but it started with a quiet commitment on that park bench, tears streaming down my face. That moment of choosing myself set everything in motion. The path wasn't easy; it was fraught with uncertainty and fear but also hope — a flicker of possibility that perhaps there was a way out.

And that was enough to keep me going.

The Breakdown of the Burnout Cycle

Burnout doesn't just show up overnight; it creeps in quietly, stealing a little more of you each sleepless night until you wonder what's left. That's exactly how it happened to me. It started with restless nights and an ever-present fight-or-flight state, whispering, "It's just stress," but that "little stress" morphed into a tightness in my chest caused by my overworked nervous system that wouldn't let go. Before I knew it, it wasn't just stress — it had become the norm and escalated into anxiety, depression, chronic adrenal fatigue, headaches, and an immune system that simply gave up on me without warning. That's burnout.

Let's talk about what burnout really is. It's not just about being tired and exhausted; it's about disconnection. I was disconnected from everything — myself, my purpose, my essence, and the people I loved. My days became a repetitive slog of tasks, meetings, and endless emails. Weekends? They turned into just another time to catch up on work I couldn't cram into weekdays. Even my downtime was haunted by guilt, constantly nagging at me that I should be doing more.

This wasn't just about being burned out; I was lost and felt hollow. Anxiety was my constant, unwelcome companion. I started dreading everything that once brought joy — my career, my relationships, and even my own reflection seemed alien to me. Society glorifies this grind — tells us to wear our busyness like a badge of honor, believing the myth that the harder we hustle, the more valuable we are. What a dangerous lie we've been sold.

The truth hit hard: I had tied my whole identity to this hustle, convincing myself that just one more push, one more achievement would make it all worthwhile. But guess what? No promotion, paycheck, or round of applause can fill the void when you're out of alignment with your soul.

And the shame — the overwhelming, isolating shame of feeling like you should be able to handle it all. I kept telling myself I was strong, and that I should be grateful for my job. But the truth? I was crumbling, my body and mind screaming for a pause, and instead of seeking help, I isolated myself even more, thinking admitting I was struggling meant admitting defeat.

I'll never forget the morning I felt I couldn't even get out of bed. The perceived weight of my responsibilities and everything I had to do felt crushing. I lay there, thinking maybe if I stayed put, the world would forget about me for just a little while.

Of course, life doesn't pause. My phone kept buzzing, and emails and meeting reminders were piling up. The guilt of not being "on" propelled me to get up, dress up, and mask up. That's the thing about burnout — it doesn't just drain you and leave you exhausted; it convinces you that there's no other option but to keep grinding. Have a triple shot latte and all will be fine. Sound familiar?

Physically, I was a mess. Ignoring the obvious signs my body was sending — exhaustion, pain, fatigue. I opted for coffee and painkillers over rest and recovery, numbing the symptoms because facing the root cause seemed too daunting. Looking back, I see how much damage I was doing by pretending everything was fine.

Emotionally, I was numb. I couldn't even feel joy in moments that should have been happy. My son's laughter sounded like it was coming from far away. Celebrations at work felt empty. I was just going through the motions, ticking boxes without feeling any sense of achievement.

Loneliness was perhaps the cruelest part. Burnout isolates you. Despite being surrounded by people, I felt utterly alone. I didn't want to burden anyone with my struggles, so I kept it all inside, but that only made the weight heavier.

Everything came to a head during a soul-sucking business trip. After a grueling day, I was berated by my boss over something that wasn't going as planned. Alone in my hotel room, I broke down. I faced the haunting question: Is this what the rest of my life will look like? The life I traded my joy for? That moment of raw honesty terrified me because I didn't have an answer. That moment of clarity sparked a slow but radical realization — burnout isn't your endpoint or a sign of failure; it's a desperate call from your soul to realign — signaling that you need a major change.

Acknowledgment was the first step out of the burnout cycle. Admitting I wasn't okay was okay. It meant letting go of the shame and opening up to help. The journey wasn't straightforward — there were setbacks and doubts—but each step forward took me closer to a life that felt genuine, fulfilling, and sustainable.

Here's the epiphany I wish I'd had sooner. I realized I had a choice: continue down this path of quiet self-destruction or step into the unknown and reclaim the woman I used to be — the wild, free, unapologetic version of myself.

So, I resigned from my job, which was both terrifying and liberating. It left some people stunned. "Why would you leave such a great job?" they asked. Their surprise only deepened my conviction. I had spent too long living for others, measuring my worth by external markers of success. I was done.

Burnout isn't just a personal struggle; it's a cultural epidemic. In a society that celebrates overwork and glorifies sacrifice for productivity, we're constantly fed the notion that success is born from relentless hustle and grind. Rest is often labeled as laziness, and our value is measured by our achievements, but what if we can no longer keep pace? What happens when the ceaseless pursuit breaks us? How many stories like mine are playing out every day? How much will it take before we recognize the cost?

My journey back to myself was anything but linear. It was filled with setbacks and moments of uncertainty. Yet, each small step forward brought me closer to the life I yearned for, and offered a chance to pause, reflect, and realign with what truly matters. This gradual, consistent progress led me back to a life that felt genuine, joyful, and sustainable — not just physically but also emotionally and spiritually.

Burnout doesn't have to define you. It can be the start of a powerful journey back to your essence, to being full of life — a life you were meant to live. It's about stepping out of the cycle, breaking free from the grind, and discovering a path that leads you home to wholeness.

The Creation of My Framework

Through my journey, my R.E.A.L.I.G.N. process was born. It was my set of actions that helped me piece my life back together. As I shared my experiences with other women, I realized these steps could serve as a roadmap for anyone looking to escape burnout and rediscover their joy.

This led me to the creation of the R.E.A.L.I.G.N. framework, a series of tools designed to help individuals not just survive but thrive on their own terms — rebuilding, reimagining, and reclaiming their lives.

R.E.A.L.I.G.N. stands for:
REFLECT, EXPOSE, ACCEPT, LIBERATE, INTEGRATE, GROUND, NURTURE

Each step is designed to peel back layers of conditioning, stories, and beliefs that keep us confined, bringing me closer to the person I was meant to be.

Now, I look back on that difficult chapter with gratitude — not for the pain, but for the invaluable lessons it taught me. These lessons taught me the cost of living out of alignment, the power of embracing my truth, and helped guide me back to myself.

If you see yourself in my story, remember that it's never too late to change your path.

You don't have to continue in a relentless grind. You can choose differently.

You can R.E.A.L.I.G.N.

You can start your journey out of burnout today.

It begins with one small, brave step — are you ready?

Stepping Into the R.E.A.L.I.G.N. Process

Hitting rock bottom was my wake-up call, the moment I realized I needed more than just a quick fix — a way out and a roadmap to find a way back to myself. I needed a profound transformation.

My R.E.A.L.I.G.N process helps you transform your life.

It's not just a band-aid solution to fix everything overnight; it's a guide to deep-dive into rediscovering who I really was. A process I developed step by step as I rebuilt my life.

R.E.A.L.I.G.N. became my lifeline, and it's structured around these seven transformative steps:

1. **REFLECT**: Take stock — a real look at where you are, what you truly want and understand your current state and desires.

2. **EXPOSE**: Identify and confront the limiting beliefs holding you back.

3. **ACCEPT**: Embrace your current reality and past decisions with compassion and understanding.

4. **LIBERATE**: Let go of harmful patterns and external expectations that no longer serve you, and free up your energy.

5. **INTEGRATE**: Build and strengthen habits that support your new path, and incorporate new behaviors and mindsets.

6. **GROUND**: Reestablish a connection with your goals and anchor yourself in your core values.

7. **NURTURE**: Continuously commit and celebrate ongoing growth and support self-care.

Let me guide you through each step in detail, and let's dive deeper:

1. REFLECT: The Courage to Confront

Reflection is the starting point of self-discovery. It requires getting brutally honest about the aspects of your life that are fulfilling versus those that feel draining. This process is not about self-judgment; rather, it's about cultivating deep self-awareness. Reflection prompts you to examine the gap between who you are and who you aspire to be, challenging you to align your reality with your ideals.

2. EXPOSE: Unearthing Subconscious Barriers

This step involves identifying and confronting the subconscious narratives that limit your potential. Common internal scripts might include beliefs like "You're only worthy if you're productive" or "Rest is for the weak." Recognizing and dismantling these hidden barriers is crucial for personal growth and transformation, allowing you to move beyond outdated self-perceptions and embrace a more empowered identity.

3. ACCEPT: Embracing Your Reality

Acceptance is about acknowledging your current circumstances without judgment. This step is critical in the journey, as it involves coming to terms with your present condition, whether that involves feeling broken, exhausted, or out of alignment. By accepting your situation, you lay the groundwork for genuine change, allowing yourself to move forward without the burden of self-criticism.

4. LIBERATE: Breaking Free from Chains

Liberation entails making decisive changes to reclaim control over your life. This might involve leaving a toxic job, ending unfulfilling relationships, or simply deciding to prioritize your well-being. It's about asserting autonomy over your life choices and setting boundaries that protect and nurture your well-being.

5. INTEGRATE: Building a New Identity

Integration is where new behaviors are consolidated into habits. This phase involves adopting and reinforcing practices that support your new identity. Whether it's through routine mindfulness practices, structured reflection, or creative outlets, these activities help solidify the changes you're making, anchoring your new self in everyday life.

6. GROUND: Establishing Stability

Grounding focuses on reconnecting with your core values and establishing a life that genuinely reflects them. It involves creating routines and rituals that reinforce your foundational values, providing a sense of stability and continuity. This step ensures that you remain rooted in what truly matters to you, helping prevent regression into old habits.

7. NURTURE: Cultivating Growth

The final step of the process, nurturing, is about ongoing personal development and growth. It emphasizes the importance of surrounding yourself with supportive relationships and engaging in continuous learning and self-improvement. This step is about embracing the journey of growth, recognizing that it is a perpetual process marked by both advancements and setbacks.

Transformation Through R.E.A.L.I.G.N.

My life's transformation was nothing short of a rebirth. I traded the exhausting grind of being an executive for the vitality of being an embodiment coach, an award-winning author, and an international speaker. I began to lead women's circles, creating a space where vulnerability isn't just welcomed; it's celebrated. My relationships deepened, my health soared, and for the first time in forever, I felt electrically alive.

The ripple effect of my journey was powerful. As I shared my story and insights in my first book, I inspired others to reflect on their lives and initiate their own changes. My openness and authenticity encouraged others to challenge the status quo and embark on their paths to realignment.

Why This Matters

This journey isn't just about self-care; it's about survival. It's about the kind of thriving that happens when your life dances to the rhythm of your true values, passions, and purposes. When you're aligned, you're a force of nature. You lead with heart, inspire those around you, and you reclaim the essence of being you.

Imagine waking up pumped for the day because everything you do reflects what's truly important to you. Imagine feeling energized, connected, and deeply fulfilled. This life isn't just a fantasy — it's within your reach, and it starts the moment you decide to truly live for yourself.

Becoming a Wild Executive: Join the Movement

The R.E.A.L.I.G.N. process is more than just a method; it's a call to arms. It's your declaration that you're over the autopilot life. You're done proving and ready to start living. You're geared up to sync your life with your deepest truths.

This isn't about piling more onto your plate; it's about stripping back the unnecessary, saying no with gusto, forgiving yourself, and dreaming outrageously big.

So, what's your next move? Are you ready to reflect, expose, accept, liberate, integrate, ground, and nurture your way to your truest self?

You deserve a life that dazzles, one that brings you joy, peace, and a profound sense of purpose. And you don't have to wait — your extraordinary life is waiting for your yes. Stop settling, stop telling yourself this is as good as it gets. You are meant for more, much more.

The Path Forward - A Call to Action

If this hits home for you, remember that change has no expiration date. The R.E.A.L.I.G.N. framework is about evolving step by step. Start small but start now. Reflect on your life, challenge those old beliefs, and take a bold step towards freedom.

Transformation is a journey, not an overnight sprint. Every little step you take builds momentum. Before long, you'll see just how far you've come.

If you're feeling like:

- **You're on a hamster wheel of endless to-dos**, sprinting toward a moving finish line.

- **You're disconnected from what once brought you joy** — your creativity, your passions, and your relationships.

- **You're surviving on coffee and adrenaline**, crashing at night only to do it all over again.

- **You're so busy** caring for others that you've neglected your own needs.

- **You're longing for more** — more purpose, more meaning, more fulfillment — but don't know where to start.

Then, this isn't just a call to action — it's your lifeline.

Stop settling. You deserve a vibrant and fulfilling life. If you're tired of running on the hamster wheel of endless tasks, feeling disconnected and drained, this is your call to action. It's time to take care of yourself and pursue more meaning and fulfillment in your life.

Begin today. Don't stay stuck in a life that no longer serves you. Reflect, expose, accept, liberate, integrate, ground, and nurture your way to growth. Let this chapter be your permission slip — the start of dreaming bigger and living true to yourself.

Because, my love, you're absolutely worth it.

You always have been.

About Tina:

Tina Kapp-Kailea is an award-winning embodiment coach, bestselling author, and international speaker. She helps high-achieving women reconnect with their authentic selves, break free from burnout, and lead purposefully. With her intuitive mentorship and personal transformation blend, Tina empowers corporate women and entrepreneurs to step into authentic and aligned leadership without sacrificing their well-being.

Her bestselling book, *CORPORATE REWILDING—A Wild Woman's Guide to Reclaiming Your Feminine Power,* won the Global Bronze Book Award. It inspires women to embrace their feminine power and live unapologetically.

Connect with Tina for coaching and mentorship to begin your journey of transformation.

Work with Tina:

Website: www.femmepreneurpathfinder.com
LinkedIn: https://www.linkedin.com/in/tinakkailea
Facebook: https://www.facebook.com/tinakkailea
Instagram: https://www.instagram.com/the_femmepreneur
LinkTree: https://www.femmepreneurpathfinder.com/instagram

RADIANT PATH COACHING LLC

Melissa Shigematsu

Founder, CEO, LCSW, Therapist, Coach

Melissa Shigematsu is a Licensed Clinical Social Worker, Therapist, Yoga Instructor, Certified Integrative Mental Health Professional and women's mindset and alignment Coach. She developed immense resilience after having been through her own trauma and adversity and realized over the years that part of her Soul purpose is to help others do the same. In her private practice she helps trauma survivors and those suffering with anxiety and depression find healing and empowerment. Through coaching she helps female entrepreneurs reconnect with their personal power and the things that give their life and work meaning while teaching regeneration from the inside out. She believes in being bold enough to go after what you want and refuses to accept limits! When she isn't working she's a single mom, dog mom, loves spending time with her family and a self- proclaimed "sassy social worker" who loves to paint, be in nature and travel!.

https://www.linkedin.com/in/melissa-shigematsu-msw-lcsw-licsw-cimhp-coach/
https://www.facebook.com/profile.php?id=61561013992424
https://www.instagram.com/radiantpathllc/
https://radiantpathllc.com/
https://www.shantiwellness.org/

Wildfire Within

A Journey Through Finding
Hope, Healing and Renewal

By Melissa Shigematsu

Born into generational trauma, and the chaos of her mother's past
Which had yet, in her own life to unfold.
At first full of hope and wonder,
Seeing the world as having much to offer,
But this vision she would later struggle to hold.

First acquainted with shame at only four,
Learning the lesson, while frozen in fear,
That no matter the truth, *she* was to blame.
This heavy darkness she began to carry,
Deep in her consciousness it would bury
Unearthed only in moments of trauma reenactment and fury.

Throughout the years the fire would grow and take hold,
Emboldened by abuses largely left untold,
Mostly unencumbered with few witness to bear.
Self-hatred scalding from the inside,
The scars showing without.

The fear that once kept her frozen now melting with anger as she felt
more lost and alone.

She was desperate for others to see the hot embers inside her
beginning to grow,
But see they did not, thinking her simply rebellious with defiance in
tow.
So on this went and the embers grew
Until the flames of self-destruction were all she knew.

The inner voice of criticism and despair grew louder still,
Feeding her insecurity, leading to reassurances sought,
The calls of which were answered by suitors and predators alike
Leaving her vulnerability to bare,
Stripped of herself, with only labels and self-loathing to wear.

The flames began raging with no end in sight,
Chaos ensued, disrupting her slumber and dampening her dreams,
Until her old high-school crush stood in front of her with a stance
that felt fated,
Only to leave her bruised, battered and jaded.
Like a twisted version of Romeo and Juliet,
She was once his secret left untold,
Now both adults, free to be open and bold.
So at eighteen and twenty-two they embarked on a toxic trail,
Red flags snuffed out by her vision and hope of the fairy tale.
In a wildfire of depravity and addiction they were quickly engulfed,
Her dreams for the future all but lost in the nightmare she was living,
Such that denial became essential at all costs.

Shackled by codependency and fueled by fear
The trauma compounded and pulled her in,
Like quicksand, wrapping her in sin.
Her days were filled with fighting and tears with only brief moments
of reprieve,
Yet somehow on this charred and burnt road,

A beautiful Angel came to be,
So soft and gentle not knowing that she, like her mother,
Was born into a pattern yet to be broken.
After one fight too many she got the courage to leave,
Her Angel in tow, the Second nestled in womb and still growing.

"Get help" they implored, hoping she'd heed,
"But I'm fine now, what for?" she retorted, not seeing the need.
But her demons would eventually come calling like sirens,
Promising to vanquish all that ailed.
She'd listen to their song until it was too late,
Her girls would be taken, seemingly sealing her fate.
She spiraled down this hellish, dark hole,
Wrapped up in guilt too tight to breathe
The wildfire raging out of control.
This was so much more than she could bear to grieve.

After some time, she and her "Romeo" rekindled,
Ignoring the pain, romanticizing the flames,
Convincing themselves this time would be different.
But the pattern played out as neither had healed,
Then a Third was to be and made her see
That history was repeating, the end already revealed.
So she left again, determined to find
The path thought lost in the all ashes,
To bring the new life inevitably born
Of wildfires and their hazardous gases.

Her decision felt guided but not without trial
As her past threatened to scorch the future pursued,
But with angels beside her whispering, "It's time"
She found the strength to face all that was dark and vile,
Finally quenching the pleas to get help and support

She blazed a new trail,
Pushing forward, determined,
Despite fears that she'd fail.

Others had doubts but she'd soon make them believe,
Proving a good mother to the son she adores,
And the pursuit of her purpose, opening doors.
As the days went on the healing took hold,
As she began to trust in herself,
Feeling favored and bold,
Signs of new life began to unfurl,
And as she set her sights forward, the embers gave way,
Reviving that strong and vibrant young girl.

She worked on herself, she even prayed,
Taking each step, day by day.
With two pieces of her heart still missing,
She focused on who they'd one day meet,
Now both back in her life,
Her heart full and complete.

Once shrouded in secrets, now open to share
How she shifted from flames ignited by fear,
To clarity and unleashing the power within.
Her days full of hope, she releases despair,
Living a life more beautiful, year after year.

This change was not easy, making courage essential.
Once a statistic whose fortune in judgment by others told,
Now spreading her wings and shattering the mold.
Guided by Spirit and learning to trust,
Evermore skilled at blocking the noise,
Walking her path with grace and poise.

The fire once scalding from within,
Now fueling her passion and lighting the way,
Her strength and her power she now conveys,
Finally understanding that in all these lessons
There was so much to gain,
And long gone are the days of writhing in pain.
Reclaiming her life and a strong sense of self,
Loving each moment to the fullest extent,
Radiating her light, her warmth and content.

She's building her business to ignite others with hope,
Creating freedom from within, agency and growth.
Once thinking her dreams had gone up in flames,
But she held steadfast to the notion there had to be more,
Turning her pain into purpose, finding alignment and joy,
Excited for what else is left in store.

One might ask, "How did she transform?"
She dug in deep, and held on tight to her truth,
Limitations she rebuked
And accepted that by her past she wasn't defined,
But rather this life is hers to design.
She called on support, when it was needed,
Embraced uncertainty and refused to hide,
Trusting the voice within that knew what to do,
Giving her strength to see it all through.
She decided that fear she'd no longer abide,
And with every step her confidence grows,
Bringing her closer to the vision she holds.

The fire within, still in spirit wild,
No longer destructive,
Burning bright from her core,

Lighting the way, blazing the trail,
Her message to others that through facing their fears
They will always prevail.

So hold on to that vision deep inside,
The one daring to hope and letting you know
That truly there IS more.
Wildfires scorch but to clear the path,
For new lessons and life that Spring forth from the past.
The smoke finally cleared, allowing her to see
All that was, is, and can be.

WARRIORHEART HEALING HEARTS

Erica Elliott

Coach, Counselor, Speaker & Author

I possess a Master's Degree in Counseling Psychology and have invested over three decades in my career as a Licensed Counselor, Certified Brain Health Coach, and Certified Health Integrative

Medicine Professional as well as military and medical experience. My expertise encompasses a broad spectrum of therapeutic approaches, such as Neurobiology, ADHD and Neurodiversity, Somatic Therapy, Energy Medicine, Neuro-Linguistic Programming (NLP), Cognitive Behavioral Therapy (CBT), Rational Emotive Therapy (RET), Emotional Freedom Techniques (EFT), Thought Field Therapy (TFT), Theology, Eye Movement Desensitization and Reprocessing (EMDR), the Gottman Method, alongside Mindfulness and Meditation.

I am the owner of WarriorHeart Healing Hearts where I champion a comprehensive healing philosophy that harmonizes the mind, body, and spirit. I am the founder of Energetic Elevation. I help people clear up the mess to discover their MASTERPIECE! Over the years, I have had the honor of empowering thousands of individuals to heal, grow, glow and soar!

Having faced my own set of adversities and emotional challenges, I understand that true healing flourishes within the framework of compassionate connections. Together, we nurture resilience and vitality, transforming our own legacies and those of future generations. Like iron sharpening iron, our collaboration fosters a profound healing journey. If you're looking for support or just want to connect I'd love to hear from you! Be Blessed and Be a Blessing!

https://www.linkedin.com/in/erica-elliott-ms-lpc-b90911150
https://www.facebook.com/warriorheartxo
https://www.instagram.com/warriorheartxo
https://linktr.ee/WarriorHeartxo

Reclaiming Joy

A Spiritual Guide to Healing from Divorce and
Anxiety

By Erica Elliott

Have you ever felt so dark and alone, wondering how it got so bad
that you would even think of driving off a bridge to end the agony?
This was my reality about twelve years ago. It was the lowest point in
my life. I felt invisible, as if no one truly knew or saw me. Despite my
outward success in my career, my home life was a dark mess. The
moment of clarity came crashing down on me like a brick: What was
I thinking? I would never leave my child in this hell.

Though I felt completely exhausted to the core of my very soul, that
moment ignited a fierce determination within me. I realized I had to
make a change, or I was going to die—figuratively and perhaps even
literally. I felt a hollowness in my being, as if I were an empty vessel.
I knew, deep down, that God loved me; yet, on the other hand, I felt
alone and abandoned. It was a tug-of-war between faith and despair.
Eventually, as I took the necessary steps toward healing, I began to
understand that God had been there all along, just as He always had.
I had just been looking for Him in the wrong places.

I want to share my story of navigating a difficult and sometimes
abusive marriage while trying so desperately to live out a Christian
walk. For years, I begged God to fix something that He had no

obligation to mend. What I mean by this is God can't, or I should say will not, make anyone do anything. We all have free will; it would be against His own law. God is always knocking on the doors of our hearts, inviting us to change, but that doesn't guarantee that the other person will respond positively. Each of us has the freedom to make decisions, and unfortunately, some choose to remain stagnant, blind, and abusive, ignoring the damage they cause to those around them.

For a long time, I worked tirelessly on myself. I internalized the belief that all problems must be mine to solve, the way my husband had painted his family was that he had an amazing Christian family and childhood, which I later learned was not all true. As a counselor, I understood the importance of taking responsibility for one's issues, and I dedicated myself to this work. However, I fell into the trap of thinking that if I did enough work on myself, my partner would eventually see the light and want to change as well. Or even as we attended church, believing surely something would penetrate his heart. Instead, I was met with the same patterns that had plagued our relationship from the start. I was manipulated into believing that if I could just change this or that, everything would improve. Then, something else would be brought up for me to change.

Understanding narcissism is crucial here. When you're in a relationship with someone who exhibits narcissistic tendencies, the blame often rests on your shoulders. These individuals refuse to acknowledge their own issues, focusing instead on your flaws. Narcissists often harbor deep-seated self-hatred, which they project onto you. The honeymoon phase can be enchanting, filled with sweet words and promises, but it's often a façade. They want you to return to a state of adoration, without having to put in any effort themselves. You become confused in the fighting because they change your words or use gaslighting, emotional withholding, and triangulated conversations.

Let me clarify that I don't believe every narcissist is beyond hope. However, I would encourage you to look for signs before entering a committed relationship. If you are married to someone with these characteristics, and they are willing to not only work on themselves and make changes but also admit to the harm they have caused, then it's possible to create a better life together. There are varying degrees of narcissistic traits, and some individuals can change. However, the darkness can easily consume anyone who believes they are perfect and have nothing to improve upon. Complacency can lead to personal stagnation, creating dysfunction not only within oneself but also in relationships with others. No matter what, it takes two people to make a great relationship.

When looking at the Bible, it clearly shows that we are to work together, loving one another equally giving and receiving from one another, treating each other with love and respect, with honor and grace.

Ephesians 5:21-3—"Submit to one another out of reverence for Christ. Wives, submit yourselves to your own husbands as you do to the Lord... Husbands, love your wives, just as Christ loved the church and gave himself up for her."

Philippians 2:3-4—"Do nothing out of selfish ambition or vain conceit. Rather, in humility value others above yourselves, not looking to your own interests but each of you to the interests of the others."

Colossians 3:18-19—"Wives, submit yourselves to your husbands, as is fitting in the Lord. Husbands, love your wives and do not be harsh with them."

1 Corinthians 13:4-7—"Love is patient, love is kind. It does not envy, it does not boast, it is not proud. It does not dishonor others, it is not self-seeking, it is not easily angered, it keeps no record of wrongs."

Ecclesiastes 4:9-12—"Two are better than one, because they have a good return for their labor: If either of them falls down, one can help the other up. But pity anyone who falls and has no one to help them."

Abuse, whether physical, mental, or emotional, is an insidious force that leaves lasting scars on the human brain. Recent research has unveiled the profound impact of verbal and emotional abuse, revealing that harsh words can create tangible changes in brain structure, while emotional torment activates the pain centers, etching deep wounds that may never fully heal. I must admit, despite my years in the counseling field, I was blind to these truths, perhaps because I had convinced myself that my situation was not as severe as others, or that my partner's stress was a valid excuse for his behavior. I clung to denial, even as close friends pointed out the toxicity of his words and actions. I remember a particular moment when I confided in my spouse about this; his fierce projection to me was a stark reminder of how unacceptable my circumstances were. Yet, fear of loneliness drove me to rationalize my partner's cruelty, attributing it to stress rather than recognizing it for what it was— abuse. I feared losing friends, so I hid things that happened. Not only did I hide things from friends but also from my family, partly because I married him rather quickly after we met, and I feared my family letting me know I should have known better. This dynamic stems from our own childhood traumas, where a desperate yearning for love and validation led to a cycle of codependency. We find ourselves trapped in familiar patterns, echoing the very cycles of abuse we once hoped to escape. It's a sobering realization that the quest for love can sometimes bind us to the very pain we long to leave behind.

One significant area of growth for me has been addressing my tendencies toward codependency and people-pleasing. I often found myself trapped in the belief that if I gave endlessly and selflessly, I would receive the same in return, as the scriptures suggest. Phrases like "with the same measure you give, it will be given back to you" created a false sense of obligation in my heart. I interpreted biblical teachings on forgiveness and turning the other cheek as mandates to endure mistreatment and keep giving, regardless of the circumstances.

However, I've come to realize that these teachings are intended to guide our relationship with God, who promises to reciprocate our generosity in His divine way. Unfortunately, not everyone adheres to these principles, which means we must protect our hearts from those who would take advantage of our kindness. It was a painful revelation when I understood that I was, in essence, casting my pearls before swine—believing that my selflessness was virtuous while being met with disregard by others.

I vividly recall my counselor's analogy: My husband was like a king who offered me mere crumbs from the table, and I would eagerly gather those crumbs, convinced that my servitude would eventually earn me more. Like the scripture in the Bible that speaks of the dog lapping up crumbs. It was disheartening to recognize that my Christian values had led me to accept this abusive dynamic, all in the hope of being a living example of Christ's teachings and getting the love I so desperately longed for. Yet, blessings can only flow when both parties strive to embody a Christlike spirit.

For anyone grappling with codependency, here are some valuable tools and tips to help break free from this cycle:

1. **Identify Codependent Patterns**: Begin by recognizing the behaviors and dynamics that characterize codependency in your

relationships. Reflect on how these patterns affect your emotional health and connections with others. Read and learn about codependency and write out your tendencies.

2. **Establish Clear Boundaries**: Create defined limits around what you will and won't tolerate in relationships. Communicate these boundaries openly and stand firm in maintaining them, remembering that it's acceptable to assert your needs. Rewrite the tendencies you came up with in a way where you put healthy boundaries in their place.

3. **Enhance Self-Awareness**: Spend time reflecting on your emotions, triggers, and motivations. Keeping a journal can help you explore your thoughts and gain deeper insights into your feelings. Go back to situations where you allowed yourself to be taken advantage of and see yourself stand up for yourself and visualize a better outcome.

4. **Prioritize Self-Care**: Make time for activities that nourish your body, mind, and spirit. Engage in practices like exercise, pursuing hobbies, meditating, or enjoying quality time with supportive friends. Use breathing tools daily and regularly, like 4/7/8 breathing, to clear your mind and keep yourself from being so overstressed and checked out that you're not aware of how you're doing mentally.

5. **Seek Guidance from Professionals**: Consider engaging with a therapist or counselor who has experience with EMDR, codependency, and narcissistic abuse. They can offer tailored support and strategies to help you navigate your challenges and heal and rewire the brain.

6. **Invest in Personal Development**: Participate in activities that encourage your growth, such as attending workshops and reading literature on personal development, codependency, relationships,

attachment and narcissism, or joining support groups. This can help you build knowledge around these areas, self-confidence, and independence.

7. **Explore Your Interests**: Discover and engage in hobbies that are uniquely yours. This fosters a sense of individual identity and helps you become more self-sufficient, enjoying and playing in life again. Many people who go through abusive relationships tend to stop having fun, playing and even isolate.

8. **Reframe Your Self-Worth**: Work on understanding that your value is not contingent upon meeting others' expectations. Cultivate a sense of self-worth that is grounded in your own beliefs and experiences. Spend some time going through the Bible, speaking with God, and learning to write out beliefs that have created problems in your life and reframe those with new knowledge and understanding.

9. **Build a Supportive Network**: Surround yourself with individuals who respect your boundaries and encourage healthy interactions. Positive relationships can reinforce your commitment to change. Remember, the right people will add to your life, and the wrong people may not be meant to be in your life. If a person is meant to be in your life, they will honor your boundaries.

10. **Practice Assertive Communication**: Learn to express your thoughts and feelings clearly and respectfully. Assertiveness allows you to advocate for yourself while still valuing the perspectives of others. A great way to use assertiveness is to start with the words. "I feel hurt, sad, mad, confused frustrated when you do this…" Then asking the individual if they would please try to do that a different way. When you start with your feelings, it helps an individual who's hearing to hear what's going on for you, and it's less triggering than if we say something like "You made me feel," or start with the act that

they did may make the person go into their head trying to figure out why they need to change their behavior.

These strategies can be instrumental in breaking free from codependent dynamics, fostering healthier relationships, and enhancing your overall well-being. Creating a healthy space for relationships.

Balance is essential in all aspects of life. Achieving harmony in mind, body, and spirit requires introspection, commitment, and courage to face the uncomfortable aspects of ourselves. Many people shy away from delving into their past traumas, fearing what they might uncover. But healing demands this introspective journey. As you heal the underlying wounds, you begin to live a life that draws others who are healthy into your life, and you stop facilitating or catering to relationships that are unhealthy for you.

True healing involves a willingness to ask, "How would I feel if someone did this to me?" This question propels us toward accountability and compassion for ourselves and others. While many people with narcissistic tendencies lack empathy, it's important to note that empathy can be cultivated. This is evident in the work done with individuals on the autism spectrum, who often learn social skills through practice.

The Bible speaks of a seared conscience—when a person continues down a harmful path and loses sight of the inherent wrongness in their actions. This phenomenon can manifest as addiction, dishonesty, or other destructive behaviors. We often find ourselves comparing one sin to another, but the truth is that any form of pride, arrogance, or self-righteousness can obstruct meaningful relationships. There's wisdom in the saying, "Judge not, lest ye be judged." At the same time, abuse is not okay and needs to be weeded out of one's life to create a healthy life and relationship.

I want this narrative to serve as a guiding light for those navigating similar struggles. It's easy to get trapped in the cycle of trauma, which can hinder us from leading fulfilling lives. As a counselor with over three decades of experience, I genuinely believe in processing trauma, but I also advocate for living a life filled with joy. If you find yourself in need, I encourage you to seek out a compassionate counselor, coach, or spiritual advisor who can help illuminate your path.

During my tumultuous journey, I grappled with the irony of being a marriage and family counselor while facing my own marital challenges. I wholeheartedly believed in the possibility of changing family legacies through honesty and hard work. However, if my spouse wasn't willing to make changes to create a healthy relationship, I was also afraid of the judgment that would come from others if I divorced. It can feel like a very trapped "Damned if you do and damned if you don't" feeling, which I don't believe God intends for us to live in. That is because of a people problem, not a God problem. Growing up in a codependent environment, I became the "fixer," the one who sought to make everyone happy. This upbringing, along with the religious beliefs of church people, conditioned me to feel like a failure if my marriage did not succeed.

Throughout our years together, I advocated for counseling, but my spouse consistently refused. This refusal fueled my internal conflict regarding faith. I held onto stories of individuals who remained in unhealthy marriages and eventually saw their partners transform. I feared that leaving would indicate a lack of faith on my part. Internally, I battled with depression, a hidden struggle that I managed to disguise well. As a counselor and prior military experience, I had learned to compartmentalize my emotions, distancing myself from my trauma.

I also fell into the trap of protecting my marriage by keeping our struggles private. I didn't realize that by hiding my pain, I was merely sweeping everything under the rug. Eventually, the weight of this façade became unbearable, affecting my mental state, physical health, and spiritual life. I knew God loved me, and I believed in His power to perform miracles. Yet, I struggled to let go of a relationship that I thought could be mended.

Years passed, and I found myself yearning for connection. I craved simple moments of togetherness, only to be met with indifference. "Can you just not talk in the morning?" he would say, or "Why do you have to be so happy?" I tried to rationalize these responses as merely personal preferences, but deep down, I recognized the manipulation at play when I let myself take off the blinders. I was often told that if I changed certain aspects of myself, everything would improve, but this was a classic narcissistic tactic designed to shift the blame.

One incident stands out vividly in my memory. A friend had complimented my appearance in front of my spouse, prompting him to shrug dismissively. Later, I was reprimanded for my friend's comment, with him stating, "Why do I need to tell you you're beautiful? I wouldn't even want to sleep with you if you weren't." The feelings of worthlessness and shame that washed over me were debilitating.

Financial struggles compounded our issues. My spouse frequently made irresponsible financial decisions, which led us into debt time and time again. I could share countless stories of the emotional turmoil, but my focus is on healing rather than focusing on trauma.

The pivotal moment came when my daughter, just nine years old, asked why her daddy never played with her or spent time with her. "Does Daddy love me?" she inquired, and in that moment, I knew I had to make a change.

No longer could I shield her from the truth; the negative impact of our situation was evident. In my efforts to protect her, I had made excuses for his behavior, attributing it to a busy work schedule. Eventually, I learned that many of his absences were due to a desire to disengage with us, and he often would lie and say it was for work reasons but choosing to watch television or sports instead.

Leaving the marriage was supposed to be a transformative moment, yet it was merely the beginning of a new chapter filled with its own struggles. My spouse refused counseling at first, but after I left with our daughter, he reluctantly agreed to attend; however, each attempt at rebuilding only led to more heartache. After several years of trying counseling on and off, it seemed to only fuel his anger outbursts and emotional abuse. His outbursts were relentless, filled with accusations that I was impossible to please, and even told me no one could ever love someone like me in a rage full fit.

Attending counseling, I opted for a male therapist, hoping for a fresh perspective and that it would be helpful for his male ego. The counselor encouraged accountability on both our parts. However, my spouse misused this opportunity, misrepresenting his progress and failing to take responsibility for his actions. Instead of confronting his demons, he dismissed his issues, claiming others had it worse and wouldn't participate in the homework assignments. The tension escalated at home, and during one particularly distressing drive, I found myself contemplating the unthinkable. If it were merely me, I was so worn out by this time I may have done it, but God and thinking of my daughter was my saving grace. I knew in that instant if I stayed,

I would die. I was already so depressed, struggling to get through the days and pretending to everyone I was fine.

I went to a mentor friend's house, pouring out my heart, laying on her couch in the fetal position, and wondering if she would hate, if God would hate me if I divorced. She was so loving and just held me, letting me know she and God would always love me. I needed to do what was best for my and my daughter's mental health. I then had the most difficult conversation with my daughter. It was then that I realized the strength I needed to move forward. I remember asking her if she understood what divorce meant and what the Bible said about divorce. We had a conversation about it. I can still remember sitting at the table with my daughter and me telling her that God may hate me for this, but that I needed to divorce her dad, and I hope that it wouldn't hurt or harm her, which is my greatest fear. I remember her saying, "God would never hate you, he loves you." Then, she said, "I hate how he treats you. It's not okay. I love you, and it's gonna be okay." Out of the mouths of babes, later I thought. Her words were a lifeline, reassuring me that I could be okay if she was okay.

Yet, amid this chaos, I felt God's presence urging me to release my fears and hold onto my faith. I had long struggled with the belief that divorce would equate to failure—not just in the eyes of the church, but in my own heart. Growing up in a religious environment had instilled a fear of condemnation, and I worried about how my actions would affect my daughter's future. I would never tell somebody that they should have these beliefs, and I worked with lots of people who had gone through divorces. I don't even know how these beliefs became such a strong weight in my head, but they did. I'm grateful that God and counseling can help to heal all kinds of marriages and even make miracles out of messes. However, I'm also grateful that

God does not condone abuse and that it's okay to walk away if the other person doesn't change.

Reflecting on my journey, I recognized the immense gratitude I felt for my daughter. In my heart, I had always longed for a larger family, dreaming of a house filled with laughter and love. But as I navigated my marriage's complexities, it became clear that my dreams would remain unfulfilled with my spouse in so many ways and I couldn't allow anyone else to suffer.

After the divorce, I started to focus on my own healing. I continued seeing a counselor individually, working diligently to reclaim my life and identity. Plus, I got my daughter into counseling. It was a process filled with missteps, and I learned valuable lessons along the way. One critical mistake I made was not securing legal representation independently. In my desire to escape without more cruelty, I didn't, which led to complications down the road.

I had hoped for a smooth transition, but that was naive. I needed to establish clear boundaries and expectations to navigate co-parenting and such. I had previously withdrawn from my retirement to cover debts accrued by my spouse, plus my parents had bailed us out a few times as well, expecting him to honor our verbal agreements. Unfortunately, many of these promises were broken, leaving me in a precarious situation.

Through this tumultuous process, I came to realize that not everyone would remain in my life post-divorce. Friends and acquaintances often distanced themselves, unsure of how to navigate the changes. I think, like grief, some people don't know what to do or what to say in these situations, so they withdraw from you. There are people who are afraid to have relationships with you, afraid that divorce is contagious or something, and they don't want that to happen to their marriage. There are also those who will be judgmental over it all because they don't know all the ins and outs. I had a young daughter, so it was not my intent for people to know everything that happened, which I believe is healthy. I also believe that there will be people who just don't wanna take sides or feel like they're taking sides if they talk to you, so they withdraw as well. Yet, amidst the uncertainty, I had a core group of friends and family who lifted me during my darkest days.

Grieving the loss of relationships was another layer of pain I had to confront. The end of a marriage often equates to multiple losses—dreams, finances, and even friendships. It's crucial to be gentle with yourself during this time.

Even as I packed up my life and prepared for a new beginning, I found myself shedding tears over the memories of good times, even in a troubled relationship. One of the most therapeutic exercises I undertook was writing down the abusive experiences I endured. This was an assignment the counselor gave me because many people continue to try to make it work in abusive relationships. This act helped clarify my thoughts and feelings, allowing me to confront the reality of my situation.

As I ventured into the world of dating, I reminded myself of the importance of healing before seeking a new relationship. It's easy to fantasize about a new partner, but rushing into another relationship without proper healing can lead to repeating past mistakes. I took the time to reflect on what I truly wanted in a partner. Writing down my desires became a guiding compass, ensuring that I wouldn't settle for anything less than what I deserved.

As a mother, I often put my needs last, but I have realized that to be the best parent I could be, I needed to care for myself and make selfcare a priority. It was okay to step back and allow time for healing and make changes that showed my daughter a healthier balanced life.

Continuing my involvement in my church community was another priority, though I ensured it was a healthy environment. I sought counsel from my pastor, ensuring that my participation would be accepted due to my divorce. I'm grateful I got to continue though I have worked with many where their church removed them from leadership which just because another heartbreaking wound when not warranted.

Sharing my story with trusted friends and family was a powerful step. Some knew, seeing us over the years. It wasn't easy to open up about the struggles I had kept hidden for so long, but it was liberating. Acknowledging the truth of my experience helped me process the pain and receive support from those who cared.

I was also careful not to burden my daughter with my story. While she experienced her own heartache, I ensured that I provided a safe space for her to express her feelings without imposing my struggles upon her.

During this transition, I made it a point to nurture healthy friendships. I had always been the one to offer help, but asking for support proved challenging. Whether it was a phone conversation with a friend while sorting through belongings or spending quality time together, I learned the value of connection and community.

Even amid the chaos, I committed to creating joyful experiences with my daughter. Just because our family structure had changed, it didn't mean we had to lose our sense of happiness. We made time for special outings and cherished moments together.

As I embarked on this new chapter, I took the time to envision the life I wanted. I began practicing my dreams, whether it was treating myself to a solo dinner out or engaging in hobbies that brought me joy. Creating time and space for what truly mattered to me became a priority.

Through this journey, I have learned that overcoming the pain of divorce is possible. It requires courage, introspection, and a willingness to seek help. Embracing the journey of healing can lead to a life filled with love, joy, and fulfillment. You are not alone, and there is light at the end of the tunnel. Your story is still being written, and the best is yet to come. I pray my story helps you if you're going through this or helps you to know how to support others who may be in these situations. God loves us and wants good for our lives, and relationships are an important part of that. Be Blessed, and Be a Blessing!

JOIN THE MOVEMENT!
#BAUW
Becoming An Unstoppable Woman
With She Rises Studios

She Rises Studios was founded by Hanna Olivas and Adriana Luna Carlos, the mother-daughter duo, in mid-2020 as they saw a need to help empower women worldwide. They are the podcast hosts of the *She Rises Studios Podcast* and Amazon best-selling authors and motivational speakers who travel the world. Hanna and Adriana are the movement creators of #BAUW - Becoming An Unstoppable Woman: The movement has been created to universally impact women of all ages, at whatever stage of life, to overcome insecurities, adversities, and develop an unstoppable mindset. She Rises Studios
educates, celebrates, and empowers women globally.

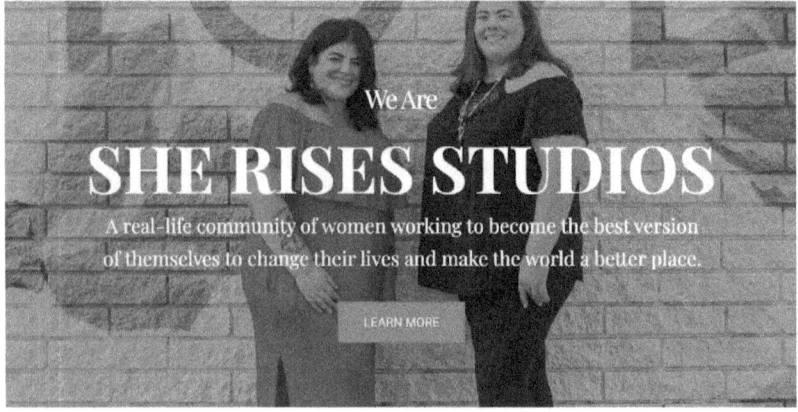

Looking to Join Us in our Next Anthology or Publish YOUR Own?
She Rises Studios Publishing offers full-service publishing, marketing, book tour, and campaign services. For more information, contact info@sherisesstudios.com
We are always looking for women who want to share their stories and expertise and feature their businesses on our podcasts, in our books, and in our magazines.

SEE WHAT WE DO

OUR PODCAST

OUR BOOKS

OUR SERVICES

Be featured in the Becoming An Unstoppable Woman magazine, published in 13 countries and sold in all major retailers. Get the visibility you need to LEVEL UP in your business!

FENIX TV
EMPOWER THROUGH ENTERTAINMENT
BE THE NEXT FENIX TV HOST AND INSPIRE A WORLD OF POSSIBILITIES!
Visit our website for more details:
FENIXTV APP

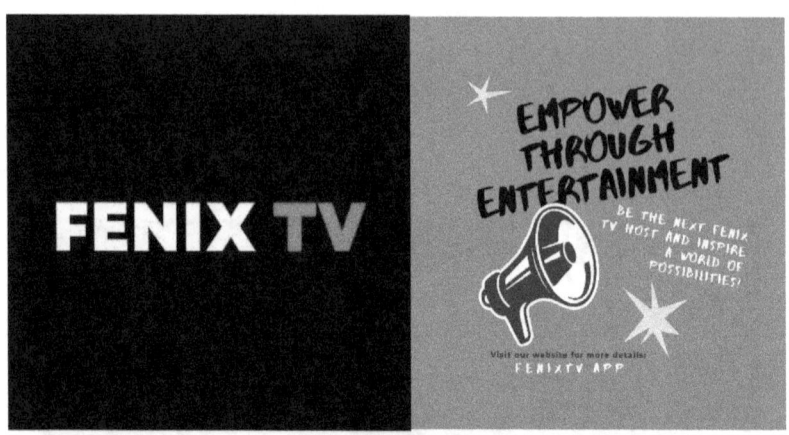

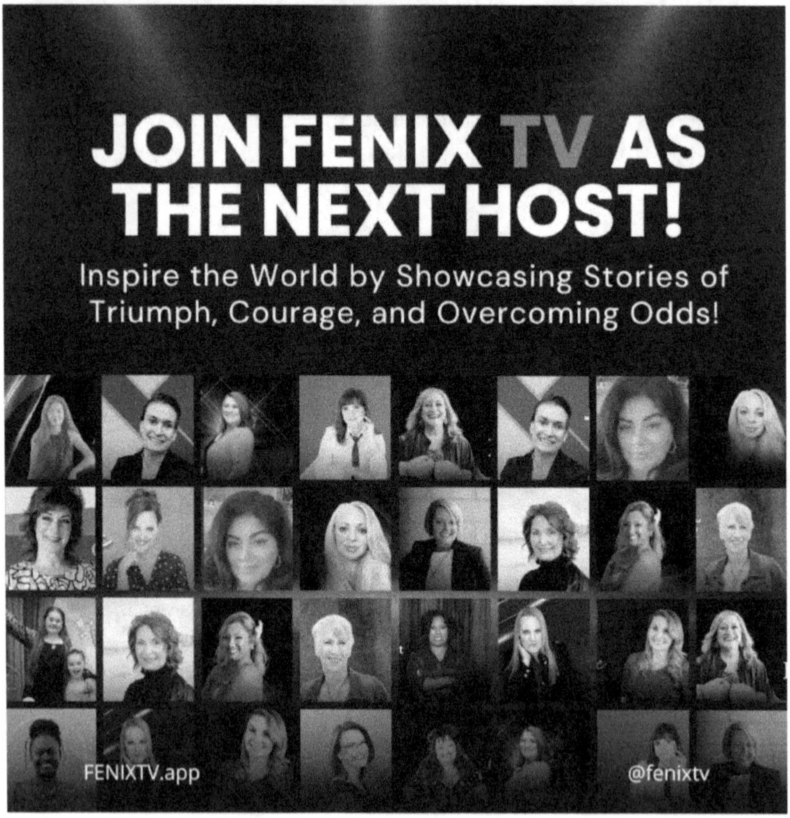
JOIN FENIX TV AS THE NEXT HOST!
Inspire the World by Showcasing Stories of Triumph, Courage, and Overcoming Odds!
FENIXTV.app
@fenixtv

Have your own TV show streamed across major platforms like Roku TV, Amazon Fire Stick,

Apple TV and more!

Learn to leverage your expertise. Build your online presence and grow your audience with FENIX TV.
https://fenixtv.sherisesstudios.com/

Visit www.SheRisesStudios.com to see how YOU can join the #BAUW movement and help your community to achieve the UNSTOPPABLE mindset.

Have you checked out the *She Rises Studios Podcast?*

Find us on all MAJOR platforms: Spotify, IHeartRadio, Apple Podcasts, Google Podcasts, etc.

Looking to become a sponsor or build a partnership?
Email us at info@sherisesstudios.com

www.ingramcontent.com/pod-product-compliance
Lightning Source LLC
Chambersburg PA
CBHW071706120626
46550CB00001B/120